SPIRIT OF ERROR

SPIRIT OF TRUTH

SPIRIT OF ERROR
SPIRIT OF TRUTH

Preparing People for the Manifestation
of God's Power in Their Lives.

L. G. BARRETT

WINEPRESS WP PUBLISHING

WinePress Publishing (PO Box 428, Enumclaw, WA 98022) functions only as book publisher. As such, the ultimate design, content, editorial accuracy, and views expressed or implied in this work are those of the author.

All Scriptures quoted in this book originated from the King James Version of the Bible. Some of the references have minor paraphrases so as to not distract the reader, such as dropping a th at the end of a word, or changing thou to you.

ISBN 13: 978-1-57921-832-4
ISBN 10: 1-57921-832-6
Library of Congress Catalog Card Number: 2005910225

To my friend Mark, who gave it his best shot, and to all those who went with me through the battle of J.U.

TABLE OF CONTENTS

ACKNOWLEDGMENTS

Val—My faithful wife who stuck by me and encouraged me through everything we experienced.

INTRODUCTION

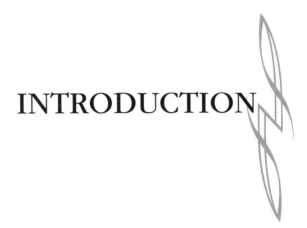

*T*his is the story of a group of people who, more than anything, wanted to know Jesus and to love Him and serve Him. It is the story of how, in their exuberance, they sometimes missed the mark and hurt each other and themselves. It is the story of what I learned by walking through these experiences and finally coming to a place of rest in my soul.

Purpose of This Book

I have three main purposes for writing this book:

1. I want to help God's people prepare for the manifestation of His power in their lives.
2. I desire to facilitate healing and restore confidence to all individuals who were involved with me in "The Battle of Jesus Unlimited" (or "J. U." as it came to be known). I want to confirm the good things that happened to them, and to separate those good things from the bad.
3. I want to help people to learn to *feel* the difference between the *Spirit of Error* and the *Spirit of Truth*. I'll take you along with me

in my experiences—to feel what I felt, to think like I thought, to be confused as I was confused, to come out of it as I came out of it. I hope that this exercise will help you to stand against the Spirit of Error successfully.

I also hope to expose leadership tactics of manipulation and abuse, expose the danger of blindly following leadership, help define correct leadership and correct following, and show the difference between a healthy respect for God and an ungodly fear of Him.

Furthermore, after you read this book, it is my hope that:

- If you move into any Christian leadership or service, you will be less likely to stumble into the darkness where I have been.
- If you come into contact with a group where the Spirit of Error is predominant, you will be less likely to support it and possibly be a factor in helping to restore people who have erred. The meek will rejoice in this message.

The Audience

I believe that this book will help the following individuals:

- **Christians** who are beginning to search for a deeper walk with God, who are part of a revival and are experiencing God's power and/or a massive yearning to know Him, who perceive that their church needs to change in some areas, or who want to help themselves guard against bad pride that is creeping in.
- **Serious seekers** who are genuinely interested in knowing more about God. There are many people who are not yet believers, but they *are* interested in hearing more about Jesus and God's love for them. They may have had contact with someone who has moved heavily in the Spirit of Error and associate Jesus with this bad spirit. I would like to set the record straight and share with these individuals how I see Jesus and how He changed a lot

of my wrong thinking about Him. Maybe by reading this book, these serious seekers will gain the faith to become believers and begin to follow Jesus.

- **Hurting people** who have had bad experiences with churches that have moved heavily in the Spirit of Error and who need to be exposed to the grace and love of Jesus, the One who always moves in the Spirit of Truth, humility, love, and grace.

Characters, Places, Jargon and Style

In the back of this book is a glossary of often-used terms, and a list of characters who play a part in this book. I have not used their real names to protect their privacy, except in the case of well-known persons or ministries. You will also find a list of the places where these events took place.

The glossary will help you learn the meanings of words I use in my journal entries. It is amazing to me how much "jargon" or Christian slang I picked up after just a few years of being a Christian. You might want to quickly skim over these sections before reading this book.

There could be many different ideas about what the phrase "The Spirit of Error" means, and that's OK. This book is simply about *my* definition of "The Spirit of Error." When I use this term, I don't mean to be creating an all inclusive meaning for the phrase. I'm simply using the term to help describe a particular spirit that voraciously came against me and my friends earlier in my Christian life.

This book is formatted mainly as a diary with commentary throughout. It is a combination of journal, short story and textbook. There are some controversial journal entries about individuals in this book. In many cases, I sought out the individuals to ask their recent opinions in order to present the clearest picture about those entries. Some individuals were either unable or unwilling to respond to my inquiries. In those cases, as in all my other opinions expressed in this book, I called it just as I saw it.

CHAPTER 1

THE UNEXPECTED HAPPENS

A PICTURE OF THINGS TO COME

This is the account of how God's Holy Spirit works . . .

(From my journal, 9-24-73)

When I wrote those words at the beginning of my journal more than 30 years ago, I had no idea what God had in store. I assumed that my writings would be full of glorious miracles, strange and wonderful happenings, and mighty accomplishments and victories. Little did I know what was really to come—and yet how true a statement it really was.

As the sun gently set on southwest Michigan one day during the winter of 1975, an unusual warm front moved in. The temperature climbed to more than 60 degrees, and shortly thereafter came a big thunderstorm with high winds. The plastic-covered wood frame addition to the Bechtel's garage was no match for the strong gusts that came late that night. It collapsed.

15

Mark Bechtel was sound asleep when his phone rang about 1:00 A.M.

"Mr. Bechtel?"

"Yes?"

"This is the Niles police department. You have a mess down the street."

"What?"

"You have a jumbled up plastic mess down your street!"

"What are you talking about?" Mark was confused as he tried to wake up. The policeman wasn't making sense to him.

"I think it's your church!" the officer told him.

The policeman was unknowingly prophetic in his statement. The church, "Jesus Unlimited," was about to become a "jumbled up mess." But this had nothing to do with a plastic and wood structure. It had everything to do with leadership and a battle between the Spirit of Error and the Spirit of Truth.

But let's go back five years to 1970, to a stuffy, crowded gym and a moment of truth for my best friend, Mark Bechtel. It was the night of our high school wrestling conference championship. Mark and I had worked hard to get here, and now our hope of taking home the first place trophy looked slim indeed.

Mark had just lost his final match. He had not only lost, but had lost badly. How could this happen? Losing was an experience I was used to, but the agony of defeat was almost foreign to Mark. He would rather suffer the physical pain of breaking a leg than go through the emotional torment of losing a match.

Shocked and bewildered, I had left the crowded gym and burst into the deserted locker room. With the roar of the crowd in the background,

I frantically searched for some way to quiet the roar in my heart. Mark had lost, and now our team would probably lose the championship. I even cried out to God, but God and I had never been on good speaking terms. About all he ever he heard from me was, "God, please let us win!"

I remember the first time I came into contact with Mark. Actually, it was my nose that came into contact with the mat during a wrestling practice as he spun me around and pinned me. He could easily tie me up in knots and had no respect for me—in the beginning. But I gained his respect when I developed my own style, grew harder to pin, and even won some matches.

Eventually, Mark and I became best friends. Now, in this agonizing moment, we shared the bitterness of his defeat. Although I had just lost two matches, I doubted if I was hurting as much as Mark was. After I settled down a bit, I began to feel compassion for him and decided that he could use a little consolation.

I walked back to the cheering crowd in the gymnasium and looked for Mark, but he wasn't with the team. He was sitting on the floor, slumped against the cold wall of the gym. His oldest brother, Phil, was rubbing his shoulders and talking to him.

Mark was in so much anguish that he was unable to receive consolation from anyone. He was also somewhat rude when I tried to comfort him. I walked away feeling hurt and confused, but did my best to shake it off and get back to supporting the team. We still had seven matches to go, and we were the underdogs in most of them.

Our team went on fighting each match of the tournament. It was a scene for the books. The outcome rested on the final heavyweight match. Then the unexpected happened. Our man was not favored to win, but in the final seconds, he rolled over on top of his opponent and pinned him flatter than a pancake! We had won! The place went absolutely wild, complete with our team hoisting up the heavyweight hero and parading him around the gym.

During the height of our celebration, my joy was doused when I glanced at Mark and saw his look of despair. It was a hollow victory for my friend. Even though he came in second, his championship loss overshadowed all the wins that had brought him to the finals. He couldn't see that each of those wins was absolutely essential to us holding the trophy of champions.

We had *all* contributed to the championship. We won by only one point, which meant that *any* performance that hadn't measured up would have caused us to lose. Every point gained was the winning point. Even those of us who didn't win a single match made a contribution. By not allowing ourselves to be pinned or beaten badly, the opponents didn't receive any bonus points. Although Mark felt like a total failure, his second place finish was a great contribution.

For Mark and me, this scenario foreshadowed many of our experiences yet to come. Unfortunately, the stakes in those experiences were much higher than a high school wrestling match. It was more like the stakes in a war. I call it "The Battle of Jesus Unlimited" (or "J.U.").

During the battle of J.U., we fought against a real enemy, and there were real casualties as well as victories. Our enemy is still at large. As I take you through this experience, you will begin to see, feel, and be exposed to this enemy. When you finish this book, you will be less likely to fall into Satan's traps. He is *not* all-powerful, and he can be defeated. He is The Spirit of Error.

CHAPTER 2

A DRAMATIC CHANGE
THE ULTIMATE REVERSAL

*A*fter Mark's conference disappointment, he also performed poorly and lost the district championship. Although he still qualified for the regional competition, it was another empty accomplishment for Mark. I tried again to console him, but once more to no avail. I was a little hurt. I could have used some consoling too. I didn't win even one match, and therefore I was not eligible to go to the regionals.

I drove more than 100 miles through a Michigan snowstorm to see Mark in the regional finals. The air in the gym was crackling with excitement. The winner would go on to the state tournament. The lights in the building were bright, and I remember seeing Mark and his opponent facing each other preparing to wrestle. But something was different. I couldn't explain it then, but the feeling was incredible. Mark looked calm and confident, not wired and fearful as he had been during the previous two championships.

When the whistle blew, Mark moved as if he had wings on his feet. He almost floated as he whisked about the mat. I had never seen Mark move so quickly or so smoothly. He was going to win and everyone knew it. And he did win, easily. He earned a trip to the state wrestling tournament. Something, obviously, had made a big difference in Mark's life.

I'm not sure why I was drawn to be Mark's friend. Maybe it was his popularity, and I *did* respect him greatly as a superior athlete. Or maybe, subconsciously, I liked the challenge of winning his friendship. Regardless of the reason, I always enjoyed his company, and he welcomed me into his world.

Mark's respect for me grew when I swore that I'd never be pinned during my senior year, and then proved it. When I faced an unquestionably superior opponent, I made it clear to the referee and the rest of the world that I would sacrifice my arm and shoulder to avoid getting pinned. I figured that the pain of a dislocated shoulder was less than the pain of loss. The referee always stopped my opponent before he seriously injured me.

Mark's and my friendship was typical of many high school kids. Mark was the popular athlete and I was his sidekick friend. I wasn't a superior athlete, but others respected me for certain lesser accomplishments. I supported Mark by honoring him, and he supported me by accepting me into his circle of friends, which brought me some prestige and honor.

Cruising around with Mark on Friday nights during our final year in high school was generally a big letdown. Even though Mark never capitalized on his popularity, all the girls liked him—but not me. This frustrated me, because I wanted to pick up girls and get to know them. But Mark always found an excuse for not "moving in."

There seemed to be a strong conflict inside him at times. Occasionally, when we went to a party and found ourselves in a compromising situation, I could see that Mark wanted to stay and have a good time.

Mark and I celebrating on our high school graduation day.

But at the same time he wanted to leave and would push me to leave with him. This was frustrating to me because I was too shy to stay and handle things myself. So I usually left when he did.

The fall following our senior year, Mark journeyed to the far reaches of northern Michigan to attend Lake Superior State College. I stayed home and commuted to a local junior college. At Southwestern Michigan College (SMC), I began to hang out with a new crowd.

I remember getting moderately drunk at a Christmas party. In a stupor, I looked around at all the people. Loud music played and laughter and conversation filled the air. It looked as if everyone was having a good time. But I thought to myself, *This is not the meaning of life.*

Mark hated college in the north. In fact, he hated it so much that he left a full wrestling scholarship to come home and attend SMC with me. He had a hard time fitting in with my new crowd, so I ended up splitting my social time between Mark and my new friends. I'd spend enough time with Mark to stay in good standing with him and enough time with my new friends to stay in good standing with them too.

I had quite a diversity of friends. There were my friends from high school, who were generally good-hearted and specialized in partying, hanging out, and looking for girls. Quite often, we found someone to get alcohol for us and we got drunk regularly. I began to hang around with Mark only during the weeknights. When weekends came, I shifted to friends who enjoyed having a little more "fun" than he did. Then there was the college crowd, who were a little more sophisticated. They dated and socialized more than caroused. I hung around with them mostly during the weekdays.

When summertime came, my life was a mixture of the excitement of doing new things and a frantic search for happiness and fulfillment. I also noticed that my will to do right was weakening. I began to feel frustrated that my willpower did not keep me from doing wrong. Smoking marijuana for the first time disgusted me, and I tried to strengthen my will by making a large bet with my friend, Lee Funt, that I would never smoke dope again.

Mark, myself and Lee at a wedding reception
just after graduating from high school.

Then came an eventful night in November, 1971. I had just started my sophomore year in college after a summer of pleasure seeking. Lee, a long time high school friend and partying buddy, spread the word about a party he was having at his parent's home after the football game. Lee's parents were away on vacation and, as usual, we took advantage of this perfect opportunity to have a good time.

Lee's house was packed. We drank a lot of beer, some of which ended up all over the floor. Suddenly, someone smashed a window. Then Lee, normally very mild and teddy-bearish, went wild with rage and yelled at everyone to leave. To make himself fully understood, he picked up an office desk and threw it across the room. (Lee was a dedicated weight lifter!)

I don't remember much more of that night or even what part of the house I slept in, but I *do* remember waking up to a disastrous mess. There was broken glass and beer on the floor. The hurled desk had landed in disarray. There was party trash all over. We faced with a huge cleaning job.

While cleaning up, Lee and I found three religious booklets, or "gospel tracts," that some girls had brought to the party. Apparently, the girls had received them from some people who had been passing them out at the exits to the original play *Jesus Christ Superstar,* that was being performed in neighboring South Bend, Indiana. Lee said the girls made fun of the tracts and left them lying around for us to clean up.

The tracts were little comic book stories about people turning to God. They had titles such as "Holy Joe," "This *Was* Your Life," and "The Assignment." Lee and I were quite moved by these stories, and after we read them, he looked me straight in the eyes and said, "Larry, I think we had better change."

I said, "Lee, I think you're right!"

As soon as I was alone, I got down on my knees, said the prayer in the booklet, and gave my life to God. I found out later that Lee had done the same thing.

Mark was overjoyed at our decisions and told us that he had given his life to God just before the regional wrestling finals. Suddenly, Mark's hard times during the early tournaments and his dramatic change at the regionals made perfect sense. It also explained why he didn't want to carouse with the rest of us afterward.

Mark explained that when he was almost pinned at the conference championship, God had been dealing with him, and he had been resisting surrender to Him. He said, "My resistance was so exhausting and distracting that I couldn't wrestle to my potential."

Mark submitted to the simple call of God, and that change in his life helped him go all the way to the state finals, where he lost a close match. However, he viewed this particular championship loss much differently. It hardly bothered him because of his newfound faith. Mark was at peace with God. He wrestled to the best of his ability, and God helped him see that being second in the state was an accomplishment to be proud of.

As for me, you couldn't see much of a change on the outside after my conversion, but some major changes happened inside. I felt that God wanted me to treat women with respect and not to lie or cheat. For the longest time, however, I was probably the most foul-mouthed Christian alive. Not having heard or read much of the Bible, I was very ignorant of simple practical truths such as *put off. . . filthy communication out of your mouth* (Colossians 3:8).

Mark was perplexed. I didn't conform to the rules of religion, yet I demonstrated a true faith in Jesus as my Lord. He had grown up hearing some good Bible teaching, but unfortunately the leadership had also taught him to conform to non-biblical expectations that some churches burden their members with, such as no television, no jewelry, no short pants, you must attend church three times a week, and so on.

Mark couldn't deny the faith Lee and I had, so he began to look closely at some of the traditions that his church, Boulder's Chapel Church of God, taught as God's truth. He began to understand much of the basics of the love and grace of God and to reject some of the hypocritical areas of his elders' beliefs. Mark was careful, however, not to criticize the church leaders. He believed that dealing positively and gently was the best practice toward resolving differences.

Boulder's Chapel had one thing that I'd never experienced before: a more enjoyable and interesting service. Pastor Allan Fletcher faithfully watched over the congregation and often preached so loudly that he would lose his voice for a time. "Brother Al," as we affectionately called him, was a great teacher, and I learned many good Christian doctrines from him. Lee and I came from Episcopal and Methodist church backgrounds, so we were not used to hearing the Bible taught and preached with so much enthusiasm. It was an answer to my prayer of several months earlier: "God, please make me enjoy church."

It wasn't long before Lee and I regularly attended Boulder's Chapel, and the three of us spent many hours in heavy discussions about God. The church laid the foundation for much of my deeper understanding about Christ. Most of the church's teaching was very good, but some of it was very bad.

This time marked the beginning of many good months. The weight of sin was now off me. Although I struggled with many youthful lusts, overall I made steady steps toward becoming the man I wanted to be. Mark's parents were helpful and loving toward Lee and me. Their house was always open for us to come and hang out and ask questions. Every Sunday after church, I would join Mark's family at dinner. The afternoons were filled with discussions and good-natured debates about God, and then we would top it off with a nice nap on their living room floor.

Often, we talked about our church and the prevailing harsh and judgmental spirit that existed. For many months, I also struggled with the hypocrisy of some people. In church, they were staunch and firm, but outside they did some things that I thought were very wrong. Others, especially some of the "pillars of the church," were outspoken and harsh toward people of other Christian backgrounds and denominations.

Mark and I were especially concerned about this discrepancy, and one night before going to sleep at his house, we prayed earnestly, "Lord, please show us what is wrong with our church." Later, at about 3 A.M., I woke up out of a sound sleep. (I was sleeping on the floor next to Mark's bed.) Looking over at Mark, I noticed that he was breathing heavily.

"Mark?" I asked.

"Leave me alone!" he yelled. It didn't sound like Mark.

"What is it, Mark?"

"Hatred!"

"Mark?"

"Yes," he answered in a rather coldly matter-of-fact voice. It was as if he wasn't really there. Then a few moments later, he yelled, "What's going on?!"

In the morning, Mark didn't remember speaking to me, and I had to tell him what he had said. He told me that in his dream-like state, he had wanted to reach over and strangle me. He said that he seemed to be fully awake and saw three demons in the upper corner across the room. One was *Hatred* and the other two were *Unbelief* and *Fear*.

The next morning, we listened to a Christian teaching program on the radio. The Scripture being taught was from 1 Corinthians 13, the "love chapter" in the Bible. When Mark and I heard the program, we knew that God had answered our prayer to show us what was wrong with our church. The message was clear: Our church clearly lacked God's type of love. We were afflicted with hatred, unbelief and fear.

CHAPTER 3

"I WANT HER!"

THE PRETTIEST GIRL IN THE CHURCH

I had never seriously considered marriage. I think I was typical of most young worldly teenagers. I'm sorry to say that selfish motives and poor intentions were what drove me most of the time. After I became a Christian, I saw that my ways were not God's ways. It was time to find a nice girl, settle down, and get married.

I pondered about this one Sunday. I was in the back of the church (Mark, Lee, and I always sat near the back), and I scanned the entire congregation from front to back and side to side. My eyes rested on Val Smith, the prettiest girl in church, sitting two rows in front of me. Fixing my eyes on Val, I prayed, "God, that's the girl I want. I want *her!* Please Lord! Would You give her to *me?*"

A few days later, I mustered up the courage to call Val.

"Vaaaaal! You have a phone call . . . it's a boooyyyy!" Val's mom enjoyed a little good-natured teasing of her "number three" daughter. Val was out in the garden picking green beans. Her family always had a garden; they were farmers all the way back to the *Mayflower* . . . probably. July ushered in the beginning of harvest and, as usual, it was hot and muggy.

Val, in her excitement and curiosity, forgot about how hot and miserable she was. "Who is it?" she asked her mom.

"It's Larry Barrett."

"Larry Barrett?" (She said it like, "Who's he, and why would he call?") Val never took notice of me, except that I was one of Mark's new church companions. She wasn't really interested in me at all.

When Val came to the phone, I asked her to go out with me. I think it was the first time I had actually asked a girl out on a date. I had gone through some blind date situations and caroused a lot, but this was the first time that ever I really showed proper respect for a girl to whom I was attracted. I hung up the phone feeling very excited and eagerly looking forward to our upcoming Tuesday night date.

I picked up Val about 6:30 P.M. She wore tan hip-huggers and a white pullover blouse. She looked beautiful. We went miniature golfing, and I won't say who won. Then we went to the neighboring South Bend, Indiana, airport for dinner and watched the planes come and go. The main restaurant upstairs had a nice view but was closed, so we ate in the little diner downstairs. We talked and talked and talked and really enjoyed each other's company. I remember both of us saying that we felt God had something special prepared for our lives—some type of special ministry ahead.

Val told me that sometimes she went on missionary trips to Haiti and often passed out gospel tracts. Many times, she stood outside special events and passed out tracts with her friends. They braved scorn and ridicule when others viewed them to be religious and "goody, goody." She even went with the group that passed out tracts at *Jesus Christ Superstar*. Remember? I gave my heart to God after reading a tract that was brought to our party by some girls. The girls had gone to *Jesus Christ Superstar* just before attending our party. *Wouldn't it be interesting if a tract that Val passed out was the one that led me to God?*

About a week later, Val and I went out on our second date. We went bowling with my brother and his wife. It was the first (and last!) time in my life that I bowled over 200! I remember taking Val home in my new silver Vega GT. I walked her to the door, turned, and kissed her for the first time. Val's lips were so soft and tender. Since that night, now more than 30 years ago, I have kissed no one else. From that night on, I knew I wanted to marry Val, and I pursued her like a young inexperienced stallion until I won her heart. Those first two dates are fixed in my mind. They were storybook wonderful!

I then traveled to Florida for a two-week vacation with my friend Lee. We visited my grandmother near Vero Beach and enjoyed the sun and surf. While we were there, we visited a little Church of God just a few blocks from my grandma's house. Of course, we *had* to go to a Church of God—back home, leadership from Boulder's Chapel and other Church of God affiliates insinuated from the pulpit that we would be sinning if we went to any other type of church. One of their favorite song verses was, "If you go 'round to Babylon, don't look around for me . . ." They called all the other churches "Babylon," which means "confusion." So we went to this little Church of God.

God really does have a sense of humor. The church turned out to be a Pentecostal Church of God, but we couldn't tell by the sign out front. Our church leadership particularly looked down on Pentecostals because they believed they were "of the Devil." There were only a few people at the first service. In fact, we almost *doubled* the size of their congregation. It was at this little church that Lee met his future bride, Ruth Ann.

A few months later, Lee, Mark, and I went back to visit my grandmother. One day, we sat around the motel room and talked about Ruth Ann, the only girl in that little church. We knew Lee was attracted to her, so Mark said, "Well, Lee, she's too young for me, and Larry's already taken, so why don't you call her?"

Lee said excitedly, "Really guys? Really? Really? You don't mind? Thanks! Thanks a lot!" Saying that to Lee was a mistake for Mark and me, because the car was hardly around after that.

The guys really made fun of me on that trip because I missed Val so much. I couldn't wait to get back home to see her. During the full year we dated, I attended SMC and worked at a grocery store. Val was an insurance administrator at the local hospital. Most of the time, I worked evenings until 9:00 P.M., and Val worked the normal 8 to 5 hours.

As Val and I became more serious about each other, we began to hang out almost daily. Poor Val! I would get off work, go over to her parent's house around 9:30 P.M., and then stay and visit until sometimes 2 or 3 in the morning. Then Val would have to drag herself out of bed early the next morning and make it out the door by 7:30 A.M. Poor, poor Val.

We began to discuss marriage early in the summer of 1973, almost a year after our first date. At that time, I still worked part-time at a grocery store, and I had just graduated from SMC with an associate's degree in science. I needed a full-time job, and I was tired of never having more than one day off at a time.

One good thing that our church taught was this: We should always be content with simplicity. We should have a simple life, a simple job, make a simple wage, buy simple groceries, and enjoy the company of friends and family. I was ready to get a factory job, marry Val, and go to church three times a week for the rest of my life.

I found a factory job in my hometown of Niles at Dayco Sheet Metal in the fabrication division. My job involved running a punch press, drill press, spot welding, and operating many types of production machines. The work was rather boring, repetitive, and sometimes involved heavy lifting and dirty work, but that didn't bother me. It was so good to have my weekends free again. But the early morning starting time was difficult for me.

Late in the summer of 1973, after much prayer and seeking God, Val and I decided to get married. Val made it clear that she had always wanted to have a fall wedding, so she said that we would have to get married "this fall" or "next fall." I really didn't want to wait for a *whole* year to get married, so we decided to set the date for "this fall." Of course, it was almost September already. How late does fall go to anyway?

The first thing I did was talk to Val's dad. I talked to him alone and sincerely asked for his daughter's hand in marriage. He was happy about it and heartily gave us his blessing. Then we announced the date: November 3, 1973, about nine weeks away! So now we began a frantic time of planning for our wedding.

CHAPTER 4

PENTECOSTAL MESSAGE SLIPPING IN
THE SHOWDOWN

*P*entecostal and charismatic Christians—those who believed in God's power being manifested today, including "speaking in tongues" (speaking in unlearned languages)—were subjected to extreme criticism at our church. We were taught that anybody who spoke in tongues was letting the Devil speak through them.

This area of criticism wasn't very important to me until my friend Lee started a relationship with one of "them." Then my *parents* began going to some charismatic meetings. I soon realized that I had to do some serious study on this subject, or else I would have to cut off all friendly communication with them. Being somewhat disobedient to the exhortations of my church leadership, I decided to go to a charismatic meeting with my parents. I had seen a definite change in my dad and couldn't deny that my parents' lives were changing for the better, so I felt I should check it out.

About 700 people met in a large, nicely finished basement of a local church. The service was led by the "People of Praise" of South Bend, Indiana. There were people from many denominations present, and I was immediately impressed with the worship at the beginning of the meeting. The lights were dimmed slightly and everyone sang familiar choruses and songs. The most moving time was when the people "sang in tongues." It was like being in heaven and hearing angels sing.

I never really saw any deviation from what I knew about the Bible. The message was sound, and the people I met afterward were very friendly and Christ-like. In fact, they were more childlike and humble in Spirit than many of the people at my church.

The only confusing thing was that some of them drank beer and smoked. I had a self-righteous attitude because of some errant teaching at my church, and so I had a hard time understanding how any of these charismatic believers could be Christians and still smoke and drink. But I could not deny their faith and love for God.

One time, I was in the midst of a small group with my parents, and one person asked another, "Have you ever tasted Coors beer?" The woman answered, "Oh yes! Praise God!" As a Pharisee (self-righteous person) in the making, that was downright astounding to me.

During the seven months before Val and I were married, Lee, Mark, Mark's family, Val, and I intensely studied the Bible with regard to speaking in other languages and the baptism in the Holy Spirit. We even visited other churches that moved in the gifts of languages (tongues), prophecy, healing, and other "gifts of the Spirit," as the Bible called them.

As word spread to our church leadership that we were regularly visiting these churches, contention grew between the leadership and us. Several other families who were seeking God in these areas were also falling from grace in the eyes of our church.

At first, there were just insinuations from the pulpit. At testimony times when people would stand up and talk, members of the congregation would give minor exhortations to be faithful to the "church." Next came more direct rebukes from the pulpit and borderline slanderous accusations of sin. As these accusations became more open, they infuriated Mark's father, Wilt, and a few other families. Then came the showdown.

One hot Sunday night in August, when testimonies were prevalent and the floor was quite open, the pastor made a comment that broke the camel's back. I don't remember exactly what was said, but it was belligerent and cut deep into Wilt's hide. The tension inside the church became as uncomfortable as the sticky humidity outside.

Wilt stood up and began to fill the congregation in on what we had been doing from our point of view. A debate developed, then a full-scale blowout, concluding with Mark's family and a few other families walking out in a huff. Wilt felt that he could not in a clear conscience keep his family in a church with that opinion and doctrine. Mark walked out in respect to his dad, but Val and I didn't. We felt the blowout was uncalled for and that the correct thing to do was to speak *the truth in love* (Ephesians 4:15) and then leave quietly.

A few weeks later after the exodus, Mark felt led to start a group to pray about what God might want to do in the Niles area. We later named the group "Jesus Unlimited," or "J.U." for short. Wilt and the other families started a church of their own. They met for a while in the Bechtel's garage and then bought a little church building on the other side of Niles. They called it the "Church of God, Full Gospel." This church is alive and well today, and Brother Bechtel pastored it faithfully until his recent retirement.

Val and I didn't leave Boulder's Chapel immediately. Because we had developed good relationships with so many people, it didn't seem right to just pull out and not associate with them anymore. We also hoped to get married at the church in a few months. But we stayed mostly because there was such a strong misconception being emphasized that anyone leaving and going to another church was in danger of going to hell.

This instilled in us (and most of the congregation) a fear of God that was incredibly powerful. We loved God, but we were afraid of hell. The leadership regularly capitalized on this fear to keep people like us from leaving the congregation. People who really love God want to please Him, and they also have a good fear or healthy respect for Him. When an ungodly fear is instilled in people who want to please God, they are quite susceptible to manipulation by their spiritual elders. This unhealthy, ungodly fear of God was prevalent in that church. The pastors commonly preached God's wrath along with Scriptures that were twisted to employ the "God is going to get you" method to keep the congregation in line.

I don't think the leadership knowingly or consciously did this as a deceitful tactic. Woe unto those who would do such a thing intentionally! The leaders themselves were probably victims of that method and were simply passing down bad attitudes and ungodly fear that they themselves picked up over the years. It had permeated their thinking.

It was the *Spirit of Error.*

So began our first progression out of the bondage of the Spirit of Error. This spirit often works within churches and good people who actually think they're doing the right thing. It took a full seven months for Val and me to muster the courage to stop attending Boulder's Chapel and dedicate ourselves to the J.U. prayer group.

CHAPTER 5
NEW LIFE AT AN
OLD CAMP
FIRST DAY, FIRST BORN

few weeks after Mark's dad started his church, I heard about a ministry near the Notre Dame campus called "The Lighthouse." There had been quite a revival going on among teens in the Michiana (Michigan and Indiana) area, and the Lighthouse provided a ministry and atmosphere that related to the younger generation. The group met in a large house that served as an informal meeting place for young Christians to hang out, pray for each other and talk about their new faith in Jesus as their Lord. There also were regularly scheduled meetings for teaching and prayer. It was a great place to gather spontaneously, learn, and grow in the Lord!

During this time, I wrote this first entry in my journal:

This is the account of how God's Holy Spirit works. Early in September 1973, the Lighthouse runners (coordinators or leaders) were impressed by the Spirit to close down the Lighthouse. Many (including myself) wondered why the Holy Spirit would impress upon leaders to stop a work that has blessed so many and has glorified God. Some said, "The work or ministry was fulfilled." Others said, "The leader is going on to bigger things." If I am not mistaken, the leader said, "God has greater things in store." He was speaking truth.

Since Mark, Lee, Val, and I were intensely studying the Bible on the subject of the baptism and gifts of the Holy Spirit, we thought about asking God for the baptism of the Holy Spirit. Our church had told us that people like those in The Lighthouse were "of the Devil" (but they didn't *act* like the Devil); that it was not God's way (although the charismatics said it *was* God's way); and that the Bible was against it (yet the New Testament is *filled* with encouragement to receive the gifts of the Spirit).

So, one by one, we began to ask those in the group who were already baptized in the Holy Spirit to lay hands on us so that we also could receive this blessing. The next entry in my journal tells about that special time for me.

Friday, September 14, 1973

It was the last night of the Lighthouse. I heard about the Calldean girls receiving tongues. I felt a bit of jealousy, but drove it away. When Lee went upstairs to receive tongues, I knew then that the Spirit wanted me to go too. I felt the Spirit tell me that I should know I was baptized in the Spirit before I got married.

Val was by my side until just before I went into the prayer room. I knew that the gifts had to come naturally, so I didn't want to be the least bit pushy. I told her to wait downstairs and pray for me, telling her that "this was the night." She was apprehensive about the whole thing and tense and uneasy from the time we parked the car at the Lighthouse. After a struggle, I spoke in another language, but not with a full release. I had many doubts.

I couldn't pray in tongues in front of Val. A man prayed for Val while I was talking to another brother. When I looked across the room and saw this man squatting down close to Val, I became jealous and went over near her until he was through. Val said that the man had told her that he had been impressed to pray for her. When he told her that, she said, "Please do." Val and I went home with a slightly different relationship. A little more close, but a bit divided as well.

I really don't like the phrase "speaking in tongues." To me, "tongues" is kind of an ugly word for a gift of the Holy Spirit. The *King James Bible* uses this word to mean "languages." The charismatic community occasionally overemphasizes this gift because it is the one experienced most often.

When I would speak in tongues, my prayer language didn't always sound like a real language. At other times, it actually *did* sound like something real. This brought doubts and some confusion on the subject. Val received the baptism in the Holy Spirit near the time that we were married.

Monday, September 17, 1973

We went to dinner at Lee's house. The whole gang was there. They told me about all the miracles and uplifting done the Sunday night before at Mark's house (I wasn't there) and about the next Thursday night prayer meeting. Then Val and I went to see about wedding flowers. I went home and tried to go to bed early.

My parents had company, a Japanese girl and her husband from the charismatic community "People of Praise." Instead of getting to bed early, we talked until 11:30. When I heard how the girl's native language sounded, it uplifted my faith. Her Japanese language didn't sound like a real language either. It just sounded like gibberish.

Thursday, September 20, 1973

Val left in the morning to go to Haiti on a missionary vacation with Mr. and Mrs. Calldean and their youngest daughter. I went to the prayer meeting at Mark's. Many people there (about 20). Our main theme was that the Lighthouse is closed and Christians need fellowship. So what shall we do?

The Lord put a burden on Mark's heart to do something for God, but he didn't want to get "in the flesh" or to do anything outside of God's will. We had a good meeting. We felt very free to pray and praise God. Mark wanted us to pray for an "inward witness" on what to do. We decided to meet again on Saturday. We sang, prayed, and exhorted until late (1:00 A.M.). The Holy Spirit convicted one of the girls after a burden fell on the group. We prayed fervently, and then someone prophesied. The girl started crying because the prophecy spoke to her heart.

After most people left, Dick Holdin, Mark, Phil Bechtel and I went into Phil's room to pray and hear from God. Unbelief was strong. Dick saw (faintly) a white cloud come through the window, and Mark also felt it as we were praying. We determined it was unbelief, but we had a hard time getting rid of it. Phil had an awful time prophesying, as flesh (unbelief) was getting in the way. We heard the mixer go on and off all by itself in the kitchen.

Mark said the mixer thing happened all the time, but it was still a little scary to me.

We prayed for a release or freedom from emotional bondage for Dick and me. I prophesied that Dick should quit his job. After praying, we all ate. Then Dick went home, and I slept in Mark's room. There were no interruptions in my sleep, except when I was just about asleep I was impressed to pray for Val.

Saturday, September 22, 1973

I went to the meeting at Mark's. Only 12 to 15 people came. Mark was discouraged, but I wasn't, and I don't think anyone else was. Mark brought out this feeling early in the meeting and got victory over it. There was no real revelation to anyone about where or what should be started. It was evident that *something* was to be started. Someone prophesied that the reason The Lighthouse broke up was to (gently) shove a few toward greater things and to split up the anointed leaders God that had chosen for greater works. There was no binding whatsoever. We had a beautiful time in Christ.

One person prophesied that we would all have a ministry in this work (whatever was to be started), and that's why the numbers were so few.

God wanted just the serious people and leaders to be present. (Gee, me too?) More than one witness determined that a work was to be started that would greatly involve the people present. It took the faith of all present to believe that these prophecies were real and not of the flesh. In many prophecies, God stressed obedience. Obedience was very necessary for a work to be started in Spirit and not in the flesh. Mark stressed before we left that we should pray for a witness about where and what. We had in mind a coffee house.

Mark later said that he never really felt a coffee house was the right direction.

The meeting mainly consisted of praying and prophesying about obedience. Also, many (including me) learned to release themselves and let the Holy Spirit take over. We felt impressed to pray *heavily* for Terry Calldean, and also for safety and protection for Val and the Calldeans while they were in Haiti.

I prophesied that this group should not emphasize winning souls or evangelizing, but rather *learning* essential truths from God—perhaps about 90 percent learning and 10 percent (or less) evangelizing.

Sunday, September 23, 1973

What a day! I got up late, picked up Terry Calldean, and went to church at Boulder's Chapel. It was not a real great service, and I was slightly relieved when it was over. The Calldean girls went to Bechtel's church. The Spirit impressed upon Terry not to move into his dorm room at Andrews University that day, but to ask me over to his house for dinner. I accepted. We put TV dinners in the oven, walked around the yard awhile, and then came back and started eating.

Mark, Sally Calldean, Melody Bechtel, and Phil came by and were elated. Before the Calldean girls went to Brother Bechtel's church in the morning, they were impressed that the 16-acre Riverside Camp was to be our place. Mark and Phil had the *same* impression the night before. The witness was confirmed. The camp was to be put into our hands for the glory of God. All our spirits and people bore witness.

The Riverside Camp was an abandoned church camp in nearby Buchanan that was owned by the United Methodist Church. Most of the buildings remained and were still in reasonably good condition.

We all felt impressed to go over to the camp. The Spirit told us that this was the reason why Terry had invited me over to dinner (instead of moving to his dorm room), so that I would be there. We took off for the camp, but we had to stop at Mark's for something. When we were there at Mark's house, all who were at the Saturday night meeting either called or stopped by, wondering what was happening. We then went to the camp in Mark's van, rejoicing as we went.

Mark's van was jam-packed. But hey, it was the early 70s.

Among those who went were Mark Bechtel, Terry Calldean, Bill Norten, Phil Bechtel, Sally Calldean, Rusty Evans, Melody Bechtel, Penny, Dick Holdin, and Cary White. The Lord impressed on me that these people would have an active part in the development or activities of the camp, provided they remained strictly obedient to the Holy Spirit. It could all change if some were not obedient—the whole camp could "go to the dogs."

Up until now, no leader had been selected. I felt that there must be a coordinator. The Spirit appeared to be resting the heaviest upon Mark at this time.

The minute we stepped on the grounds, we felt the Spirit moving and assuring us. We went down to the vesper bowl immediately, praising and singing with absolutely *no* bondage. The vesper bowl was a cement amphitheater facing the large, winding St. Joseph River. There was a large wooden cross made from a telephone pole at the bottom by the river.

My heart had never felt so free in all my life. There was a drawing of the Spirit toward praise and singing and prayers of thanks. We prayed and laid hands on the ground and dedicated the place to God. Mark prophesied, "Thus saith the Lord, I have given this land into your hands for My glory. Be obedient and faithful, and it shall come to pass."

This occurred in early fall on a warm and beautiful day. The camp seemed to be totally abandoned, and we felt no reason why we couldn't just go walking around the place. Only a few buildings had locks on them, and many of the cabins still had mattresses on the bunks. The huge cement swimming pool was empty and had lots of leaves and sticks in it.

We went to the tabernacle, praising and singing with freedom and unity all the way. When we entered the tabernacle, we felt the glory of the Lord upon it. We also felt a burden of prayer. At different times, we spontaneously shouted and lifted our voices to God in one accord. We laid hands on the building, dedicating it for the saving of souls and for the church's edification. Some prophesied about God being well pleased and that if we were obedient, He would take us through the process one step at a time.

We then split up, walking around the upper level of the camp and talking before gathering again to pray at the top of the hill. Terry read the "love chapter" from 1 Corinthians 13, we shared what was on our hearts, and then we dispersed. Some went to picnic tables and some gathered in twos or threes nearby on the grass.

Earlier when we had come to the camp, I felt that we would meet someone outside of our group and that something was going to result from it. I saw a young boy walking on the other side of the camp on the top level. I was alone and immediately felt impressed to talk to him. At the top of my mind was a feeling that this boy would have a big part to play in acquiring the camp for God. I was impressed to tell him what we were doing here and what the Lord said He was going to do. The preaching of Jesus was in the back of my mind, but I didn't have the faith that a 12- or 13-year-old would accept Christ (truly) into his heart. That age group seemed too hard to reach—too young.

As I walked over to the boy, I noticed that Terry was right behind me. He caught up and said, "I think we ought to go over and tell that boy about Jesus."

As we approached, the boy seemed uneasy, with a meek *what do you want with me?* kind of attitude. We told him about Jesus and also about the camp God was going to give to us. Terry did the majority of talking.

We prompted the boy, "Have you been converted?"

He said he was Catholic. Then Terry explained about being born again, using the story in the Bible about Jesus talking to Nicodemus. When Terry was through, we asked if the boy wanted to have a deeper relationship with Jesus. He said, "Yeah."

So I said, "I'm getting down on my knees. You don't have to, but you can if you want."

Immediately, the boy was on his knees, with his hands folded and ready to pray. Terry and I laid hands on him and rebuked any spirit that would bind him. We thanked God for him and prayed a salvation prayer out loud so that he could pray with us. When we stopped praying, Terry asked the boy if he wanted to say something in prayer to the Lord. We then put our hands on him and thanked the Lord quietly while we waited for him to speak.

"Thank you, Father, thank you, Father," he said. The burden was lifted off Terry and me. The boy was saved! His name was Chris Stokes.

We went rejoicing in amazement down to the vesper bowl where the others had gathered. We told the group, and they rejoiced openly and loudly, giving thanks. Terry introduced the boy to everyone and then sat down and quietly instructed the boy on a few things that were going on. We walked up to the van, praising God for the newborn believer. Some felt that this was a go-ahead sign: *first day, first born.*

We gave Chris a ride home, and when he got out he said, "Be sure to come back and see me!" He seemed so wondrously saved that it astonished me. I never doubted his salvation. His faith was like a rock. I knew that he would be an instrument in getting the camp, and I told this to several people so that the Devil couldn't later say it was my imagination.

We all went home rejoicing, and then went to church. Terry and I went to Boulder's Chapel. The others were going to a Baptist church so see some of the members of the group get baptized. Terry and I really wanted to go, but we both felt a commitment to go to Boulder's Chapel.

The service that evening at our church was pretty lively. The "Group," a quartet from the church, sang a special song. When they sang, "When you go around to Babylon, don't look around for me," some people got overjoyous and walked around the church, hugging each other. Brother Al requested that verse be sung again along with some other similar verses.

The rest of the gang went to the Baptist church. Some of the group needed to be baptized, and they were hoping to be baptized that night. However, the minister wouldn't baptize them, so they all went to the Christian Center Church in South Bend, Indiana, instead.

It's probable that the minister wouldn't baptize them because he didn't know some of them, and rightfully considered the responsibility to spend some time with them before administering that ordinance. Also, some of the guys had rather long hair, which at that time was not acceptable to most Bible church ministers.

The message at the Christian Center Church was on faith and seemed to be directed towards our group. At the end of the service, the congregation all went into the prayer room to pray. When Pastor Murphy, the Christian Center's associate pastor, saw the glorious praises of our group, he was astonished. Sally Calldean, said he was dumbfounded as he watched everyone praising God.

Mark went to talk to Pastor Murphy about the camp and asked him if he would like speak to our group sometime.

Brother Murphy said, "How about Saturday?"

"All right," Mark replied. "Where?"

Brother Murphy answered, "At the tabernacle. Go by faith!"

Mark tested the spirit . . . "Yeah!" he said.

Brother Murphy said that he would advertise the meeting on the radio and perhaps even on television. The thing that was so frightening was that we had no permission to use the campgrounds. That was sort of a mountain to overcome, as the Methodist Church owned it.

The relationships between the churches in our area have changed so much since I wrote the above entry. I didn't think the Methodist Church would rent or loan us the tabernacle. I looked at them as competitors, and I figured they also looked at J.U. as a competitor. Although that spirit is still around, it isn't nearly as prevalent as it was back then. My competitive thinking was partly due to my own sinful nature and also due to the lack of good teaching from church leaders.

I think today the average pastor still deals with the fear of losing members, because when they leave his church, they take their financial and ministry resources with them. But the attitude that is growing among evangelical pastors today emphasizes concern for the welfare of the individual members, and de-emphasizes where they go to church.

Monday, September 24, 1973

This day was the start of miraculous happenings. There was not much excitement all day at work in the factory. I eased off my spiritual high and wasn't quite as burdened with the camp.

I got home from work, and at 4:00 P.M., Rusty Evans, Bill Norten and Mark came over in the van. Mark said they had the name of a man who was a camp coordinator for Riverside. Mark was flabbergasted, because he knew the man from way back. They were to go over there about 6:00 P.M. I felt an impression that I should stay home. Although I wanted to go with them, I had some wedding things to do. I told them I didn't know if I should go and asked if we could all pray for direction. We prayed, but I still felt that I should stay. However, all the others felt I should go. So I went.

On the way, we praised God and really prayed everything would work out. One time, we all spontaneously started praying out loud together in other languages. By the time we got to the camp coordinator's house, we knew that he *would* be home and that we *would* have the victory. The man recognized Mark, but he didn't know what he could do to help us. He said that he really had no say in the matter—it was up to the caretaker, who lived at the camp. He didn't give us any indication as to whether we could use it or not.

So we decided to go to the camp. All four of our spirits bore witness. We sang and praised God all the way. When we were almost at the camp, we spontaneously broke out in other languages and prayer that ended in victorious faith. When we pulled into the driveway, Rusty praised God. He wanted a witness as to whether we would have the camp. He prayed, "If he is home, we know that God is with us and for us."

When we drove past Chris Stokes' house, he saw us and ran inside as if he were going to ask permission to see us. As Rusty and I got out of the car, we immediately felt impressed to go across the street to his house. But when we I got to the door, we both got cold feet and felt uneasy. We were two seconds away from walking back to the street. Immediately, we felt impressed to pray whether we should be there or not.

At the end of the prayer, Chris came out slowly, with his mother right behind him. We were worried, because we didn't know what kind of people they were. We didn't know how they would react to a group preaching salvation to their son, getting him saved, and filling him with "nonsense" such as God promising to give the camp to some young kids.

The woman, Mrs. Stokes, came out with a pleasant looking attitude, although somewhat strained and concerned looking. "Hello," she said.

We said "Hi" and also felt very strained. It was a "what do we say now?" feeling. We told Mrs. Stokes our names and that we had met Chris over at the camp the previous afternoon. We told her that we were Christians and that God had given us assurance that He was going to put the camp into our hands for His glory.

She asked us if we were Pentecostal. Immediately, I felt like we were being put on trial. I wondered if she was thinking that we were some of those "holy rollers." So I backed off slightly.

"We are nondenominational," I answered.

"Are you charismatic?" she then asked.

We backed off again. "We go to some charismatic meetings," I said. I felt slightly convicted for not being more definite with our answers. But I reasoned that we didn't want to scare her with the deepness of the gifts.

Then something completely opposite to what we expected happened. The woman said that she and her husband went to charismatic meetings in South Bend. Praise the Lord! What a relief! But then I felt sort of bad that I had beat around the bush and not stood up fully for what we stood for. I still wonder what we should have said. She told us that she was a born again, Spirit-filled Christian. Our spirits bore witness, and we were overjoyed.

She invited us inside. Later, when Mark came and joined us, he told us that he had received permission to use the place! Mark said the caretaker was *very* apprehensive about the whole thing and that we just *barely* made the deal. The woman was very surprised, because she knew the caretaker and said that he was very touchy on these things. He almost never consented.

Then she filled us in on a glorious account of that Monday morning. She said that on Sunday, they had not seen Chris that afternoon or night, because they had been in Kalamazoo. When she spoke with Chris on Monday morning, he told her of his experience and all about the young people, the singing, and how God had given them the land. She told Chris that the city was going to buy the camp. Chris said, "No, they aren't" and insisted God had given the land into the hands of the young people. When she heard Chris talking like that, she felt something was happening and was concerned about him riding home in a car with strangers. But there was also a feeling inside that told her that this might be the result of true born again Christians praying with her son.

She had felt impressed that morning to call the caretaker and ask about us. When she talked to the caretaker, he said that he wasn't at the camp on Monday, and he became quite concerned about the whole situation. Then Mrs. Stokes felt impressed to say, "You ought to give these young people a little more credit."

At that point, we could see God's hand in the picture:

1. We had felt impressed to go to the camp;
2. We had dedicated the camp to God;
3. Chris had become saved;
4. He had told his Christian mother about us;

5. The mother had then called the caretaker and softened him up; and finally,

6. We received the caretaker's permission to use the camp.

We shared a few other things with Chris' mother, and our spirits really bore witness that she was a child of God. We then went back to Mark's, shouting the glory of God and praising His name.

Isn't it exciting to see a plan come together with God's help? When Brother Murphy encouraged Mark to go by faith and start planning a meeting at the camp for the upcoming Saturday, we had no idea how God would work out the permission problem. However, this was not a problem for God.

This is not to say that we didn't have some surprises coming. When we called Brother Murphy to tell him that the plan had come together, we found out that he had been called away for the weekend and couldn't make it. Not to be discouraged, we immediately decided to host an evangelistic meeting in the Tabernacle at the camp. We had no experience in these types of things, so we had our work cut out for us. We decided to call the meeting a "Jesus Rally."

CHAPTER 6

MIRACLES CONTINUE

SALVATION AND
ANGEL SIGHTINGS

Monday, September 24, 1973 (continued)

When we got to Mark's at 7:00 P.M., we called up the gang to have a meeting. There was great unity, and I was praising God.

Then Sally Calldean came and reported, "When I was leaving the house, I looked up and saw Terry working on the roof. Slowly, *an angel appeared just behind Terry.* I was astonished and said in a low, calm voice, 'Terry, there's an angel behind you!'"

Terry replied nonchalantly, "Praise God! I don't have to see to believe."

Earlier in the day, Terry had heard someone call his name while he was on the roof. He answered, "Yes Lord, your servant hears You."

When I heard this story, a spirit of depression, jealousy and covetousness immediately came over me. It took away all the praise from my heart. I thought, *What's the matter with me? Am I out of God's will? I would have been so grateful to see an angel. Why couldn't I see one? I'm not doing anything for God. Am I saved? Am I going to be in on this thing? I'm just not good enough. I'm missing out. I'm all messed up.*

While the rest of the group praised God from their hearts, these feelings plagued me for more than an hour and a half. Then I decided to let the people pray for me. I must have had enough discernment or faith at the time to realize that something wasn't right. I look back and cannot see that I had any more faith than usual, except that I knew that two hours before I had been praising God, and then I had heard the angel story, lost my joy, and become depressed. I decided this feeling could not be from God. I was sure it was from the Devil.

I told everyone that a spirit of depression was upon me and that I wanted hands laid on me to cast the Devil out. I didn't tell them why the spirit was there, although I did tell Dick Holdin later about my jealousy and oppression because of Sally Calldean's and Terry's experience.

When they prayed over me, I really didn't feel anything. I could hear them all praying, and I was praying too. I don't remember just what I prayed exactly. It was just the usual prayers such as, "I command you, depression, to leave in Jesus' name." The praying lasted about 20 seconds, after which I said, "It's done. Thank you, Lord," even though I didn't notice any change. I really didn't expect any. I got back up and sat in my chair, forcing a smile, worried that I might not look delivered. I *did* notice that I had a feeling that *something's missing.* But then, after a minute had passed, the realization suddenly hit me: I had been delivered! I couldn't even remember what the feeling of depression felt like.

I immediately told the group with great joy. Some must not have expected anything either, because when they saw how happy I was, they all shouted and glorified God and praised and sang. I had never felt so free to praise God in all my life. *I can't express the joy that was bubbling over in me.* I felt like a new man. I had never been in a prayer meeting that was as joyous as that night when I was delivered. Later, several times during the night, I felt a little hint of the depression coming back. But it was *very* small, and it went away promptly when I rebuked it in Jesus' name. What a joyous time!

That night someone had prophesied that by spring, the camp would be ours.

Tuesday, September 25, 1973

During the day, I prayed for Val's receptiveness to all the things that were happening. [She was still in Haiti on the missionary trip.] I also prayed for the whole situation with the camp, and that I might do what the Lord would have me to do.

At around 6:35 P.M., I arrived late for the prayer meeting at Mark's house. I felt slightly bound after walking in. Mark was not there, because he had to be at work. I met a new brother who had come with the editor of the *Jesus Paper* (a local monthly publication). People got extremely bound up, especially when we tried to play and sing. Melody Bechtel and Penny then went to pick up Penny's cousin, a girl about their own age.

We tried to bring the awkwardness we were feeling out in the open, talk about it a little, and pray, but it was all to no avail. While praying, Dick Holdin, Cary White, and another brother came in. Now present at the meeting were Dick Holdin, Melody Bechtel, Terry Calldean, his sister Sally, another one of his sisters, the brother who wrote for the *Jesus Paper*, the new brother, Phil Bechtel, Bill Norten, Rusty, Jeff Bechtel, a girl and her baby, one other brother, and me. The praise was bound. The singing was bound. Sometimes, we would break through, but only for a minute. I spoke a prophecy about letting others bind us, about cliques, and about accepting the new brothers. We were relieved for a while.

Then Melody and Penny came back with Penny's cousin. She seemed very out of place. We still felt bondage—there just seemed to be a lack of attention. Penny's cousin left 30 minutes after she arrived there, and Penny took her home. We again prayed, and Terry spoke about love. Then, remarkably, Penny called to tell us that she and Melody had just led her cousin to the Lord, and she had become saved! We thanked God, and the binding soon eased up. When the *Jesus Paper* editor and the new brother left, the binding eased up more. We prayed for one of my coworkers at Dayco. I felt impressed to go home and write.

I distinctly remember feeling God say to me, *Go home and begin writing a journal, because someday you will write a book about this experience.* I had written a little bit the day before, but at that time I didn't feel a real calling. It was just a personal desire to document what had happened. This particular night, however, I sensed a strong calling to not only document what happened, but also to eventually publish and share these experiences with others.

As I was leaving, Penny and her cousin came back in. The binding was almost gone, and we praised God. Terry felt impressed to lay hands on me for my writing. I wanted to stay and hear about Penny's cousin, but the Spirit said no. I prophesied that God would greatly encourage the group for the remainder of the night.

Dick wanted a ride home, so he left with me. He told me of the depression he had been experiencing the prior two days. He thought that the Devil was working hard because great things were about to happen. We went outside the house and prayed. We cast out all binding at the Bechtel's house. I dropped Dick off at his house, and then went home.

After Dick and I left, Mark came home from work and joined the prayer meeting. I heard that they had a great time in the Lord. Rusty took Sally Calldean home at around 11:30 P.M. and was on his way to work when the Spirit said to him, *Don't go to work. Go to the tabernacle. Don't go now by yourself, but go to the Bechtel's first. And don't drive yourself—have someone drive you.* Then the Spirit impressed on Rusty that demons were infiltrating the camp and that God wanted them cast out. At the Bechtel's, everyone felt impressed to go. They prayed and cast out the Devils. They left the house, picked up the Calldeans, and then went to the tabernacle.

The group prayed and praised God at the camp until 5:00 A.M. At around 3:30 A.M., some of the group began seeing angels. One person said, "I'll bet the angels are rejoicing with us."

After that, Mark thought he saw an angel, but he passed it off as just his imagination. Then he thought he saw its wings unfolding and spreading out. He still doubted what he was seeing. Finally, a girl next to him said, "I see an angel with its wings spreading out." Mark was flabbergasted.

Most of the people who went to the tabernacle that night saw at least one angel. Those who said they saw angels included Sally Calldean (25 angels), Mark (several), Penny (one) and Rusty (one). They all went home rejoicing in the early morning hours.

Wednesday, September 26, 1973

I went to work feeling as if I was losing the burden for the ministry at J.U. I then thought, *I am a part of the work started, yet I haven't asked the Lord to tell me what to do.* So I asked God to indicate to me what I should be doing.

I felt that He said, *Put ads in the newspapers for the upcoming Jesus rally at the camp.*

I wanted to know what I should put in—something that was good and catchy and wouldn't sound stupid. He said, *If you put any Scripture or words on paper that lifts up My name, no matter how it sounds or how many technical mistakes there are, that paper shall not go out void if you pray. My Word bears witness with that.*

Then God gave me the Scripture, *Come unto me, all ye that labour and are heavy laden, and I will give you rest* (Matthew. 11:28). I thought that there should be more, so I added, *I am come that they might have life, and that they might have it more abundantly* (John 10:10). I wasn't sure about the second verse, but the first one was definite. I decided to put the ad in two newspapers. I prayed and asked God how big the ad should be.

God said, *place a 2"x 2" ad and a 4"x 4" ad. Put the smaller one in the* South Bend Tribune *and the bigger one in the* Niles Daily Star.

I spent my workday trying to arrange the ad in my mind. I came home from work, planning to catch up on my writing. I went to pick up Terry Calldean. He wasn't home, but I heard about the Tuesday night/Wednesday morning angel experiences.

Immediately, depression came over me again. I thought, *All those people saw angels. I wasn't impressed to go. Does this mean that I'm not involved or led? Why wasn't I impressed to go? What is the matter with me? I must be doing something wrong so that God can't use me. I'm not doing anything for this work.*

On the way to church, I was so depressed that I started to cry. I really began to think that there was something seriously wrong with me. After all, I reasoned, I'm never around when the miracles start happening. If I were in on the deal, I would see miracles as well. The depression became so great that I could not cast it off. I didn't know whether it was the Devil or if something was seriously wrong with me.

I went to Boulder's Chapel so burdened down that I could barely sing during choir practice. I really had to strain to do it. Once during a song, tears filled my eyes and I felt the urge to go to the altar. I was close to bursting out crying, but I fought back the tears, because I didn't want to show my feelings. (What? Start crying in public?) After a few minutes, the teary feeling went away. I wondered whether the Lord wanted me to speak, and I began to worry. During the rest of practice, I tried to get the teary feeling back. It never came, although I felt burdened with what I was to speak or do.

I went back to my seat after practice with a heavy heart. At 8 P.M., I felt impressed to ask for prayer for the rally. After the prayer, Terry Calldean walked in and sat down beside me, and then told the group that he had to speak. I could really feel the Spirit when he began to talk. He spoke about the rally Saturday night and about the angel experience the night before. He mentioned tongues. As Terry spoke, Brother Al was very stern looking—maybe even a bit sick looking.

Then Terry asked for hands to be laid on him for college and for doing God's will. I didn't want to lay hands on Terry, but I felt the Lord wanted me to do so.

After Terry sat down, a few people who appeared to be against what Terry had said stood up and indirectly testified against him (among them were Brother Al and one of the prominent women). Then Penny's aunt got up and said that we should pray for the rally and not condemn it. She told about her daughter getting saved at the Tuesday night prayer meeting.

About five people wanted hands laid on them for healing. The Lord told me to be obedient and lay hands on them. I didn't have faith, but I felt the Lord said that if I were obedient and laid my hands on them, He would supply the faith. After the prayer, no one appeared to be healed. However, I noticed that after we laid hands on the second person, Val's younger sister had gone to the altar crying. She had become saved! She later said that Penny's Aunt's testimony about her daughter getting saved was the prompting message.

I remember going back to my seat after laying hands on people and feeling very embarrassed that no one seemed to be healed. I screamed out in my mind, *I'll never do that again!* I had gone up and laid hands on those people because I felt that God said to me that if I was obedient, He would heal them instantly. When that didn't happen, I was shamed and frustrated. But then I felt God say to me, *If I ask you to do something like that again, you will know it is I as if I spoke to you in a literal voice.*

Several times over the years, when I have felt an inward push to do something that was not accompanied by a clear belief that God was going to move, I remembered this past experience and decided that I wouldn't step out and act on that compulsion. I am still waiting for clear direction. I believe someday I will hear clearly from God, act accordingly, and see the mighty hand of God's deliverance toward people who are afflicted with diseases and lameness.

When we sat down, there were a few testimonies. I suddenly felt impressed to say, "The two in the wheelchair will rise up and walk. God has shown me this through the gift of prophecy. We can't imagine the things God can do."

There were two regular attendees at Boulder's Chapel who were confined to wheelchairs. One was a grown married woman and the other was a 10-year-old girl.

One of the older brothers then stood up and testified, "We need to follow through with the things that God has shown us. We should be Christian enough to pray with people in wheelchairs and get victory after we have preached to them. Yet the young brothers are overly enthusiastic and should be careful to be in the Spirit when they testify.

After the service, I went to Terry's house for a bite to eat. At 10:30 P.M., I was supposed to take him to his dorm room at Andrews University, but I knew that I should be getting the ad ready. Earlier in the evening, I felt impressed to see a friend of mine who was an ad salesman to get the ad set up. But I figured that Terry needed a ride, and that this was a good thing to do. I reasoned that the ad could wait. I'd get it done the next day after work.

As I was eating, I felt uneasy. I felt that I should go over to the ad salesman's house right away, so I told Terry as much. He said that he understood. As I was getting into the car, the phone rang, and it was for me. People at Bechtel's had felt impressed to place a big ad, and they said they had a lot of money for it. I replied that the Lord had shown me what size and what to put in, but that I might need their financial backing. So I went to the ad salesman's house. He was just getting ready for bed, but we got the ad all set up.

Then I felt impressed to go to the camp, even though it was past midnight. When I arrived I felt the Lord say to me that He would instruct me on salvation. Earlier in the day, I had realized the reason why I had so much trouble preaching salvation to others and closing the deals (praying with them to receive Christ as their Savior):

I didn't know the correct path or way of salvation. *I knew that I was a born-again believer and baptized in the Holy Spirit, but I could not explain the plan of salvation.*

I was scared as I walked all the way down the hill toward the vesper bowl. Sometimes, the fear was so great that it felt as if there was a great weight on my chest and it would collapse. I could hardly breathe. I'm still not sure what to think about the whole experience. I stayed at the vesper bowl and prayed until 3:00 A.M.

While in prayer, a voice said, *Sin is doing anything you know without a doubt is sin. To be saved, a person must stop doing all things he knows to be wrong and be willing to follow Jesus. He must be willing to repent of things that are brought up before him by God.* The Word says, *Repent. . . . believe on the Lord Jesus Christ, and thou shalt be saved* (Acts 2:38; 16:31). *All things are lawful* (1 Corinthians. 10:23). *He that doubts is damned if he eat* (Romans 14:23). *I will chastise you for doing things that are not beneficial for you.*"

While praying and seeking God for understanding about salvation, I was struggling to reconcile some of my legalistic ideas with what the Holy Spirit was trying to get through to me by His gentle leading and speaking.

Friday, September 28, 1973

I went to work as usual at 7:00 A.M., not so tired (although I should have been tired) and not so high spiritually. I did light work on a machine. As I worked, I prayed and praised God all day. I still didn't feel that I understood salvation, so I prayed that the Lord would instruct me before the Saturday night rally, as there would probably be people to counsel. I went home spiritually high, putting most of the burden on the Lord.

The last two hours at work I had butterflies so bad because I thought Val might surprise me with a phone call. Every time the phone rang, I ran to it, hoping that it was she. I began writing at 3:30 P.M. that afternoon. Val called at 6:30. I was so glad to hear from her, because I was concerned.

At about 11:15 P.M., I went back to writing, but I quickly tired and fell asleep. At 11:35, my head jerked up as if something had grabbed me by the hair. *What is it?* I wondered.

The words came clearly to my mind: *Go to the tabernacle.*

I said, "I went there Wednesday and nobody was there."

A voice said to me, *Many will be there. Now go!*

I replied, "Before I go running around again at night, I'm going to make sure."

I called Mark and the Calldeans. No one answered, so I got dressed and headed over to the tabernacle, praying in tongues all the way.

When I arrived, I was relieved to see people there. We got in a circle and praised God. I prophesied that Mark would enter the ministry of an apostle, Sally Calldean—prophet, Phil—teacher, me—miracles, Dick Holdin—healing. Also, I prophesied that the Lord would instruct us that night.

We prayed for Mark, and then we went down to the vesper bowl. It rained on us after we prayed that it would not, but the rain stopped shortly afterward. Then we went back to the tabernacle for one hour of prayer and praising God. I was waiting for instruction. I thought everybody else was too, but they all decided to go home about 1:30 or 2:00 A.M. I stayed in the tabernacle and waited for an angel or Jesus or to be instructed by the Word.

I couldn't stay awake, and I couldn't keep my mind on the Word. I wasn't afraid at all, but I did not want to go outside. It rained all night. The Lord released me about 7:00 A.M.

I said, "Lord, I wasn't instructed."

He said, *Thou hast been instructed, whether thou knowest it or not.*

I went home baffled and went straight to bed.

Notice in the above journal entry that I was hearing God speak to me in the older style of English used in the *King James Version* of the Bible. There was a time when God spoke to me that way. I also used to prophesy in this type of English. It is a tradition that I have grown out of, and now I chuckle when I hear it used. I shudder when people try to convince me that it is the *only* way to prophesy or pray.

So, does God really speak in this older form of English? Yes, and He also speaks in "new English" and any other language that one traditionally feels God would use. It makes no difference to God. I think God looks at our amoral traditions with enjoyment, as long as we don't impose our traditions on others as His commandments. He speaks to our hearts, and we do our best to relate to others what we think we hear.

Think of it as water coming through a hose. When we drink water from a hose, it usually has a "hose taste." When we hear God speak to us, and as we try to relate to others what we think He is saying, we often add our own flavor to it, like the water coming out of a hose. I *will* say that the less hose taste, the better.

Saturday, September 29, 1973

I got up about 2:00 P.M. and started writing. I worried all day that I didn't understand salvation, so I prayed that the Lord would instruct me. At one point, I felt impressed to find my Bible and read it. When I walked into a room and saw my Bible opened up, I said, "Lord, show me something right now in the Word." I felt that there was something on the opened page that was for me. I believed it by faith.

As I studied the page, my eyes were drawn to certain Scriptures at once. They were: Jesus said, *Come unto me, all ye that labour and are heavy laden, and I will give you rest. Take my yoke upon you, and learn of me; for I am meek and lowly in heart: and ye shall find rest unto your souls. For my yoke is easy, and my burden is light* (Matthew 11:28–30).

Nothing else on the page leaped out at me or was special to me. I went back to writing.

Shortly after, a Scripture in 1 John about sinning came to me. Another passage, Romans Chapter 14, came to me about what sin is. Also, I was directed to Isaiah 55, which I had never read in my life. I don't even remember how I came into contact with that chapter. As I wrote down these Scriptures and my thoughts, I began to understand salvation (basically), although I still had some questions.

I left for the tabernacle at about 5:00 P.M. As I went through downtown Buchanan, the Lord told me to stop and pass out a few fliers about the rally. I felt that I had to be obedient and pass them out if the Lord was to bless us. When the fliers were gone, I went to the rally.

There were very few people at the tabernacle at 6:00 P.M. It was raining, and things looked pretty grim. I felt the Lord had allowed this to test our faith. People started rolling in about 6:45. When about 50 people were there, we started with singing and sharing testimonies. I felt extremely free to clap, praise God, and say a prayer of blessing.

Around 7:50 P.M., I felt that I should speak. I realized that there were many unbelievers attending the meeting. I felt that a salvation message was in order. My breathing became heavy and my heart started pounding. I wondered what I would speak about. In fact, I was still not sure that the Lord wanted me to speak. Then the Scriptures came: The third chapter of John, about Nicodemus and being born again; and Isaiah 55, about forsaking the ways of the wicked.

I said, "Lord, I have never gotten up in front of a group."

He said, *Step out and believe.*

I had always been so afraid to get up in front of people and talk. But when I was sure the Lord wanted me to speak, I started to get a strange sensation. A group was singing, and then Cary White gave a testimony. It lasted about 15 minutes. All this time, the sensation I was feeling grew stronger. I felt *hyper*, as if I were being filled up with fire. The sides of my hands tingled, sort of like they were falling asleep, but not really numb. It wasn't an unpleasant physical feeling, although I did get a bit scared when the tips of my nose, ears and mouth started getting tingly as well as my arms.

I rebuked the physical sensation, hoping that the Holy Spirit's anointing wouldn't leave with it. The tingly feeling left my face and half of my arms, which was enough for the fear to subside. When Cary White was through talking, I walked up front and went behind the pulpit to deliver my message.

I must give God the glory. Every one of the words came clearly. I had never felt so unafraid to get up in front of a group in my life. I had always had trouble with losing my train of thought while speaking, but this time I didn't even have to think or set one up. The phrases and words came by the verse of Scripture. I never got ahead of myself or behind.

When I gave an altar call, two girls came up. I sat down feeling great. Mark and Terry Calldean also gave talks as the altar call proceeded. Three more people asked for salvation. After that, we praised God for a while. Next, the singing group came up and sang. After that, we all just sat around talking and praying.

I left shortly afterward and went to meet Val, who had just returned from Haiti. I had missed her so much. Val and I had a good reunion and talked until 2:00 A.M. We were not divided over anything that happened in my life or in hers. Praise God!

CHAPTER 7

STORYBOOK
WONDERFUL
VAL AND I GET MARRIED

*V*al and I were going to be married soon and we frantically searched for a place to live. We had no living essentials (silverware, appliances, linens, furniture) and had many things to do to set up our household. I had hoped to buy a house, but nothing seemed to be right for us. I remember crying out to God about it and getting the impression that He wanted us to rent. I really did not want to rent and resisted all leading in that direction.

I finally submitted, and on October 1, one month before we were married, we heard about an opportunity to house-sit for Mrs. Larson, an elderly lady who went to my parent's Episcopal Church. She was going to California to be with her son for several months. We would live in the house rent free (paying only utilities) in exchange for watching over it.

Tuesday, October 2, 1973

Val and I went to see Mrs. Larson. The house was much brighter and better looking than what I had remembered. I realized that watching it would be a great responsibility. I told Mrs. Larson we'd pray about it.

Later in the evening, Val and I talked to an older Christian couple, who told us about the experience they had with Riverside Camp. The husband said he had "lost his mind." This set me back, and I decided to relax for a while and not get so involved. Earlier in the week, I had been thinking about spiritual things, and it seemed that I was starting to lose touch with reality. Not a lot, but enough that it scared me. When this couple told me of their experience, I decided to relax and just watch.

The couple had become involved in the Riverside camp ministry many years prior to its closing, and for some unknown reason the husband had "lost his mind." The couple didn't elaborate on the details of their bad experience, but their testimony sobered me up a bit. These wonderful people lived a long and fruitful life, ministering and contributing to many Christian ministries. They never again experienced a problem after leaving the camp. I decided to be more careful in my movement in and around the spiritual gifts and to be aware of possible excesses.

Thursday, October 11, 1973

I just got back from the prayer meeting at Mark's. The Lord told me to get back to writing, telling me, *If you're too busy to write, you're too busy.* I confessed that I hadn't been keeping up and told the Lord I would be faithful.

I was slightly bound at the beginning of the prayer meeting, but by the end I felt completely free. I sensed that the binding was my chastisement for not keeping up with my writing. After I confessed my unfaithfulness, I was blessed.

At the prayer meeting, I thought I was supposed to say that God chose Mark to start a work in or around Niles and that he would be (or should be) the chief coordinator. Was that the Lord's leading? I didn't say anything about that. I did talk privately to Mark about it later.

Wednesday, October 17, 1973

Val and I went to Mrs. Larson's at 6:00 P.M. She will be leaving for California tomorrow.

The prayer meeting at Boulder's Chapel tonight wasn't that good for me. I had a tough time staying awake during prayer. There were testimonies and choruses. I don't know how long I can stay at Boulder's Chapel with no edification there for me. I find myself looking at the people's faults. One thing is for certain: we could have a great revival if we all would let go and love one another.

Thursday, October 18, 1973

I went to the J.U. prayer meeting at Mark's house. There were many people there, mostly strong Christians. The message of the night was that we need to get a bit more organized and also that the Lord would reveal the part of the body where each person should be. I was slightly bound or spiritually down at first, then I grew free, especially while laying hands on people.

Friday, October 19, 1973

After work, Dad and I went to look at a farmhouse that was for sale, but we couldn't find it. I went to Val's after that around 6:30 P.M. I felt a little nervous, jumpy, and restless. I couldn't relax. Although Val and I are moving our things into Mrs. Larson's house where we will live after our wedding, we will still need to find a place to live when Mrs. Larson returns from her stay in California. Should we rent or buy? Some thoughts:

Regarding the farmhouse, I think the Lord is trying to teach me about His leading of the Spirit. When Val and I were looking for a place to live, the four or five houses that we were serious about buying caused me much strife when I began trying to work out the details. I sensed that the Lord wanted us to rent, but I didn't want to, and neither did Val. I felt uneasy whenever anyone would mention renting. But when we were serious about a house, I prayed, "Lord, if You want us to get it, make it possible. If You don't want us to get it, let it go out from under us." All the houses have gone right out from under us.

As our wedding day drew close, I prayed, "Lord, You know we need something to live in. Please supply something!" I was getting worried. We had so many things to get to set up our household, but no place to put them. We had nothing but a refrigerator, rugs and two beat-up end tables. My brother gave us a good start, but we still needed much more.

Then when Val and I yielded to renting instead of buying, the opportunity at Mrs. Larson's opened up. There, we would have everything we needed for four months.

So the Lord provided for us a month before our wedding. We would have a three-bedroom home, furniture, television, cooking and eating utensils and everything else needed for a very comfortable household.

Friday, October 19, 1973 (continued)

The farmhouse that Dad wants to show me is giving me strife already. I have faith that if God doesn't want me to have it, it won't work out. I wonder about the Bible verse, *Seek ye first the kingdom of God . . . and all these things shall be added unto you* (Matthew. 6:33). Does that mean I don't have to look for a house, but that God will supply these needful things easily and without strife, just as He supplied Mrs. Larson's house to us? I believe the verse means that the answers to my needs will come to me rather than me going looking for them. Of course, the majority of Christians would say that I have to do my part, but I think all I need to do is relax, seek the Kingdom, be open to the Spirit where He leads, and let God supply.

I have decided to let God prove Himself on this truth. I don't know whether I'm wrong or not. I want God to be glorified in this. I'm not going to seek a house. I'm going to let God bring it to me and dedicate my time to serving Him. If I'm wrong, it will cost me an expensive apartment when Mrs. Larson gets back. If I'm right, God will be glorified and my belief on this critical subject will be strengthened. I feel a need for some land, but I don't know if that is the Spirit or flesh. I just want a small house that is easy to take care of and inexpensive, for which I will praise God!

There are three or four things I must do on Saturday that are scheduled at the same time. I am supposed to go to revivals, visit my brother, witness with Mark and the others at the Niles Apple Festival booth, and attend Val's family reunion. I wish I could learn to understand the Spirit's voice. I feel as if I would be sinning unless I did them *all*, and of course, that's impossible. I know that souls are in need and that the booth probably needs help, and I want to be there. I have always had trouble witnessing, and so I feel the need to step out in faith. The world needs Christ!

Why, Lord, must I be in this bondage? I want to be a witness for you! I want to be quick to say to others, "Jesus loves you." Why can't I do this? Please Lord, release me from this bondage. Why am I afraid to carry a Bible into the shop? I do not want to be afraid. Please help me, Lord.

I believe the Spirit is leading me to go to Boulder's Chapel Church and to be faithful in writing and in reading the Word. I cannot understand this, but I do it. I cannot be edified at Boulder's Chapel with the lack of love and the division that exists there. When Mark and the J.U. guys tell me how God is teaching them about hitting the streets and witnessing and that people are getting saved, it makes me feel bad that I'm not on the team or doing anything for God.

God knows I'd give Mark and the gang a cup of cold water and wouldn't be a bit convicted for doing only that little bit if that was what He wanted me to do. But I crave the smile of my Savior! When Mark talks about the world going to hell and how few people do anything about it, I hurt inside that I'm not with them and helping out. Oh, my God, if this is just a learning period for me, help me to realize this. Take away the hurt.

The Lord says to me now: *We all are parts of the body of Christ. Some sow, some reap, and some give drinks of water to the prophets. All receive the same reward, as long as they all do the Lord's perfect will.*

I went to a revival service at Boulder's Chapel. I really didn't learn anything that I didn't already know. But it was refreshing to see a Church of God preacher who is humble enough to bring out the fact that they are lacking. He is still dwelling on the "Church of God" message, which I feel is the major problem. They have left their first love. They preach so much about the Church, Church, Church of God instead of Church of God, God, God.

My whole problem of bondage is the fact that I do not understand *grace and the love of God.* I know Christ is the answer, but my salvation has been burdensome. It's been a lot of "do this" and "do that." But I *know* I'm on the right track. Praise the Lord!

Their "Church of God message" was originally a doctrine by D.S. Warner, that basically said that we should not cut off fellowship from believers of other denominations, but should "reach out in fellowship towards all blood-washed believers." This group of Church of Gods eventually separated themselves from all denominations, and formed independent, individual churches. The message morphed to say that all church denominations were a part of Babylon, and that church membership was a sin. They actually became what D.S. Warner preached against, and although they didn't have ties to a formal corporation, they certainly became a spiritual denomination. As they often said: "If you go 'round to Babylon, don't look around for me . . ."

Sunday, October 21, 1973

I went to church at Boulder's Chapel. The service consisted mostly of singing and testimonies. I felt miserable through most of the service. I just can't rejoice in that church because the majority of people seem to get their joy out of the fact that they're in the Church of God.

The Church of God is in need of repentance. There is an excess of pride and a lack of love. The people rejoice because they belong to the church, not because they belong to God. I firmly agree on the church's basic doctrine, but the mistake is to let pride come in and then dwell on that subject too much.

I feel God is dealing with all of these Church of God affiliates through the last days charismatic push and move of the Spirit. Their preachers sense a falling away of their own churches, but they are not able to help them. There is too much hypocrisy. God must move in an unusual way. Praise God, He will!

Monday, October 22, 1973

I got up around 9:00 A.M. and studied the Word. I was (and am) distressed about the situation at Boulder's Chapel. I want to get grounded in some things, although I don't know just what to study. I have studied a little on elders, but I'm not through. I must know whether or not I should go against the pastor of any church. Remember Saul and David and "the Lord's anointed"? *Who can stretch forth his hand against the LORD's anointed, and be guiltless?* (1 Samuel 26:9).

I stopped studying at about 10:30, feeling discouraged that I hadn't been shown anything. However, looking back, I now realize that I was being shown truth, mainly from this Scripture: *The elders which are among you I exhort. . . . Feed the flock of God which is among you, taking the oversight thereof, not by constraint, but willingly; not for filthy lucre [money], but of a ready mind; Neither as being lords over God's heritage, but being examples to the flock"* (1 Peter 5:1–3).

Friday, November 2, 1973

I went to our rehearsal dinner. I felt OK spiritually, but I didn't have much time to read the Word. Before going to bed, I prayed for a Scripture to ease my nervousness. I was very uncomfortable and had butterflies in my stomach. It took half an hour to find a comforting verse: Psalm 55:22, which says, *Cast thy burden upon the LORD, and he shall sustain thee.* Then I went to sleep.

Saturday, November 3, 1973

I woke up at 7:00 A.M. I was sort of nervous. I spent some time reading the Word and then had breakfast with Mom, Dad, and Grandma.
After that, I packed and cleaned the car until it was time to get ready
for the wedding. By keeping busy, I was able to not get nervous even
up to the time of the wedding, mostly because of the Scripture I read
last night in Psalms.

The wedding went as perfectly as could be expected. After the reception, we went to Val's for a change of clothes. We couldn't find the
car keys. After we changed clothes and prayed, we found the keys in
the glove compartment. Then we went to my house to get some shoes,
and then off on our honeymoon!

I was sort of upset when I found out that someone had hidden our
car keys. But then I felt bad about being angry when we prayed and
found them. I give God the glory and thanks for all joy. I had trouble
keeping my mind on God, but still I prayed a lot.

Really! I had just gotten married! I think God understood. God
said in Ecclesiastes, *To every thing there is a season, and time to every
purpose under the heaven . . . a time to embrace, and a time to refrain
from embracing* (3:1, 5). This was God speaking in his Word! Lighten
up! God also said in the book of Deuteronomy, *When a man has taken
a new wife, he shall not go out to war, neither shall he be charged with any
business: but he shall be free at home one year, and shall cheer up his wife
which he has taken* (24:5).

Val and I had a wonderful wedding. I have been to a lot of weddings
in the past thirty years, and I still think that our wedding was the nicest
one I have ever attended. The church was packed. They had to put up
extra chairs along the aisles. Pastor Al Fletcher still tops my chart for
the best minister at weddings. His message was excellent. Everything
went great and in my opinion—storybook wonderful. Thank you Val,
moms and dads, and everyone else who blessed us!

Mrs. Larson's house, the home God provided for
Val and me just a few weeks before getting married.

Val and I joyously exit the church after our
"storybook wonderful" wedding.

Val and her family had decorated the fellowship hall for the reception in fall colors and decor. There were *so* many gifts from people who loved us that we had more than fifty left to open when we had to quit. It was getting late and it was time to go! I had to take Val by the hand and lead her out. "Come on, Val!" I said. "You don't have to help pick up and do the dishes!"

We made several different stops and visits on our honeymoon, and we had a *great* time in the Smoky Mountains! And, yes, there are more journal entries on the subject, but they are censored. After a week, we had to come home to real life and get back to work.

CHAPTER 8

SOULS SAVED, DEMONS DEFEATED
GROWING PAINS

Thursday, November 15, 1973

I see a change in the meetings. They are getting more formal and structured: singing, prayer, testimonies, and then the lesson. It is good to do all these things, but I have a suggestion: Instead of Mark planning to do things as 1, 2, and 3, why not plan to do them in whatever order seems right at that time? We would still get the same things accomplished without the form or formality. It is evident that with the growing number of people, opinions, and doctrines, a greater amount of order and leadership is now required. Mark feels that more structure is the way to handle it. I agree, but I feel that we could *plan to get the same things done* and be less formal by not sticking to any set order of events.

Now, people are not feeling free to give a testimony, sing, pray, or give the lesson at a time when it is "not generally" done at that time. If the prayer group switched to this system, Mark would have to get the group back on track if he felt it was getting out of the Spirit.

Wednesday, November 28, 1973

At Boulder's Chapel, Al looked and acted as if he was down. But he tried so hard to get everybody up. I could see he was having trouble and the words just wouldn't come easily to him. He spoke about the "Judases" in the congregation. I have a strong feeling that he was speaking about me. I pray God will remove every bit of hidden malice and contempt I have for Al, because I don't feel God will use me in this situation until it is removed.

When prayer time came, the church was pretty lively, especially the women. Four women in particular really got to whooping and hollering. After the prayer time, Brother Al was "up" enough to preach on what he really wanted to preach at the beginning of the service. He cut down Billy Graham and Pentecostals. The church really got a blessing over that.

It grieves me to see people getting a blessing from words that snap, rhyme, and have a sarcastic attitude. Even worse, I see so many loving followers of Al that are being deceived. They laugh at every punch line—usually parables of some situation that happened to the church. But the Word of God is never used. I pray that this situation will be over with soon.

I have been feeling very high spiritually lately. My faith is growing. More and more, I am realizing that God is with me.

Saturday, December 1, 1973

Mark made a few statements at the Thursday night meeting that didn't seem right. Maybe I misunderstood. He said that if we don't keep growing, God will stop moving. Mark must be praying a whole lot, but I cannot see in the Word where we must grow in order to keep God moving.

I think the leaders of this movement should be concerned about evangelism, but there seems to be *too* much emphasis on it. Also, it worries me to see us letting down our principles in order to try to get more of an evangelistic punch. For example, not letting the people sing along when a group sings because it supposedly lessens the effectiveness of the evangelistic thrust of the song.

It worries me to see Mark so noticeably burdened. I have heard of and talked to people who did so much for God that they went into a frenzy and were compelled to do more and more for Him until they cracked.

Here are some of my observations about the group in general:

- It's growing. Many are getting saved.
- A few younger members are clap dancing [clapping with artistic and sensual motions]. There's also a cliquey and "this is cool" attitude. Terry Calldean noticed this too, but he said not to worry about it.
- We are now a bit more structured and formal.
- The leaders *must* get together and pray in unity.

Friday, December 7, 1973

I have been getting very close to God these last few days. Miracles are not very far off. They don't seem so impossible anymore.

Things at Boulder's Chapel are getting worse. I feel the people in the church are pointing their fingers at Val and me because of our association with Mark and J.U. I definitely feel things are coming to a head.

I had a great prayer meeting at J.U. last night. I really praised the Lord! I am getting freer every day. I feel that after being in the wilderness for two years, I am very close to crossing over the Jordan into a Promised Land. I think the Lord is telling me to fast and pray concerning Boulder's Chapel. I really would like to be free from the bondage that is there.

Things are really happening at J.U. Demons are being defeated and souls are being delivered from demon possession and won to Christ. Earlier in the week, Mark went to a dope party hoping for an opportunity to preach. He was able to preach, and souls were delivered.

During the week, Mark and Rusty went to Buchanan to check on a girl who was struck by Satan. It appeared that she had become demon possessed. When they couldn't find her, Mark and Rusty split up to look for her. After a search, Rusty and another Christian found her at the camp, but she took off running. Rusty commanded Satan to stop running away, and the girl fell down immediately. When they got to her, she was cursing God. Rusty laid hands on her to free her. She fell limp at his touch. They commanded Satan to leave, and he left. She was delivered and praised God.

Mark is still expounding the Word like a saint. It is really uplifting. A few others, including me, agree with Mark that we *must* get together and get hold of God in prayer. I believe God is anxious and ready to really let things happen, such as seeing more souls saved, the purchase of the camp, and miracles.

A hot topic of discussion, study, and debate has been on the subject of spiritual warfare and confronting demons. The Christian bookstore is filled with all sorts of books on this subject.

In the middle of the night shortly after Val and I were married, I woke up to find her wide awake and shaking. Her heart was beating wildly, and she was very frightened. Val had no idea what was wrong with her, except that an uncontrollable fear was engulfing her. We had been studying spiritual warfare for about a year, and it was clear to me that Val was under some kind of demonic attack. It seemed that now was the time to put our knowledge to good use, so I said, "Satan, you spirit of fear, I rebuke you in Jesus name."

In my spirit, I clearly heard a voice come back at me, speaking quite belligerently, sarcastically and confidently, *By what authority?*

I said, "By the authority of the Word."

The evil spirit said, *Where?*

I couldn't think of a single Scripture to quote. I was speechless.

Val and I got through the rest of the night. In the morning, I sought God about the incident. I felt the Lord say that I must be so well-versed in the Word that it is second nature to quote the correct Scripture to my adversary. When you are driving down the street and a car pulls out in front of you, you automatically swerve or slam on the brakes. You don't have to think about turning the wheel or stepping on the brakes because it is second nature—a well-practiced reaction. In the same way, God was telling me that I needed to know His Word so well that responding with Scripture would be second nature.

I felt the Lord say that the evil spirit would indeed come back soon and that I should be ready for it. So I memorized James 4:7, *Resist the Devil, and he will flee from you,* and Mark 16:17, *In my name shall they cast out Devils.*

Sure enough, after about two weeks, the same thing happened again in the middle of the night. This time, however, I was ready. I rebuked the Devil and the spirit of fear and quoted the Scriptures immediately. The fear left Val instantly, and that spirit has never bothered us since. That was more than thirty years ago.

Another remarkable demonic experience came later in the spring when Mrs. Larson returned to live with us. Being newly married, we enjoyed our privacy and were a little apprehensive about living in the same home with an eighty-year-old person. We knew that we would likely have to give up a great deal of freedom in directing our own household and that this could lead to trouble because our lifestyle was such that we often came and went and visited a lot with friends.

When Mrs. Larson came back from California, things went well for a few weeks. Then suddenly, she became very grouchy. This went on for a week or two, until the situation became unbearable. We could hardly have a conversation with her at all because she acted so irritated at us and was really rude.

One evening, after what must have been the last straw, I decided to pray about the situation. Mrs. Larson had gone into her little bedroom and closed the door. I went into my bedroom on the other side of the house and began to talk to God. After praying for a few minutes, I came to the conclusion that this was an attack of the Devil. I had *no* doubts: Mrs. Larson was acting irrationally and was not her normal self. We were all miserable because of it. *This was the work of the Devil!*

I stood up in my bedroom and faced the other side of the house where Mrs. Larson was. I pointed my finger towards that bedroom and said, "You foul spirits that are working through Mrs. Larson to torment us, I rebuke you in Jesus' name and command you to desist in your maneuvers against us right now!" I immediately felt the assurance that the job was done. Mrs. Larson didn't come out of her room for the rest of the night.

The next day, she was a totally different person, even more gracious than her normal self. A day later, we were all eating dinner together and she asked me, "Does God speak to us?"

I said, "Why yes, He does."

She said, "No, I mean *really* speak to us."

I said, "Yes, He really does speak to us."

Then she got even more serious and said, "No, I mean does He speak to us . . . in a *literal* voice?"

I said, "Well, yes, He does, but not very often. Most people go through their whole lives without hearing God speak in a literal voice. But He does occasionally speak that way."

I thought we were enjoying a nice theological discussion at the time, but then Mrs. Larson became even more dramatic and said, "Two nights ago, I was in my bedroom and was all upset. You see, I had been spending time with some friends at my church, and they had been getting me agitated by some of the things they were saying. They said that you and Val were just using me, that you were ripping me off, and that I should tell you to leave. I was thinking about what my friends had been saying to me, when God spoke to me."

She put out her hand and extended her crooked eighty-year-old finger at me and exclaimed, *"In a literal voice!* God said that you and Val were *not* using me or ripping me off and that I was not to tell you to leave. God said that my friends were wrong, that I should continue to help you and Val, and that I wasn't to listen to those old ladies any more!"

Saturday, December 8, 1973

I have been less depressed lately than ever before in my Christian life. Jesus is becoming more and more a *Friend* rather than a condemner.

This evening, the Lord showed me that I should not say anything that would turn away innocent Christians when Val and I leave Boulder's Chapel. He showed me that I should be informative on what I'm doing, but that is all, and especially that there should be *no condemning of doctrine.* I am to be loving and kind to all present, including Al. Praise God through His Son Jesus Christ!

Thursday, December 13, 1973

At the J.U. prayer meeting at Mark's, there was a girl downstairs with a demon.

I spoke very freely in tongues, but I would often get feelings such as, *I sound better than Lee. I sound pretty good. I really sound like a real language.* Despite these thoughts, I believe God revealed to me that unbelief hinders the casting out of the Devil. I still crave approval from others, especially Mark. I must get off of this and look directly to God.

Wednesday, December 19, 1973

Mark called me at 7:00 P.M. and told me about some of his demon experiences that he had been having lately. He said that he's been talking to and casting out many, many demons. Last Sunday night, Mark was at the Glory Barn, and his chair floated a few inches back and forth. It was not his imagination. A girl next to him saw it.

Mark also said that recently he turned off the light to go to sleep and a few minutes later his Bible slammed shut on the nightstand. Moments later, his covers were pulled half off. He called in Terry Calldean, and they rebuked Satan. Mark says he hates casting out demons and coming into contact with Satan, but that all this phenomena is for his learning and strengthening.

Last Friday, I felt God told me that I would be living at the camp before summer and that soon I would quit my job and work for Him full time through J.U. I'm ready right now! I sent a letter to the Methodist Church camp director, John Beal, asking for the caretaking job and also about buying the camp. I believe I will live in the caretaker's house before long.

I got sick at dinner tonight, so we decided not to go to Boulder's Chapel. Mark called shortly after that decision. I wanted to go to church, because I didn't want them to think I am falling into a pattern of backsliding. After Mark called, I began to feel better. It is clear that God didn't want us at Boulder's Chapel tonight, and I should *not* worry about what might be said about me. It is clear that when I don't listen, God intervenes.

In other words, it appears that when I am not listening to what God wants me to do, He intervenes and causes circumstances (such as sickness) to divert me *into* His perfect will.

Saturday, December 22, 1973

I just got back from the J.U. prayer meeting. Mark reported that he hasn't been getting enough sleep lately. People come to his house and talk all hours of the day. The people who need deliverance burden him down the most—it takes quite a bit out of a person to cast out demons.

Yesterday, he got to bed around 5:00 A.M. after casting demons out of a few girls. He had to get up at 7:00 A.M. and was in a haze from the lack of sleep. Then, after working from 8:00 A.M. to 1:00 P.M., another girl came needing deliverance. He had only slept two hours the night before. It is wearing Mark down.

I believe it is time for Mark to appoint elders or deacons to assist him with the many responsibilities. He *must* let the group know that he has confidence in those appointed. I pray that God will get my mission at

Boulder's Chapel accomplished *soon* so that I can give myself more to things pertaining to love, charity, and camp business.

About this time, Mark gathered a few of the guys together to ask them to help out in the different aspects of the meetings. Mark didn't feel comfortable publicly appointing us; he simply wanted us to step up to the plate and start doing more of the ministry. But from this time on, we started to openly refer to ourselves as "elders."

Monday, December 24, 1973

It is becoming increasingly clear that the leaders of J.U. are falling slightly out of the *perfect* will of God. On September 22, I gave a prophecy that J.U. was to focus on *learning* rather than on evangelizing. Because this prophecy was not well received, I assumed that I had given it in the flesh. However, situations in the group that have arisen are pointing me to the conclusion that the prophecy was of God. For instance:

1. Mark continuously has to counsel new converts to the point that he has no time for uninterrupted study.
2. Many of the elders are dealing with demons to the point of exhaustion.
3. Many elders (especially Mark) *are not* getting proper rest due to the continuous flow of new converts who need counsel or deliverance.
4. The elders are not getting together enough, as they did at the beginning.

Evangelism is a good thing, and it pleasing to God. J.U.'s main task or mission right now is evangelism and following up with new believers. However, I am convinced that Satan has been unable to kill the zeal of the elders or sidetrack the elders through sin. Thus, in order to make the total mission (especially the end result) of J.U. less effective, Satan is using this good thing of evangelism to sidetrack the elders during this prophesied learning period.

The Bible says: *Study to shew thyself approved unto God* (2 Timothy 2:15). So, can we expect God to use us in a great way until we've studied the approved amount? Sure, J.U. is doing something good right now. But the end result or *total number* of souls saved may be *seriously hindered* by this slight deviation from prophecy. Jesus accomplished more in the last three years of his life than the previous thirty. However, in order for that to occur, it was imperative for Him to seek to know His Father better for those thirty years.

Thursday, December 27, 1973

I love my Lord Jesus more today than I ever have. Every day gets better. If there's anything in my way to prevent my walking in His will, I pray God will remove it or make it very clear to me what it is.
A girl from J.U. started a tabernacle fund. She was going to put it in her name, but Mark said he planned to step in and put the account in four men's names: Phil, Rusty, Mark, and me.

It seems that everybody wants to do the same jobs. I talked to God about this, and I have decided what I'm going to do about it. First, I'm going to make sure that at least one other elder agrees with what I think God wants me to do, unless it is *very* clear to me. If there is strife or disunity with any other brother or sister concerning anything God impresses me to do, or if another is set on doing it, I'm going to let him or her do it in order to keep love and unity flowing. I'm going to rely on God to get me where He wants me to be. I am so eager to do things for the group that I must watch myself. I crave authority, so I must be *absolutely sure* it is God who impresses me to do things.

Walking in the Spirit cannot be as hard as it seems to be. Going places late all the time (such as the continuous tabernacle meetings late at night) and always doing things that are hard on me. I talked to God about it, and I'm going to learn the Spirit's voice. I'm going to concentrate on *not going* where I shouldn't be. When I master that, I'll be ready to go where I should go and know *when* I should go.

Thursday, January 3, 1974

I have noticed lately that Terry Calldean is developing pride. He has a withdrawn look on his face. His subject matter is becoming very deep, and I am worried about him. When getting into deliverance a week or two ago, I could really see this pride coming to him. I feel division between us. I felt it first last Saturday when I told him we needed to get together for a leaders' meeting. He said (lovingly), "We're here often, almost every night."

Last Friday and Saturday night, Terry and Bill Norten dealt with a woman who was demon possessed. They worked with her almost all Friday night. According to Terry and Bill, they cast 2 million demons out of her. When she was in her right mind, she wouldn't accept Christ.

Just before the Saturday night meeting, Terry brought the woman to Mark's house. Terry wanted Mark to get someone else to take over the meeting and to help with the woman, but Mark refused. After the meeting, Rusty, Bill, Mark and Terry dealt with her all evening until 11:00 P.M., but there was little or nothing accomplished.

Several days before this, Mark had stayed up late dealing with demons in a person. Then a day or two later, some girls came over, and Mark helped them until late casting out demons. When Friday night came and others wanted him help a woman, Mark began to catch on. He realized that the Devil was running him and some others ragged through the process of attempting to cast out demons. Only a few were delivered, and the exorcist was becoming exhausted. The demons must obey God's people, but they can go right back into the victim if the victim invites them back in (see Matthew 12:43–45).

This was an exciting time. We were seeing people come to the Lord, learning about the Holy Spirit, and dealing with the demons. But what I learned from this time is this: *We can do no exorcism successfully unless God wants it done.*

CHAPTER 9

ORGANIZING THE "ARMY"

J.U. BECOMES A CHURCH

*T*his was a time when the young men and women were looking for mates. Most of the leaders were dating and making plans for marriage. Within a year and a half, most of the leaders got married. Phil Bechtel married a young lady named Sandy, Melody Bechtel married Jim Flood, Val's sister married Mick Ahrens, and Rusty Evans married Penny.

Lee missed Ruth Ann so much that he went down to Florida to court her. After they were married, he and his bride came back to be a part of J.U. Mark began to date a young girl named Christi. She was quite young and still in high school at the time. Christi loved the Lord and was dedicated to serving Him. It wasn't long before Mark and Christi too made plans to get married.

Thursday, January 3, 1974 (continued)

There is not much unity among the leaders of J.U. Maybe it is just me, but I feel strife or resentfulness from Phil Bechtel. Bill Norten is not realistic or serious. And lately, I've been feeling a separation forming between Terry Calldean and me. It's as if he thinks he is really serious and I'm not.

I just got back from the J.U. prayer meeting at the Bechtel's. At 11:00 P.M., Cary White, Phil, Terry, Bill Riggenbacher, Rusty and I met in the basement to discuss business. Mark was taking Christi home to Buchanan. As I thought would happen, Phil and Terry cut down the idea that God gave me about the board and corporation for the camp. Rusty, however, was on the same channel as I was. For 25 minutes, we rather bluntly bickered about this. There was no yelling or losing of tempers, but Phil and Terry told me they didn't like the idea. Then I gave my side of the story. I had received an answer from God. They hadn't prayed yet, thus there was no direction from God and no unity.

Phil went upstairs and prayed for a witness from the Bible. The Lord gave him the Scripture: *In the multitude of counselors there is safety* (Proverbs 11:14), which confirmed the corporation and trustee idea. Phil soon apologized and I was overjoyed at the unity of our spirits. Everyone else then bore witness also.

We then prayed for:

1. How to buy the camp (this was answered at 11:30 P.M.)
2. How much to pay for it.
3. Finding a lawyer to finalize the purchase.

Tomorrow, I must find a lawyer and set up J.U. as a corporation. The group questioned my leading about the caretaker's job. I must let God handle this situation, or I'll be worried to death.

Sunday, January 6, 1974

Last week, after the Lord showed me to be careful of diversionary tactics of the Devil, Nick Fisher proposed establishing a halfway house for drug rehabilitation that he said could "turn out bigger than the camp." Although a work like this would be commendable, most of the J.U. elders saw this as just a good thing that could get us away from the camp burden.

Nick Fisher was our elder by about five to ten years. He was reportedly a member of a local Church of Christ where some of the J.U. people were going to church on Sundays. J.U. never met on Sundays. People went to local churches on Sunday and came to J.U. during the week. At this time, J.U. was viewed as more of a Christian support ministry than a regular church.

Understandably, Nick was probably concerned with our youthfulness and lack of depth. He probably felt that our direction to buy the old Riverside Camp was not feasible, and so he offered his help to put together another ministry in which he could be involved. Only the Lord knows for sure whether his motives were pure or selfish.

A few weeks later, a strong rumor began to circulate that Nick was a "narc." Mark and several other elders came to the conclusion that Nick wasn't really concerned about our ministry at all, but that he was only using us to find druggies. As far as I know, he never found any regular attendees involved with drugs.

Friday, January 11, 1974

Today I met with an attorney. I was disappointed that I did not have the opportunity to preach the gospel to him. When I invited him to a J.U. meeting, he politely refused, suggesting that we get together sometime with all the elders. I am slightly confused as to what is to be done about setting up a corporation, but I'm trusting God that it will work out. My biggest concern is that we set up the corporation according to biblical principles with Mark having most of the control and the chief advisors having the remainder of the control.

Control. Hmm. I think someone should write a book about that word and its place in the body of Christ. But here's a hint: In the above entry, something was definitely wrong with my thinking.

Sunday, January 13, 1974

By the conclusion of my talk with the lawyer, we had established the following:

1. He will check up on some laws and gather some information concerning the government of our corporation.
2. I will get information concerning the governing body and an idea as to how we want it set up.

This is what Mark, Rusty and I came up with after discussing establishing J.U. as a corporation on Saturday night:

1. The governing body is to include only Mark, Rusty and me.
2. Mark is to have the majority of control, with Rusty and me having the remainder of control.
3. There will be no replacements to the elected board without Mark's approval.
4. Rusty and I may impeach and oust Mark if we feel the need to do so.

The reason for having only the three of us on the governing body is that only we three have true unity among us. More importantly, we also have a burden for the camp. We all are sensible, responsible leaders in wisdom, sincere, and are willing to give all to Jesus.

A little modesty wouldn't have hurt either.

Thursday, January 17, 1974

I talked to the lawyer today and received an outline for setting up the corporation. It looks as if J.U. will be set up as we planned: with simplicity and based on biblical principles, because at this time there is little written law concerning church organizations.

When a few of the guys questioned me tonight about the lawyer's meeting, I hesitated to tell them much because only Mark, Rusty, and I are involved. God has chastised me for this, because it shows sneakiness or a lack of assurance in direction. So I am now telling it like it is. I'm a lot freer when I don't try to hide things.

Tuesday, January 22, 1974

In order to be a teacher on Thursday nights, I must dig harder than other people. In my digging, I have come to understand why Jesus had to die. I am learning so much. Full understanding of salvation is just around the corner.

Because I'm getting clearer on salvation, I'm getting freer at Boulder's Chapel. Brother Al is really trying to get the congregation on fire, but to no avail. I don't know if God wants me there much longer.

I never did warn the leaders of Boulder's Chapel publicly. Although I felt that God wanted me to warn them, I also felt that He would tell me the right time to do it. I *do* remember a key word I received at the time: *When I speak with you, then you shall say, "Thus says the Lord . . ."* Even in hindsight, I think that commission *was* valid, *is* valid, and may *still* happen. The warning is to repent from legalism, condemning true believers, resisting the manifestations of the Holy Spirit and, in general, moving in the SPIRIT OF ERROR for selfish purposes. Remember, a warning from God is usually full of love and concern for the people involved. This includes people who are acting selfishly, but who may not be fully aware of their own motives. Harsh criticism is only for true hypocrites, those who *know* they are doing wrong.

Sunday, January 27, 1974

Well, we sent the forms to the State of Michigan today. We believe that if we're wrong, God will burn it up on the way. I became aware of a deeper sense of responsibility when I signed the papers.

Brother Al mentioned in church that he had talked to one of our neighbors in the hospital. The neighbor told Al that he's been watching Val and me and was impressed that God was with us. I had no idea that the neighbors have been watching us. It is neat how God is using these types of things to speak to Al. I can also see how our coming to Mrs. Larson's house was not coincidence, but God's invisible direction.

Thursday, January 31, 1974

No word yet from John Beal or the state. This past week and a half has been quite nerve-racking. I see so many problems in my life and J.U. When I want to commune with God, my mind just seems to wander at times. I long to commune and meditate with God. I want to know Him better, but I don't know where to start.

There appears to be such a spiritual lack in me at times that I wonder if I am ready to do anything for God in J.U. I had such a battle yesterday reading my Bible in front of the guys at work. It shouldn't be this way, but I don't know how to get over it. Mark has the same problem.

On Monday, we had a baptismal service at the Church of Christ. When the pastor took over and preached false doctrine, I had no idea what to do. Should I speak out hard against this church or be passive? Time will give me wisdom.

Remember, for the first few years of my Christian life, I attended a legalistic church that believed and taught me that they had the corner on all the truth of the Bible. Too often, I heard about other churches with "false doctrine." There were too many "false doctrines" to list. Some doctrines the church taught me were good, and much of what it taught me I still believe to be true. But the spirit in which those doctrines were taught was often mixed with a spirit of exclusiveness and pride.

The false doctrine that I specifically referred to at the end of the above journal entry was the idea that you must be baptized to be saved—no exceptions. I didn't (and still don't) believe that the Bible teaches this idea. If a person becomes a follower of Jesus, he or she should *then* be baptized as an outward sign of something that has already happened on the inside. If a person happened to die between the time of conversion to Christ and the time of baptism, that person would still be saved by faith through the blood of Christ, not by the work of baptism.

I now have some high priorities that I remain dogmatic about. Some of them are:

1. The shed blood of Christ is necessary for our forgiveness.
2. Fellowship and communion with God is important to Him.
3. Jesus is alive, well, and still directing the Church in its ministry.

I am sad that I jumped on so many legalistic bandwagons and hurt people in my younger Christian years. I am sure that I still have much more to learn, but I think we all should continue to call it as we see it and trust the Lord to correct us if we're calling it wrong. I believe the Church of Christ would wholeheartedly agree with these particular priorities of mine, which gives us firm ground for fellowship and worship of God together. I have many friends who go to that Church of Christ today, and we have great Christian fellowship when we get together.

Monday, February 4, 1974

I heard from our lawyer today, and our papers came back. We will probably adopt our by-laws on Friday.

I also heard from Mark and Rusty about Nick and the Church of Christ. It appears that Nick has changed his colors since the baptism last Monday night. It may be that he never did trust us. Rusty said that Nick was against tongues, but that he told Mark he agreed with the gift. Now he appears to be totally against J.U., saying that one of our leaders is demon possessed. If what Rusty said is true, and not a misunderstanding, Nick is a liar, a deceiver, and is treading on quicksand.

If this turns out to be real persecution against strong Christians, I am sure that it is training for the later years when a mistake may mean a jail sentence. God is surely using this as conditioning for that time. I believe that J.U. will be one of the last evangelistic outreaches that will fulfill the prophecy, *And the gospel must first be published among all nations* (Mark 13:10). We will not be politically recognized (not working through governmentally recognized church corporations) and will do most (or all) of our outreach underground.

I still believe that what I stated in the above paragraph is true in many respects. As the world continually grows more evil, I suspect that the Church will be pressured to follow suit. True worship and activities at church will become increasingly more politically incorrect and under more and more criticism. I suspect that someday our church organizations will actually weigh us down in our service to Christ until it will no longer be beneficial to maintain them. For hundreds of years, Jesus and the Early Church did many great things without the benefit of ecclesiastical corporations (governmentally recognized church organizations). I think we may end up doing the same.

Tuesday, February 12, 1974

I have heard no word yet from John Beal about the camp, and I am itching to write another letter. But God hasn't given me a definite witness to write, therefore I won't.

God told me today that the proposed by-laws are satisfactory. But I (not really sure that it was God) changed a few minor details (such as specific names).

Val told me that a few girls felt left out of the camp "business" and that they were getting together to pray Friday night. This worried me for a while, because I was afraid of losing a bit of authority. But I realized this is a wrong attitude. I am not doing this to be in the camp business, but because God wants me in this position. If the girls should have more to do and it's God's will, so be it. If I have a wrong concept on a woman's place, I want to be corrected.

I am still concerned about emotionalism at the Friday night prayer time. I'll just trust God that whatever the girls come up with will be proven by the Word and Spirit to Rusty, Mark, and me. If their answer is not of God, I'll trust God that it will come to naught.

Man! So many insecurities! I don't remember exactly who the above-mentioned girls were, but they were probably my age (about 18 to 22). The question about a woman's place in Church government has been a hot topic in Christian circles for about 2,000 years. The women's liberation movement that started in the late 60s was still picking up steam at this time, and I was trying to work through that issue. Then there were my own insecurities to deal with, which complicated the matter. Trusting God for appointment and position in the body of Christ is the right viewpoint. However, one should not ever be preoccupied with gaining positions of authority or leadership. We should be concerned only with *serving*.

Tuesday, February 12, 1974 (continued)

The problem with Nick Fisher appears to be dying down, although fresh rumors about J.U. are springing up all over—such as sacrificing cats in the basement, Devil worship, and an underground drug ring. God will have to protect us. I understand that Nick is moving out of the state. An act of God? Or a trick?

Wednesday, February 13, 1974

It appears that Mark has trouble sticking to what God has told him to do. Because of this, Mark has structured and restructured the meetings many times. Three weeks ago, he felt impressed to teach on Saturday night. Three days ago, he wasn't sure whether that should be the teaching night or not. I realize that Mark is carrying the responsibility and that I probably would do worse, but I am learning by Mark's mistakes. It must be that the restructure is only temporary. Nevertheless, Mark shouldn't get so burdened when God tells him to do something and it doesn't turn out the way we would like it to.

Sunday, February 17, 1974

Something interesting happened yesterday. A few weeks ago, I prophesied that J.U. would become well known in the surrounding area and that support would come in from all over. Yesterday, Mark, Rusty, and I were asked to give a testimony at the Full Gospel Business Men's meeting. Rusty talked about deliverance. Mark and I talked about J.U. and the army.

The phrase "raising an end-time army" would eventually be used to describe our commission from the Lord. About a year prior to this, Mark and Lee had gone to a prayer meeting at Christian Center Church. I was not there, but they later told me what happened. During prayer, one of the ministers came over to Mark, laid his hands on him, and began to prophesy. Mark said that this prophecy hit him like a ton of bricks and pointed him in the direction of leading J.U.

Mark said the prophecy went as follows: "I [God] have called you to raise up an army of young people who will go forth in these latter days. They will cast out Devils, heal the sick, and raise the dead. They will go into the bars and the hellholes of society and will proclaim the gospel of Jesus Christ. They'll go forth and defeat the Devil and his angels." Mark took this personally as his commission from God, but at the time he didn't have any idea what to do about it or how to proceed. Much of the future direction of J.U. hinged on this prophecy.

Lee had a slightly different take on this Word from the Lord. Lee felt that the prophecy was more general in its direction, and that the wording went more like: "There is an army of young people who are being raised up in these latter days. They will go forth . . . ." Lee later told me that he was somewhat confused about this commission, because Mark took it so personally.

Saturday, February 23, 1974

Today, I remembered that Val and I need to have a place to live soon as Mrs. Larson comes home in three weeks. I keep trying to get a go ahead from God to write again to John Beal, but there's no witness. So I'll just wait. I have had no word from the caretaker or about getting the caretaker's house. I know God can work it out in a short time. And He may have to do just that!

The leaders of J.U. *must* get together and pray in one accord. *We must* because God revealed to me that *prayer is the moving force of J.U.* There has been little prayer in unity since the beginning. I'm calling up Mark now to talk about it.

98

Like most of us today, the leaders of J.U. were more about talking than praying. No one really stopped us from praying—we just didn't do much of it at this time. We all have an enemy who wants us to pray as little as possible. Distraction is the main tool he uses against us.

Monday, March 4, 1974

I picked up some forms Friday from our lawyer on tax exemptions. I was very distressed about all the IRS stuff that I had to know. I must let God give me an answer on what to do.

There is not much is happening at Boulder's Chapel. I feel that I should tell Al about what I'm doing. He won't understand, but I don't want to seem sneaky.

The thought came to me today that I am still not baptized in the Spirit. The reason I think this is because I have no real power. However, when I spoke at the Jesus Rally, it was with great power. I wonder if the tongues I have are based on emotionalism or in reality? I have no doubt that we can have the Spirit and power and gifts, but I see little of that power in my life. I am happy and content in the natural, but my *desire is to be closer to Jesus!*

The *diagnosis* for this problem is either:

1. I am not acting in obedience;
2. I am not praying enough;
3. I have not allowed myself to be broken by God;
4. I have not been baptized in the Spirit.

There are probably many other reasons why we don't experience God's power in our lives. I think the main reason is that we usually get puffed up with pride when God moves powerfully through us. He doesn't want us to get hurt by our pride, so He just holds back.

Saturday, March 9, 1974

I just finished praying in tongues for ten minutes, and I expect a result today. The last few days, the elders of J.U. have begun to realize how lacking we are in the area of our personal crucifixion. We are seriously lacking in obedience to the Spirit. This all has to do with the breaking of our outer man. I have a big problem with the things at hand. I long to see God manifest Himself through me and others, but I now realize that I am not responsible enough to be entrusted with a gift of healing or miracles. All the elders of J.U. have come to this realization at the same time, and I believe we'll have a breakthrough soon.

I recently learned something that has given me a great peace: I should not *strive* to attain authority or *maintain* authority, but simply trust in God. If He wants me out of a certain role or situation, then praise the Lord. If He wants me in, no one can take me out.

I am going to see Brother Al today to inform him that Val and I are leaving Boulder's Chapel.

The meeting with Brother Al went smoothly. Al accepted our decision to leave, and told me he would keep us in prayer.

Monday, March 11, 1974

Saturday night, Mark spoke of selling all that we have and giving it to the poor. The Holy Spirit confronted me to lay aside every sin and *weight* that so easily besets me (see Hebrews 12:1). The last few weeks, the Spirit has dealt with me about laying aside unneeded things that cause strife, such as keeping such a detailed ledger of home expenses.

Each day when I come home from work, I always plan on praying and reading, but somehow I always get sidetracked. I have sensed God dealing with me on this issue over and over again for the past four or five months since J.U. began. And now this: *Lay aside every weight and sin that gets in your way of praying.* This is a command from the Lord to me tonight. I must get guidance on what to keep and what to sell. I decided to get rid of everything but what I need, and now the message is clearer than ever. Lord, help me distinguish what *I really* need.

This is where I am right now:

1. I'm called to active duty in J.U.
2. I'm not sure what ministry I'll have. Miracles?
3. I am a representative of J.U.
4. I'm not called to quit my job yet.
5. I am committed to loving my wife as Christ loves the Church.

What I feel the Lord is saying to me is this: *Lay up no treasure on earth. Have no bank account or stashes.*

I wouldn't say that God tells everyone to get rid of his or her bank accounts. But I had the problem of trusting in my stored up riches for my security. I felt God told me to get rid of those things, so I did. Val supported me on these decisions. In hindsight, I still think it was the right thing to do.

Sunday, March 17, 1974

So far, God has instructed me to get rid of all my stashes: silver and abundance in my bank account. I should have my coin collection sold by Tuesday. Then I must know where to put the abundance of my bank account.

I had prayer with Calldeans about my weights. They said not to sell everything, because that takes up lots of your time too.

I feel a sense of urgency in the air to be obedient, because there's little time left to work. *God help me to get victory over these weights!* Mark dreamed that he, Rusty, and I were laying hands on people and raising them up.

I knew when this thing started that Brother Wilt was going to be tried and torn up by jealousy or something. I believe that Brother Wilt is scared to death of Mark. He's afraid that Mark will pull kids out of his congregation and that they will start their own congregation. Well, the time is about here. It has been impressed upon a few leaders, including Mark, to meet once a week as a body. They say we must become a body. I have no command of the Lord myself, but it seems needful and in order. Mark will talk to his father soon about it. I pray for them both. Wilt is going to have a big trial over this. It will cut his congregation in half.

I struggled over whether or not to leave the above entry in this book. It seems like a rather negative statement against Brother Bechtel, but I think the dynamics of the situation need to be revealed. When Brother Bechtel started his own church after the big walkout at Boulder's Chapel, the group met in his home in the beginning. Several months later, he moved the meeting place to a nice little white church building on the other side of town, and by this time, the church was comfortably full.

Brother Bechtel has been a faithful friend and a "non-stop" pastor for all these years, and he deserves praise along with anything negative said about him. In the above entry, I zeroed in on some negative motivations that I still think are accurate. However, I would now use the term "threatened by Mark" instead of "scared to death of Mark."

We have all felt threatened by people at times, for all kinds of reasons, both good and bad. Being a relatively new full-time minister, I think Brother Bechtel *was* concerned about the size of his congregation (that was about to become significantly smaller), and *that* created some selfish motivations on his part. But I think Brother Bechtel was also legitimately concerned for Mark and his "followers." In hindsight, his concern was appropriate.

Monday, March 25, 1974

I haven't gone to Boulder's Chapel since last Sunday night. The people *must* be suspecting something by now. I still am greatly lacking in my Christian walk. *I am so dissatisfied!* I can't be bold for Jesus. I want to, but I just don't have the guts. God, help me to be a true witness with joy and radiance!

Several of the J.U. leadership went to a Full Gospel Business Men's Fellowship International Convention in Indianapolis. We stayed at a motel and enjoyed going to meetings, hoping to learn more about and see God's power. The first night, I went to the altar to help pray for people who came up. I was awed by a lady who came up to help.

Wednesday, April 3, 1974 (First Night of Convention)

I met a lady with wisdom at the altar. *She had so much love radiating from her.* She said that when she was living behind the Iron Curtain and was baptized in the Holy Spirit, she received the English language. She said she did missionary work.

This is what this lady said concerning me:

1. It was no coincidence that we met each other.
2. I haven't begun my ministry yet.
3. Had I heard about the story of Goliath? (She had an "if only you could imagine" look on her face that was mixed with love and wisdom, indicating that God has great things in store for me.)
4. I was chosen from the time of my birth.
5. Every situation in my life has been under God's control.
6. I will see Jesus.

She also said something to the effect that I am walking through a valley. She seemed to give the impression that the situation could get worse before it gets better. I might be wrong about that. I hope I am.

The woman said each of these things matter-of-factly and with love in the midst of our conversation. When dealing with a man at the altar, she said kindly, "God wants you to get rid of your cigarettes." Later, he pulled a wadded pack of cigarettes out of his pocket, and put them on the altar. I had tried to help the same man, but my efforts didn't seem to help him at all. She came up and talked sternly and with so much wisdom and love that it downright astounded me.

I include the above journal entry in this book because the contrast between my way of helping people and her way was so apparent to me at that time. My way was cut and dried and full of the Law, intermingled with my own need to "score." I'm sure that there were some good motives in my desire to help people back then, but this woman's way was *clearly* laced with so much love and pure motives that it strongly drew me and other people to Jesus. I wanted to help people the same way.

Thursday, April 11, 1974

I have still heard no word from John Beal. God must be testing me.

I am learning about faith and anointed healings. My faith is growing. One thing I have learned is that we *must stand on chapter and verse* in order to have victory in faith, healing, or spiritual warfare.

Wednesday, April 17, 1974

Last Saturday night, a local Methodist minister told us about the Methodist Church Camp Board meeting in Grand Rapids and the upcoming sale of the camp. I'm going to Grand Rapids this Saturday to bid for the camp. We also heard that the American Canoe Association (ACA) is interested in buying the camp. I am only a little nervous. I realize any fear I have is of the Devil. I plan to put down at least $1,000.00 for a hold on the camp. I don't think it is out of the question to get the camp for nothing. I feel fairly confident that we will attain the camp on Saturday.

Monday, at work, I prayed to have boldness to speak the name of Jesus freely. Around 11:00 A.M., I heard a funny noise and looked behind me to see the foreman lying on his *stomach* with his arms *and* legs arched up off of the floor. He was obviously in pain and moaning "Oh no, oh no." He was jolted by 440 volts of electricity, and when I saw him lying on the floor, God gave me the boldness to kneel and pray for him until the ambulance arrived. When it was over, I prayed that God would glorify His name through this accident. Already I've talked seriously with one person (Paul), and I can definitely see a change or conviction on others. I also can see a deeper respect for me from others. Praise God!

As Mark, Christi, and I made plans to go up to Grand Rapids to bid on the camp, we were counting on receiving much help from Brother

Murphy and the Christian Center. But Brother Murphy gave no indication that he was led to say anything or help us in any way. All we have is about $2,000.00 and a little faith.

Tuesday, April 23, 1974

Things didn't go as I thought they would last Saturday when we gave our bid for the camp. When we went into the room to talk to the council, both Mark and I had shaky voices. Also, Christi never said a word. After leaving, I didn't feel at all satisfied. I wonder whether I should have submitted a list of the names of the residents who live around the camp who support us.

We'll know who is getting the camp by next week. God may give it to us after the American Canoe Association buys it. Who knows?

Wednesday, April 25, 1974

I received a letter from Mrs. Larson today. She'll be home tomorrow. By May 25, we'll have the camp and I'll be living in the caretaker's house, according to what I felt God told me last December 19. Praise God! I am not really looking forward to living with another person in the house, but I trust that *all things work together for good* (Romans 8:28).

Saturday, April 27, 1974

Something miraculous happened yesterday! Jesus Unlimited has been assured of receiving $70,000.00 by the first of June. Praise God! Mark told John Beal from the Methodist Church, and now we're sitting back to watch the glory of the Lord.

Somehow, Mark came into contact with a man who said he could get us the $70,000.00 we needed to buy the camp. Details were obviously sketchy, but I was told that we were going to be given the money.

Saturday, April 27, 1974 (continued)

This is what has happened so far:

1. The Lord said that we'll get the camp before summer (in the springtime).
2. The Lord told me that I will go into full-time ministry before summer and that I will move from Mrs. Larson's to the caretaker's house within thirty days of Mrs. Larson's return home.

The man who told us that we would be given the $70,000.00 was someone from the Christian Center Church. What he *really* meant was that he would put us into contact with the owner of the new Christian television station in South Bend, and that he would personally help us with a telethon to raise money from viewers. We contacted the owner and set up an appointment for Mark and me to visit and discuss the situation. We were very disappointed to find out that the owner had no intention of putting us on the air. This was not at all what we had expected.

Tuesday, April 30, 1974

I just got back from the TV station. We learned not to shoot off our mouths until we've heard from *the* horse's mouth. The owner of the TV station gave us advice on raising money. It was good advice, but not what we had hoped for. Besides that, Mark already told the Methodist Church that we would have $ 70,000.00 by the first of June. God's going to glorify Himself. He has to, or we're cooked!

CHAPTER 10

REAL MINISTRY
PRAYING AGAINST ATTACKS

*B*y now, all of us at J.U. were fairly certain that God was calling us into a major ministry. The beginning excitement had now worn off, and we began to regularly experience leadership frustrations due to the rising number of people coming to the meetings. We also felt an uncomfortable urgency that I believe was not from God. We not only felt the leading to fulfill a commission, but also the guilt and shame for not pursuing it to the level of our own expectations. I don't believe that this spirit pushed only one person. It worked on all of us, pushing us to trust in our own efforts to accomplish the commission that was forming.

We clearly felt the call, but what could we do other than follow the path of what we perceived as normal church growth? None of us had any formal training. None of us had any extensive knowledge of church history or church governments. All we had was our own experience of growing up in church and being involved with a few different churches since we became Christians. Our experience mirrored traditional church history, so we began to move forward in a way similar to most churches that were growing from scratch.

We began to feel that in order to go forward, we had to start doing something and to be serious about it.

Monday, May 6, 1974

Yesterday, when Mark and I went to the camp and prayed, the Lord told us, *More people, more organization. One worship and one teaching meeting a week.* It seems that only Mark and I have any burden for organizing J.U. It seems that no one else can do any administration. So now we're going to give a statement of purpose at every meeting.

I have heard no word from the Methodist Church. I heard one minister say on a tape, "Don't worry how God is going to do it." Maybe that means He will provide money for the camp.

Wednesday, May 15, 1974

I found out Monday afternoon that the Methodist Church decided to sell the camp to the ACA. The decision didn't really surprise me, because I feel that God is *really* going to glorify Himself. I still believe. I've got approximately two weeks to move into the caretaker's house. God can and will do it! Praise God! Doubts come here and there, but only when I look at the situation. When I look at God and Moses and Joshua, I say, "God will do it. Behold, the salvation of the Lord!" Mark and I have gone out on a limb for God. *God, manifest Yourself!*

Thursday, May 16, 1974

We had our first worship service tonight. It really wasn't very good. One of the guys seemed out of order, while the prophecies and tongues were erratic and non-edifying. Something is wrong with Jesus Un-limited! I don't know what it is. I think Jesus is telling me that the leaders need to seek God for guidance more. I seem so disorganized, and I don't know where to start. Also, very few funds are coming in. I put an ad in the Niles paper. People will now start thinking about Jesus Unlimited.

Sunday, May 19, 1974

It appears from the natural that God isn't doing much, but *I know* He's doing something. Val feels a fervency to pack and be ready to move. Also, lately I have felt impressed to *act* as if the camp will be ours in about a week and a half. I haven't prayed much for guidance. Lord, help me. I must pray for guidance. I will!

Rusty, Penny, Val, and I were down at the cross in the camp this afternoon, and I saw a patch of light on the cement walk not two feet from me. We saw it while discussing love. It appeared for a second, and it then vanished. Later, Penny said she saw it up in a tree. Val also saw it out of the corner of her eye. There were no physical explanations.

I believe that I have seen the first vision into the spiritual world. But God has definitely made it clear that I must not dwell on these supernatural visions and discernment. I must stick to the Word.

This truly was a supernatural manifestation. I have thought about all the possible natural explanations for it, but I can't think of any that could produce what I saw. It was like a spotlight—round and about two feet in diameter. It appeared out of the corner of my eye, and then I looked right at it just before it disappeared. We were in broad daylight. The patch of light was much brighter than what a strong flashlight beam could produce.

During this time, Mark and Christi got married, and Mark became the full time pastor of Jesus Unlimited. His salary was $100 a week, with utilities paid by the church. They lived with Mark's parents.

Thursday, June 6, 1974

It sure is easy to doubt, but right now I feel a surge of faith. We've done all we can, and now God has to move. We are at our wits end. Yet I know that is when God can get the glory.

I have proposed a covenant to God. I know that my God is a powerful God, but I have seen very little of His supernatural manifestations. I know that my God can do more than I've seen! According to the Bible,

God can *really* manifest Himself. I'm going to be careful not to fake God's manifestations or to try to "help" God. I will be obedient.

Saturday, June 8, 1974

Right now I am terribly discouraged, but I know God will help me. Lately, as I have been giving the announcements at J.U., I have had an uncontrollable fear come on me so that I lose my train of thought. I stutter and look very nervous. Then tonight, after we prayed for it *not* to rain, it rained and I got soaked. To make matters worse, two crazy people came and disrupted the meeting. I didn't know what to do about them.

But I know that *all things work together for good* (Romans 8:28). However, I can't help but wonder: If God wants me in a position of authority, why doesn't He help me? I've learned my lesson. *I can't do anything without Him! Help me in Jesus' name, Father!*

Sunday, June 9, 1974

I just got back from Jeff Bechtel's house, where Mark and Christi, Jeff, his wife, Val, and I did some serious praying. I went out to pray this morning, being distressed over last night's meeting, and God seemed to say to me that J.U. has a veil of Satan over it that is binding it and oppressing it to a point of stalemate. The only thing that will get us out of this mess is prayer. Not necessarily individual prayer, but praying together at one time with unity.

Mark, Jeff, and I talked most of the afternoon. When we started praying fervently at 10:00 P.M., we were blessed. We have bound the evil rulers of the darkness and expect to get the camp within a short time. I feel it will be in three days—a number that popped up while I was praying. I feel that we should pray fervently for three days to keep heaven hopping. The battle truly is not ours. It is heavenly. We must keep faith and pray.

I felt the Lord say, *You cannot have any person in the prayer group who has the least amount of dissension with Mark or you or anyone in the prayer group.* So far we have only four: Mark, Rusty, Jeff, and me. We also discussed about me going full-time.

Monday, June 24, 1974

Lately, I have been super oppressed. I have no joy and nothing to add to the meetings. I seem to have no power over the oppression. Even during last night's meeting at another church, I had no praise until Steve Hill spoke. I still suspect satanic oppression. Christi, Mark, and I talked tonight about Christi and me being obsessed by fear. But why can't I take authority over it? *God, help me!* I'm afraid that if God doesn't give me *complete* assurance that I should go full-time at J.U., the pressure will crack me, especially if it is not in His perfect will. I'm ready to humble myself. If I am not ready to minister, I'll go back to being ministered to and confess my mistake.

The meetings at J.U. have generally been dead, except when Mark speaks. I think I know what has oppressed me. I have been trying to muster up help for Mark at the meetings, without the necessary burden. How do I get it?

Monday, July 8, 1974

The meetings at J.U. remain super dry and we have been at a standstill. Nothing is really going on, such as rallies or special events. For the past month, the leaders have been praying and asking for direction, but things are still up and down. Starting last week, however, the elders of J.U. have been gaining unity. Phil and I got unified. I talked with him last Sunday morning and today. I confessed that I was elbowing in.

Here are some of the problems with which we are dealing:

1. There is still no word about the camp.
2. Nothing is happening at J.U.
3. There is friction between Mark's dad's church and J.U. because of J.U. officially becoming a church body.
4. There is no room.

What do we do? We must *step out.*

1. I will go full time as the administrator for J.U. in three weeks. (We decided this tonight).
2. We will get more room.
3. We will get organized.
4. We will raise an army of young people to defeat the Devil and his angels. This is what we have defined as our purpose.

God gave me the assurance, so I'm ready. He said, *I told you last January that you will go full-time in the summer.* I'm expecting God to manifest Himself greatly soon. For the past few weeks, I have been aware of acting as if I have little time left at the Dayco factory.

The next day, I gave Dayco a three-weeks notice and started working out the details of going full time at J.U.

Tuesday, July 9, 1974

I just found out why J.U. has been dead. On Friday, December 14, 1973, God told me to give up all and follow Him. We would then move into the camp after Mrs. Larson got home. I didn't move then, and we still haven't moved. If I had done what God said, we would have been organized by the time we were to buy the camp. We are now six months behind. I repent! Time is *short* for working for Jesus. We must be obedient!

Saturday, July 13, 1974 (After a Meeting)

I have learned a *great lesson* in the past two days. Here is the answer for victory in Christ: *A bold confession* of who we are in Christ, mixed with praise to God for our redemption, mixed with praise for what we *expect* God to perform following our prayers. This is the key to victory. For example, instead of praying, "God, give us a good meeting," we should be praying, "God we *thank You* for a good meeting tonight!"

I have been boldly confessing victory for J.U. meetings, and it really works. Not only have we had powerful meetings, but I've been very uplifted and not fearful. By the way, I found out yesterday that the

ACA is having trouble with zoning for the camp. They are thinking of backing out of the deal. Hallelujah! Funny, I don't feel exuberant, but I still believe and thank God for Riverside Camp!

Tonight we had a super meeting! Mark was anointed, and at the end, ten people wanted to be filled with the Spirit. Some were slain in the Spirit, but some didn't receive. There was a lot of confusion up at the front and a lot of newcomers were afraid. So I feel that we should be more structured to avoid confusion and hysteria.

Saturday, July 27, 1974

A lot of things have happened in the past two weeks:

1. Services at J.U. have been powerful. I believe bold confession is the key.
2. I go full time on Monday, and I am excited.
3. Last Sunday, God told Mark to act like a man of God and put away childish things.
4. As elders, we decided that we should dress more neatly for the sake of man. We realize that it makes a difference in how people treat us.
5. We also organized how the altar calls will be conducted. Although they are now much better, I still feel they need a bit more organization.
6. I feel Mark, as leader of meetings, should be giving more direction to the people at the meeting and not letting so many kids get up and talk out of the Spirit. He told the group Saturday night that no one was to do anything special without first talking or conferring with him. I feel Mark also should delegate authority to spotters and organizers in front of the group.
7. We went to talk to the ACA about the camp caretaking job twice last week. They don't think I qualify, but Val and I need a place to live, and I believe God will supply.
8. Mark and his dad got into a heated discussion Thursday night, and Mr. Bechtel had a change of heart. Mark is going to live there and fix up the basement. My office will be also be set up at the Bechtel's house by Monday.
9. The ACA is having troubles socially and politically and also trouble with the Methodist Church. No papers have been signed. Recently,

with all the confusion of what we are going to do, I made a petition to God for what we need. The key points are:

- We need a place to worship and meet, three rooms for counseling, and so forth.
- We need a permanent location for the offices.
- We need housing for Mark and Christi, and Val and me.

10. Mark and I feel that the old hotel at the camp is the best bet for J.U. Therefore, I'll send a letter to the ACA stating, in order of preference:

- We would like to buy the upper level of the camp.
- We would like to buy the hotel and parking space.
- We would like to lease the hotel and parking space.
- We would like to rent it in the meantime.

So, I quit my day job and went into the ministry full-time as Business Coordinator at J.U. My Mom and Dad bought me several suits, ties, and dress jackets to help me look the part. I did everything I could to fulfill our commission, as I understood it. This job change thrust Val and me into an exciting time of our lives, as we worked "heartily unto the Lord."

For my office, we fixed up a small (and I mean small—six feet by seven feet) porch-like room next to the living room in the Bechtel's home. Mark had his office in an extra bedroom. Brother and Sister Bechtel had their bedroom on the main floor. Mark and Christi had their bedroom in the basement.

Brother Bechtel and his wife were quite generous about opening their home to us. After a few months, they moved into their new church parsonage across town. Mark and Christi continued to rent the home.

J.U. meetings were being held in the garage, which was too small, so we added on a plastic structure to the front of the garage. This structure was like a clear plastic tent, with the plastic stapled to the outside of a wood skeleton frame. This plastic structure and the garage held about

The Bechtel's house where it all started. The plastic structure extended out from the garage and over the grass to the right of the driveway.

150 people, packed in like sardines. We used this structure for another six months through the rain, snow, and cold.

Wednesday, August 7, 1974

I'm at my desk at the Bechtel's. I have just prayed for 20 minutes, and I feel settled. I believe God for revival in Niles, Buchanan, and the South Bend area.

I have really accomplished nothing yet as an organizer. I think I am trying to get ahead of God. One thing is for sure, however: We need a meeting place. God *has* to pay up. We've claimed it. But in the meantime, we are seriously hindered in our outreach. We look like a bunch of kids.

Last week, I felt God wanted Val and me out of Mrs. Larson's house, so I looked for an apartment. I asked the Lord if I could live at the Briarcrest apartments near Mark's house. The manager moved a one-year waiting list, and we got a beautiful one-bedroom apartment. Glory to God!

It really seems that J.U. is scatterbrained about a lot of things. We can't even get a retreat organized. Mark and I change our minds, or we don't think on the same level. The result is chaos. I think it stems back to getting guidance from God first.

Tuesday, August 20, 1974

Lately, I've been feeling a *desire* to tell others about Christ. This is exciting! No word on the camp yet. God must do a miracle for the winter meetings.

Wednesday, August 21, 1974

One of the girls who attends J.U. just came back from a vacation in New York. While visiting a church there, a man told her that she belonged to a body of believers in Niles and that an army was going to be raised up. He also said that she should be back at that place and work in that army. She never told him about what was going on in Niles. The man was anointed by the Spirit.

Tuesday, August 27, 1974

Last Friday night, about twelve of us gathered at the Binks's home to pray all night for the body. Since that time, a group has met there together every night to pray. Now, things are starting to happen.

Back on June 9, God told me that a veil of Satan was covering J.U. and that the only thing that would lift it was prayer. At that time, no one else felt this revelation was of God. Two months later, we are starting to lift the veil through group prayer.

Jeff Bechtel and Jim Flood had visions. Rusty, "Furry Curry," Ron Binks, Jeff Bechtel, and Bill Riggenbacher were delivered from oppression, all because we are stirring up heaven by praying in unity as a group.

We called Greg Curry, "Furry Curry," because Greg had a head full of long dark hair and a full beard. At this time, Greg's hair was bushy, giving his head more of a round appearance. Greg was gloriously saved from sin and drugs at J.U. and displayed an intense desire to walk with God. He was tall, dark, and strikingly handsome. Greg could have played Jesus in a Hollywood movie.

Wednesday, September 11, 1974

Last Saturday night, a few girls gathered at Melody Bechtel's house to pray and the Spirit fell, giving two girls a ministry of intercession. Since then, they have regularly fallen into the Spirit of intercession. In addition, ever since the August 27 prayer meeting, Jim Flood and Ron Binks have been given the ministry of travail. It appears that God is giving J.U. the first steps toward revival.

About this time, several people began to report having visions. These visions were usually of Christ, but also about J.U.'s commission and direction. We all believed in these types of things, so when people started reported having visions, I had no reason not to believe them. It was inconceivable to me that anyone would lie about something like this, but I still questioned if people really saw their vision as clearly as real life. They all said that it was as clear as if I were standing in front of them.

Wednesday, September 25, 1974

Last Saturday night, Devin Stockbay fell under the Spirit, talked to Jesus, and shook hands with Michael the archangel! Jesus said we're just now starting to pick up the sickle. Devin will go full-time under J.U. Then, on Monday night, he prophesied, "The leaders are blessed. They *will* yield. Stay away from worldly lusts and pleasures. We have all of the gifts of the Spirit."

Also, last night Mark and I went to talk to the bigwigs in the ACA. They still don't legally own the camp. They gave us full priority of the hotel-cafeteria on the top level of the camp to rent for our meetings. Now there is the legal junk to go through.

I set up an appointment today with the building inspector. Although we spent many hours cleaning up the hotel-cafeteria and getting it ready to use, the building inspector nixed the use of it because, as he said, "the main floor didn't have enough support for a large group of people."

Friday, October 4, 1974

A few things have happened that should be written down.

In June, 1974, I knew that if I went full-time at J.U. without a vision (a clear understanding of our commission or task), my mind would be stressed. In late June, the vision of our commission hit home: to help build an army!

On September 27, we started Friday night prayer meetings. Bill Riggenbacher and Phil were interceding. Bill was travailing and Phil was speaking in tongues. It was clear that these two were being used hand in hand. Three or four times when Bill would travail, I could actually feel a burden, heaving or a great urge to cry within me, although a full release of crying never came. I had never felt that before. I had a sense that Bill and Phil were praying for me. During the last period of travail, Mark noticed my reactions and asked whether I was all right. I went over and told him that I thought they were praying for me.

About thirty seconds later, Phil said, "Larry . . . Larry Barrett," and motioned for others to lay hands on me. I knelt down. Phil laid his hands on my head, and he prophesied to the effect, "[God said] *I am going to give you a knowledge of the business world. You will be a manager of millions of dollars.*" Phil also said that God had given me a ministry to the businessmen in the area.

On Thursday, October 3, 1974, at the elder meeting before the service, Mark told us to each give an exhortation to the assembly that night. When he said that, a great fear struck me. It was overwhelming! I cannot even describe it. It was almost paralyzing! I felt like running away. I rebuked the feeling, but it still stayed.

Then God spoke to me. When one of the women at the meeting spoke in tongues, I had that same manifestation as last Friday—a heavy burden and the urge to cry. The same woman interpreted half of the prophecy, and a black lady finished it. The words plowed into my spirit: *I love you. I'm with you. Go forth and do that which I have set thee to do!* The words anointed me, and the fear left. Well . . . at least *most* of the fear left, but I rebuked it successfully. After the teaching, I spoke two times unhindered.

Tuesday, October 22, 1974

Since September 21, when Devin Stockbay talked to Jesus, four days later Furry Curry danced with Jesus and then, last Thursday and Friday night, Mindi Lander was caught up into the heavens. She says the Lord even put His arm around her. She was impressed with His friendliness. When she suspected that it might not really be Jesus, she asked Him to tell her about the blood that was shed at the cross and the work that was finished there. He had no inhibitions about the finished work. It was Jesus!

As for me, I haven't felt down much at all and have had very little jealousy. There has been a little confusion about intercession. I still have problems getting up in front of people, but I will get over it! The Lord *is* giving me confidence and faith. Some additional things that have happened include:

1. More travail and intercession since August 27.
2. Mark was asked to speak at the Full Gospel Business Men's dinner on October 19.
3. Legs grow—October 19–20.

One of the main "happenings" at charismatic services back then was to ask the congregation if anyone had legs of unequal length. The minister would call these individuals up front and have them sit down on a chair. The minister would have them stretch out their unequal legs and pray for them (usually pulling slightly on the short leg), and the short leg would grow out. We had a few meetings in which Mark did this. I don't remember being up front and seeing any leg unquestionably grow out, but some said they saw it happen.

Tuesday, November 5, 1974

Things are really tense here at the Bechtel's house. There is special stress on Christi. This morning, I had a letter to give to Bill Norten, who was in conference with Mark in his office. I didn't want to interrupt, so I waited until there was a break. As I talked to Sister Bechtel in the hall, Christi went into Mark's office. I felt this was an opportunity to give the letter to Bill, since I had it in my hand and they had already been interrupted. I thought I could just slip it in. Immediately after the door closed, I opened it slightly and reached the letter through. Christi *snatched* it from my hand and *threw* it down. She was *very* rude.

Needless to say, my feelings were hurt. I try my best to make things go smoothly, and then I get jumped on by the pastor's wife. I was humiliated. This was the second time that she has done this to me in front of other people. It is not good. May Jesus supply grace to her.

About this time, Christi and Mark found out that she was pregnant. It is easy now for me to see why Christi was so stressed. Can you imagine how she felt? She was young, crammed into the basement of her in-laws' house, her husband was struggling with juggling the responsibilities of a ministry and family, and now she was feeling the special needs of being newly pregnant.

To add to this stress, Christi was concerned about delivering her baby. When she was a child, she had been injured in a car accident. The injury made a normal delivery difficult, if not impossible.

Friday, November 8, 1974

Well, we're still under the plastic structure at our meeting place, and now we're putting up more. It's possible that serious negotiations with the ACA may begin Monday.

There has been a big uproar of problems lately. There have been people against intercession, people against Mark, division over submission, division over whether the girls should be wearing veils (when they pray in meetings, according to 1 Corinthians. 11:5–6), division over prayer meetings, and so forth. The leaders are seeking God this weekend.

I still have trouble getting up in front of people, but I have learned one thing that has really helped: When ministering to people, you *must see the need* to preach effectively. Otherwise, all you're doing is trying to entertain. God wants us to preach to the need. We should ask God to show us the need, get down the points that we want to get across, and use Scripture to drive home the points. This will provide the solution of the need to the people, setting them free.

Friday, November 22, 1974

I must learn to have a constant burden. Tuesday night, Mark was looking for an elder to speak at the girl's prayer meeting. My first response was that I felt inadequate to do the job. I feel that I must change my whole attitude in order to minister. *I must learn to always keep an attitude of ministry!*

Last night, Kelly Garber talked to Jesus. A few days ago, Jesus told Mindi Lander that the gifts He had given to J.U. would manifest shortly. Then He went before the throne and prayed for the blessings to come to J.U. Jesus told Kelly that the camp was ours.

Before the meeting, I drove by a Baptist church that was for sale. It included thirty-three acres of land. I thought maybe we should try to buy it. Mark seemed to feel that was unbelief with regard to the camp. But I feel J.U. will be *big*! I don't doubt the camp, but we need facilities *now*! Even if we got the camp today and started fixing it up tomorrow, it would still be months before we could move in. However, I do see the futility of *buying* the church. Maybe we should think in terms of renting it.

Wednesday, December 4, 1974

"We must confess the camp daily!" The last few days, Mark has been drilling this into me and the others. I believe it is true. Right now, Mark is confessing to others in the house. We must keep heaven hopping!

Since the beginning of J.U., we had steadily increased in attendance. Now, there were over 150 attendees at every meeting. We had been experiencing a true revival spirit, with many people giving up their drugs and wild lifestyles to follow Jesus. More than half of the attendees came to know Jesus through the ministry of J.U. We felt clearly called to teach sound biblical principles and to continue expanding the outreach.

As I wrote earlier, we had to build a plastic tent-like structure onto the garage to accommodate all the people. The floor was the grass and cement driveway. There were rows of chairs with an aisle down the center in both the garage and the plastic structure. We put the pulpit in the garage doorway so that when the speaker had his back to the doorpost, he could face everyone.

Sometimes, Mark's dog would find his way into the plastic area and leave large dumps of you know what. Many times before a meeting, Mark and I would have to go out and clean up the dog messes and prepare the meeting place. When it rained or snowed heavily, the plastic would fill with water in the center of unsupported areas. We had to reach up and push the bulges up and direct the water to the edges to drain it off.

After a few months, the grass died, and all we had left was dirt. That is, until it rained—then the water came in under the tent and made a big muddy mess.

I think it is amazing that the neighbors, the building inspectors, and the city officials never bothered us. I suppose they couldn't deny the good that was happening there, so they winked at the minor building infractions and the inconvenience of cars parked down the street in front of the homes for a quarter mile.

Then came the storm that blew down our plastic structure. For the next two weeks, we still met in Mark's home. (Mark's mom and dad had moved into their parsonage across town by now.) We crammed into the living room, the garage, the bedrooms, kitchen, and even the basement. With the help of a little speaker system, we all were able to hear and have good meetings, with more people giving their hearts to Jesus.

Tuesday, January 21, 1975

Things are really in an uproar at J.U. now. Two and a half weeks ago, we felt that we should cut off the Thursday night meetings so Mark could concentrate more on setting up a training program. We would then only have the Saturday night meetings. Then, ten days ago, the plastic-covered extension to the garage blew down. The next day, a building on Front Street opened up for $400 per month. We told the owner that we could only afford $200. He said he'd have to think about it. So here we sit, no place to meet, waiting on God to supply. He will!

Ever since Terry Calldean came home, there has been trouble. [Terry had been doing missionary work overseas.] I don't know what it is about, but he is giving off a bad spirit. This spirit begins to dominate everyone that he gets close to. First it was Ron Binks, then Bill Norten, and now Mick Ahrens has been affected. Ron is back in the fold now, and after having a talk with Bill Norten and Mick last night, they are also returning. Yet they are still confused, mainly about marriage.

This week we hired Mick Ahrens, Jim Flood, Bill Norten, and Ron Binks for prayer ministry and maintenance. For the last two weeks, the Lord has been giving us wisdom in organization for the simple reason that if He doesn't, we're gonna sink!

Now, with the division coming in because of Terry, we are in a *very* shaky place. We need organization and unity, but we have division. I believe that God is going to work this out. Terry will have a change of heart, and there will be no more disunity!

I have been very worried about hiring on before there is more organization, but everyone else feels it is of God.

Thursday, January 23, 1975

Mr. Tuff just called and offered the Front St. building for $300 per month. At first I wavered, not knowing what to do. Mark, the prayer ministry team, and I talked it over. Mark felt an inward witness for $200. I had to agree. I'll call Mr. Tuff tonight and tell him that we can pay $200 per month for four months, and then we'll negotiate a lease for June.

Tuesday, January 28, 1975

8:05 A.M.—Mr. Tuff called last night while I wasn't in. He's going to call here today. The Lord has told us to pay $200. We're going to stick to that. If Mr. Tuff asks anything more, we won't take it.

Terry, Mark, Bill Norten, Mick Ahrens, Cary White, and I had quite a talk the other day. We found out that Terry was teaching false doctrine about marriage, which was contrary to the leadership and causing the disunity problem. First, back when Terry was in Greece, he wrote a letter to Cary about the teaching. Then when he came home, Cary shared it with Ron Binks, Mick, and Bill Norten.

Mark and I had asked God to show us the root of the problem last week. One night last week, Mark woke up out of a sound sleep. He looked up and saw two demons. Then his wife started crying in her sleep. When Mark woke her, she said, "I feel like I'm not needed, that you don't want me, and that I'm holding you back."

The next few days, many girls came to see Mark because of Terry's teaching. So we had the meeting, got understanding, and things are good now. Bill Norten and Mick openly admit they were deceived. Terry and Cary are holding back, but keeping it to themselves.

Terry and Cary were teaching that it would be better for a person to remain unmarried than to get married. They said there are many troubles and concerns of married life, and therefore it would be easier to serve God if people remained single, as they were. Now, I can't disagree with the basic logic, because there is truth to it. Any marriage partner will attest to that. But there are also things in marriage that *help* people in their walk with God.

The Bible talks of both the advantages and disadvantages of marriage and clearly blesses the institution of marriage. But the real message that was being portrayed by Terry and Cary was this: "You can get married and still love and serve God, but if you *really* love God, you will remain unmarried." This is a good example of how twisting a little truth can bring people into bondage. Here is the truth of the matter: If you have the gift of singleness and can remain happily unmarried, you should feel free to do so and serve the Lord undistracted from the duties of marriage. But if you feel the need and strong desire to be married, you should do so and serve the Lord together with your spouse.

By the way, both Terry and Cary are now married, and each has three or four children. Last I heard, Cary is busy serving the Lord overseas as a missionary in eastern Germany. I don't know what Terry is doing.

Tuesday, January 28, 1975 (continued)

9:05 A.M.—Mr. Tuff called this morning and agreed to give us the Front Street building for $200 per month. But he threw some cold water on the agreement: He says we'll go on his word for four months. No lease. We are debating whether or not this is God's will. I don't know what to do.

I called Mr. Tuff at 3:00 P.M. and asked for a lease. He agreed to write a note of agreement. So, we have the Front Street building for $200 per month for four months. Just what the Lord said would happen two weeks ago. But it never would have come to pass without our following the inward witness. The next step is the camp!

The lesson I have learned from this is that there are two reasons for inaction:

1. Unbelief of God's Word or inward witness.
2. Acting out of want and not out of God's perfect will.

When we step out to do some good thing for God that isn't in His expressed perfect will, we will experience fear, because our inward witness will be telling us we are going in the wrong direction. How can we have faith for $400 when God's price is $200? Fear will *always* be present when we step out beyond our inward witness. Sure, God would be able to supply the $400, but if He wants us to take the property for $200 and witnesses that to us, our God-given faith cannot exceed that amount. Below is a word given to me by the Lord as I was trying to figure out what to do after the Lord said to get a lease:

Prophetic Word: *I am leading you against your mind purposely in order for you to understand your inward witness. There will come a time when a decision must be made for My kingdom's sake, when time is an element. Time is no element now, but the time is coming when I must have servants who will know My voice and be able to act on it with great speed. Keep searching, and I will lead you into this realm. I have a holy calling for you. You must learn My inward witness.*

Friday, March 14, 1975

We have been going through the heaviest trial since the beginning of J.U. We are in the worst dry spell. However, some great gains have been made in the last few days. The problems started right after we hired on four leaders in prayer ministry. Soon, there seemed to be a breakdown in maturity and unity. We still are not completely through this trial.

The Front Street building, simple but functional.

We are also not yet over the problem that seems to be the greatest threat to J.U. Last month, Terry Calldean began teaching doctrine contrary to the stand of leadership with regard to marriage. It brought strife and division to the leadership. We had to do something about it. Mark was continually distressed about it, and he finally called a meeting to find out where the leaders stood.

Mark declared, "If you do not feel that I have been called to lead you, and if you do not think that we have gone forward as a whole from the beginning until now, then God has told me I must go elsewhere, find new disciples, and leave you to do what you feel is best." After saying this, Mark left the house, telling us to judge him while he was gone and to be truthful. He wanted to find out who was really for him and who really submitted to him. He also stated that if we judged him to be led of the Spirit—and that as a whole we have been led forward—then the ax was going to come down on us for the problems we've been having.

After he left, it soon became clear that ten of the leaders were behind Mark. Terry and Cary felt we had been led astray. It also became clear that the body could still go forward despite their complaints, even if they were valid and never resolved. It was clear that Terry and Cary simply gave place to a complaining spirit, dwelt on a few specific complaints, and became obsessed with a spirit of division or disunity. I don't know why they gave place to these spirits, but it is clear that any such obsessions are the result of deeper problems of insecurity.

Friday, March 28, 1975

So much is happening so fast that it is hard to keep track of everything. I preached last Saturday. The message went well. It was the Lord! I almost started smiling, because I felt so free and my mind was so clear. It was really a miracle for me. Last Thursday night, the Lord spoke to Christi in a literal voice and said that spirits were working through unruly people in the body. He told her that until these people are put in their place, the body will not go one step forward.

So, Friday and Saturday, Rusty, Greg Curry, Bill Norten, and I got some Scriptures together to fight this problem. The Lord revealed truth about delivering over to Satan *for the destruction of the flesh* (1 Corinthians 5:5). When unruly and immoral people are in the body and we know it but don't do anything about it, they are under our covering. We protect them from Satan. When we openly rebuke them according to Matthew 18:15–17, 2 Thessalonians 3:14, 1 Timothy 5:20, 1 Timothy 1:20, and 1 Corinthians 5, we deliver them to Satan, uncover them, and withdraw our protection. They will then be at the mercy of the Devil, who will buffet them. Hopefully, this will jar them to Godly sorrow, as 1 Corinthians 5:5 says, so his *spirit may yet be saved in the day of the Lord Jesus.*

Word of Wisdom and Prophecy: *These spirits are especially prevalent among people who go from church to church and stir up strife and division because they think what they believe is more important than the way the shepherd is leading. Instead of going through the correct channels, they talk to the sheep, who then lose faith in the shepherd when they become obsessed with the same spirit. Unless this spirit is controlled in a church body, within a short time that body will be dying and stagnant, with disunity and strife being very evident. There will be occasional outbursts of love and manifestations of the Spirit, but the relief will be short-lived. The shepherd will be the one most hit by this problem, and he will be hindered and full of anxiety. It can cause a complete loss of zeal. It may cause him to take drastic measures to get rid of the problem—measures that are unwise and hurtful to the body. For this reason, these spirits must be taken under control! Thus saith the Lord!*

CHAPTER 11

THE MAN-CHILD
REVELATION
THE BEGINNING OF THE END

The Man-Child revelation. The beginning of the end of the revival joys.
I remember the first day I heard about this. I came back from lunch
and was walking down Mark's driveway when I met Mick Ahrens and
Mark. Mark looked rather serious and talked with a hint of exaggeration.
He was trying hard to motivate me to some higher level of seriousness
and dedication to our calling. He began to explain how our calling related
to the Man-Child mentioned in the book of Revelation.

Apparently, Mark and/or Mick had a revelation about the Man-
Child the day before, and they had been studying the Bible to establish
the doctrine surrounding it. As Mark began to tell me about the Man-
Child revelation, I had a feeling of something that I couldn't quite put
my finger on. I can pinpoint this feeling now—it is called "trying to
motivate people by using an ungodly fear of God." I also had a feeling
of something new creeping into our mind-set, something I call "exclusiveness," a type of "cultish pride."

Monday, March 31, 1975

Last night, Mark brought forth the revelation of the Man-Child. It
pierced me. I feel that Revelation 12 and Daniel 12 are related. I still

don't understand about when the child is "caught up" and no one else can enter in—everyone else is left as the "woman." As I write this, my insides grind from time to time. Why? It's the same feeling I had as before the meetings. Should I seek the Lord? What should I do? Prevail?

Mark said, along with Mick's vision, that J.U. had missed the gate but had one more chance, because Mark held on and prayed for the body. That one more chance was the Man-Child revelation.

It is amazing how powerful the written Word of God is. Start with a portion of truth from the Bible, twist it slightly, mix in a bit of fear to motivate people toward a cause, then add to that blend a bit of self-importance and . . . presto! You have a great Bible-based "truth" that can bring people into tremendous bondage.

The Man-Child revelation was typed up and distributed to all of the faithful followers of Jesus Unlimited. I must admit that I saw a lot of truth in this revelation and that I do not intend to mock the basic doctrine. But I *do* intend to expose the added untruths and bondage that accompanied the doctrine being taught during this time at J.U. The revelation was four pages long, but I will try to sum it up in a few paragraphs.

In Revelation 12, there is a story about a woman who brings forth a man-child. The woman is the Church of Jesus Christ—Christians of all denominations. The Man-Child is an unknown number of Christians who are exceptionally gifted with faith and a belief that Jesus will use them to deliver the world from the bondage of Satan.

They will "rule the nations with a rod of iron." This rule will be a spiritual rule, affecting the world's events through prayer, preaching, teaching, healing, and proclaiming the gospel of Jesus. The Antichrist will begin his rule during this time, because Satan has been cast out of heaven. The man-child will do God's bidding on Earth to facilitate the final call to Jesus, and he will have power over all the power of the Devil.

But God's plan isn't just an assault on the Antichrist to topple his rule. It is also to give the nations a chance to see the difference between the Devil's way and the way of Jesus. All persons on Earth must choose either Jesus or the Antichrist during this time. A large portion of Christians (the "woman") will break ranks and choose the Antichrist because of the horrible persecution and because they haven't built up enough faith to make it through the hard times. A smaller portion will choose Jesus. The end of the age will come shortly after this time, and the Devil will be totally defeated and cast into hell.

That is the short version of the Man-Child Revelation. One of the added parts of the doctrine that contributed to excessive pride and exclusiveness was the teaching that after the Man-Child was "sealed," no one else could get in. Now, there could be a little truth to this except for the fact that anyone who *couldn't* get in really wouldn't *want* to get in anyway. But that type of added information produced great fear and bondage to those people in J.U. who already had a healthy fear of God.

The revelation also implied the thought that if you rejected the ministry of J.U., you would be sealed out and never be able to get into the Man-Child. This was the big kicker into bondage. This put too much weight on Mark and J.U., because deep down we really wanted to do the right thing. If Mark, the other leaders, and I knowingly brought this tactic in, we could have more easily have borne the weight. But all of us *were* seeking the truth and wanted to do the right thing.

I think that we were on track in many ways and were bearing good fruit in many areas. This made our enemy mad, and he began to work overtime against us to lead us into deception, one little twist at a time. It was at this time that the SPIRIT OF ERROR began to move in like a flood. One quote from the actual Man-Child handout said:

The Lord told us that once the Man-Child is sealed, no one else can get in because there won't be enough time for them to be raised up into sonship. This sealing takes place sometime during the revival;

133

however, it is an individual thing in every person's walk. Some who have come to J.U. have already been sealed out. They have rejected God's Spirit and calling and have left.

Portions of this passage *could* be true. It *does* take time to learn God's ways, it *does* take some hard times to learn the pitfalls of pride, and it *does* take time to learn how to responsibly administer gifts of the Holy Spirit. If a person came to J.U. and heard the simple message of Jesus, understood it, and made a firm and *lasting* decision to reject that message, then that person *would* be doomed.

So why, then, does this part of the Man-Child doctrine carry so much weight, and why is it so full of bondage? Because there is some *strong* truth here with some untruth mixed in. I see three specific *un*truths:

1. *It takes time to be raised up into sonship*: Normally this is true, but with God all things are possible (see Luke 18:27). He holds the keys to spiritual growth.
2. *Some have already been sealed out*: The implied message here is that the leadership at J.U. knew who had been sealed out and had judged them as infidels. But who really knows whether a person's decision to reject Christ is with full understanding? Who really knows whether God's Spirit may draw that person again at another time? No one.
3. *If you come and hear our messages and don't receive those messages as totally from God—or leave and go to church elsewhere—you will be sealed out of the Man-Child:* The implied message here was that the J.U. doctrine was correct, and all other doctrine was false. You had better stay with us, accept our teaching, and stay in good standing with the leadership, or you would be sealed out of the Man-Child.

Soon we began to fear and follow the leadership in an ungodly way. We also were afraid of being left behind. We began to look at the leadership as a group of elite men whose actions and teachings could not be questioned. Everyone fell into this bondage, including the leadership itself.

Two months later, we established four levels of leadership: bishop, elders, pastors, and deacons. Mark, as the bishop, had an ungodly fear of God and a wrong perception of how to lead. The elders were next, and they feared Mark's disapproval because he could demote them or put them out of leadership entirely. The pastors and deacons were considered equals. They feared both the elders and Mark, although they *did* look at Mark as having the higher wisdom and authority. Occasionally, when we disapproved of an elder's opinion, we would go and appeal to Mark.

Hey, we were young, trying to please God and be bold for His cause. We were babes in the jungle, Mark included. None of the leaders recognized this ungodly fear. I suppose it is imbedded in most people due to some cultural conditioning. But it is an unfortunate cornerstone in portions of the Christian world that I hope to expose and bring to light.

Tuesday, April 1, 1975

> Sometime last fall, the Lord said we failed to prevail against Him as Jacob did. After the gifts were poured out, we went slack. I am determined to be blessed of God, to prevail, and to take what was bought for me at Calvary. I think that when my innards grind, it is time to seek the Lord and find out what is cooking!

Here are two phrases that you will begin to see more and more: "The Lord said . . ." and "God said . . ." Mark began to gravitate toward the people who were having visions and literal words from the Lord. When J.U. started, I was Mark's best friend, and we were very close. But as things progressed, Mark began to pull away from me. I seldom had any literal visions or literal words from the Lord, while Mick Ahrens and Rusty Evans began to have them regularly. The literal words were much more important to Mark than my simple inspirations, and I was not invited to spend as much time at night praying and seeking God with Mark.

I would always question the people having visions. "You said you saw Jesus as plain as day," I would say. "Did you *really* see Jesus as plain as day? Did you hear that Word the same as you hear me now?" Soon, I was soon looked on as a hindrance to the supernatural because I was skeptical of the words coming forth. I believe in the supernatural and all of the gifts of the Holy Spirit, and I do expect to see them operate more often as my life goes on. But I think it *is* healthy to ask the hard questions of the people who are reporting supernatural experiences. Resistance to this type of questioning is a warning signal that something is wrong.

I think that Mick and Rusty subtly began to be competitive concerning the revelations they received from the Lord in order to be closest to Mark and to be on his good side. This increased the temptation to exaggerate and report more and more visions and revelations.

Tuesday, April 1, 1975 (continued)

Greg Curry and Rusty were added as pastors yesterday. I was leery of them for a while—not because of any sin, but because I feared they didn't really have what it takes to be pastors and go forward. But I think my thoughts were premature and probably partly due to my fear of not making a salary. *We are going to go forward together!*

Friday, April 11, 1975

It was God's leading to expand the staff. Mark's witness was correct. It was the other people (including myself) who let him down. If we would have persevered and prayed through rather than becoming perplexed and quitting our prayers, we would have found the answers to our confusion. Mark, Bill Norten, Mick Ahrens, Bill Riggenbacher, and a few others are fasting. Maybe I should too. I have had a great burden for the camp since last Sunday night.

It looks as if we're going to put our seriousness into action tomorrow night. A new attendee has really been unruly, and we are going to have to rebuke him publicly for being a "railer." Three days ago, he railed on Greg Curry, rudely complaining about some disagreement. When

Rusty and Greg went to see him Wednesday, he was even more ready and willing to cause trouble. He is determined to bring accusations before the body against the elders. He said, "No one is going to stop me." This will be a training ground for all of us.

Lesson: When a person has a grievance against an elder, he should pray and persevere about it. God will either show him or the leadership the answer. Or God will tell him to leave the body in a respectable manner.

We never saw the above-mentioned person again, and he never caused any more trouble.

Tuesday, April 15, 1975

I had a talk with Terry last night that I sure hope changed him. He has been teaching foreign languages to his parents, Cary White, and a brother from another church. Then my sister decided to be taught. I warned her, and she told Terry. Then Terry called me.

I said to Terry, "There is to be no teaching languages at this time to any J.U. people except your family and Cary White." I also said, "It is advised that you stop all emphases on languages and concentrate on learning how to cause revival and seek a personal relationship with God." I told him that I, along with the brethren, feel he is getting off track—if he feels God wants him to teach what he has been teaching, it is a wrong interpretation of his inward witness.

I said that we felt that he has a strong spirit that causes his students to become obsessed with languages, Europe, and world evangelism, so that the short-term goals and the current leading of the Lord take second place in their walk, which causes them to err. I told him that this was the most important reason to lay off the teaching.

I also said to Terry that it was now *his* responsibility to prevail in prayer for an understanding between leadership and himself. I told him, "If you prevail, God will show either you or us." There will be no excuse for a continuous misunderstanding on such an important problem.

God lifted us up last Saturday and forgave us for backsliding. But He warned, *Be careful not to slide back into complacency when things are going well.* Mark also prophesied, *Some are being sealed tonight!*

I still don't understand all the loose ends of the Man-Child doctrine—some sealed now, and so forth. But I know that if I persevere and cry after wisdom and knowledge, God will reveal the truth.

I have taught and preached several times in the last few weeks and, hallelujah, the fear of man is leaving me. I am getting bolder in the Spirit. I'm not sure what the solution was, but I believe it may have been in persisting and hearing from God. When I've heard from God, it is much easier for me to speak in front of a group. At the meeting last Saturday, I was supposed to speak, but I knew that salvation was in order. One of the brothers interpreted a salvation tongue, and I went to the pulpit knowing that the message I had prepared was not to be preached. We simply waited on God. Jim Flood preached instead, and twelve people got saved! I felt full of authority. No fear. Amen and praise God!

Saturday, April 26, 1975 (After a Meeting)

All afternoon, a grinding in the pit of my stomach grew stronger. I looked for a prayer closet but found none. I wanted to get in line with what the Spirit had for J.U. tonight. I really didn't get down with God at all, but fervently looked for a meeting place. When it came time to go to the meeting, I went walking, just to get alone with God. Nothing.

All during worship, the grinding in my stomach was still there. I knew the sheep needed to be fed, but no Scripture came to mind. Why? Then confusion set in as many people spoke and prophesied. First, a burden for the body, then salvation, then the body, then this, that, and confusion. No word went forth to feed the sheep. At dismissal, the people at the service were depressed and confused.

Every minister and ministry occasionally experiences dry times or confusing services. Mark and J.U. were no different. I was noticing one of these times, and was wondering if maybe I could do a better job than Mark.

Saturday, April 26, 1975 (continued)

There wasn't much leading all through the meeting. I think I could have done a good job leading, but something happens when the pressure is on me. Is it my flesh leading me to emcee, or God? We need order, but does that mean I'm supposed to do it? Please, God, make it clear. I know I can do it if You tell me to and help me.

Thursday, May 1 1975

For some reason, Mark does not give others enough trust to work their positions effectively. The problem may be incompetence in myself and others, but if so, Mark has no business giving responsibility to others until one is found who is capable. This is what must be running through Mark's mind: *They're not capable of handling their position, so I must constantly overrule.*

The others are really concentrating on setting up one aspect of their ministry, and then Mark jumps on them for not being efficient in another area. So they break their train of thought and become obedient and concentrate on this new area. After they begin, Mark then jumps on them again for another area. So they stop and go on to a new area. In the end, nothing gets done efficiently and everything that is done is scattered.

It's not that I'm mad at or disgusted with Mark. I realize he's got hang-ups and problems that need to be worked out like anyone else. I realize that he *is* called to lead me into the fullness of Christ. And I realize that this problem will be solved sooner or later. But it seems to me that until this problem of disorganization is taken care of, I'm no good for J.U. It's still a one-man show. I don't care about position! I care about going forward! Why go on to new projects when we can't efficiently take care of what we're doing now? Why not "drop back ten and punt," trusting God to hold the enemy while we regroup and organize? Then we could pick up the ball and work as a *team.*

It seems that I'm getting like Cary and Terry, but I'm not. I have faith in God leading Mark, and I believe sooner or later it will be worked out. I *know* I'm called to J.U. I know that I am right where God wants me to be at this time. I *believe* we will triumph together.

I don't disagree with Mark's "Spirit storms" (inspirations for going forward). *Very* seldom do I get a negative reaction. But the presentation always comes when I am concentrating on another area.

Terry and Cary always wanted something Mark *hadn't* ordained. But all I want to do is set up something Mark *has* ordained, one area at a time. I really don't know if I'm out of line writing about this. I *dare* not touch God's anointed. Now that I have begun to understand the problem, I trust that Mark will hear God when I pray.

Notice here that I am very reluctant to criticize or question Mark's leadership. At Boulder's Chapel, we were taught that it was a mortal sin to touch God's anointed or say anything against God's chosen leaders. The text in 2 Samuel 19:21 says, *But Abishai the son of Zeruiah answered and said, "Shall not Shimei be put to death for this, because he cursed the* LORD'S *anointed?"* And 1 Chronicles 16:22 says: *Touch not mine anointed, and do my prophets no harm.*

Although the Bible speaks on this subject in the Old Testament, the J.U. leadership added an ungodly fear to the doctrine, making it almost impossible to engage in constructive criticism. This mind-set had a tendency to encourage the leadership to build a wall of pride that resisted questioning.

I did not expect anyone else to ever see this journal account in which I vented my frustration about Mark's leadership style. I still don't know how Mark got in a position to read my journal. But somehow Mark, and maybe a few of the elders, read the above passage. It seemed to cause Mark to have even less patience with me.

CHAPTER 12

THE SUPERNATURAL INCREASES

MORE VISIONS AND MIRACLES

Tuesday, May 6, 1975

Two weeks ago on April 20, the Lord gave us three prophecies at an elder's meeting. He said, *Unite, become one flesh (soul), and lay down goods at the apostle's feet.* We planned on doing it, but we were too slow. God didn't manifest Himself or bless us even in prayer during the last two weeks. Then, when we realized we were out of His will and began to distribute and lay down our goods, He really gave us a good meeting Saturday night, with legs growing and other miracles and healings and testimonies that were glorious. I haven't felt so free in a year!

We started an apostle's fund among the leaders. It was not tax deductible, and it could be used for any purpose without reporting it. Eventually, the fund grew to well over $12,000.00.

Tuesday, May 27, 1975

We have been going through quite a shaking time. Christi had her child last Saturday. Mark said that he made a mistake and took Christi to the hospital the night before. With the fear of the place and the

141

pushiness of the doctors, Christi gave in to having a C-section. Fear and unbelief swept over her at the crucial moment.

Even though Christi's childhood injury made it dangerous for her to have a normal delivery, Mark and Christi felt that God was going to do a miracle and allow her to have a natural birth. They even considered doing a home birth. Christi felt that she had let Mark down because she had given in to having a C-section, and Mark felt that he had let J.U. down. They both felt terrible about it. However, the upside was that Christi gave birth to a beautiful baby boy. Even though Christi was quite young, she was a very good mother to their son.

Tuesday, May 27, 1975 (continued)

I preached last Saturday about the time of shaking, foundations, and faith. Up to the time of the preaching, I really felt anointed. My hands were tingling, and most of my fear went away. It was the same last week, even though I didn't preach. But when the altar call time came, I didn't know what to do. For an hour, the anointing was spasmodic. God told Mark on Saturday that He wants to do mighty miracles but that the elders are stopping Him. I suppose it is fear. When I saw a crippled person come in, it made me fearful. But the message came forth pretty well.

After the Man-Child Revelation came forth, the Calldeans left the body. Then a week ago, one of the assistant pastors from the Christian Center called and acted very sarcastic and rude. It was terrible. Apparently, the Calldeans gave them a story that was not true. I would think that other Christians would first think no evil and check us out, especially full gospel Christians.

Several weeks ago, Jesus told Mick Ahrens that a sword was being drawn through the body of Christ because of the call to a deeper walk with God in prayer and dedication. I have a feeling that this is just the beginning.

Tuesday, June 3, 1975

For the past three or four months, God has bestowed much grace upon this body. He has granted so many visions and revelations that it is really astounding. He has used Mick Ahrens the most. Mick has talked to the Lord many times during this last month.

Several months ago, God told Mick that He was soon going to tell about every elder's position. Three days ago, Mick was caught up and the Lord told him about church government. Instead of nine elders plus Mark, there is now one bishop, three elders, three pastors, and three deacons. I am designated as a deacon.

When this was brought forth, I felt cut off from Mark, whom I have been close to from the beginning. But I'll get over it. I'm going to learn and do my job—and do it *well!*

The deacons were in charge of the physical aspects of the organization: business, maintenance, and other technical jobs. The pastor's main responsibilities pertained to counseling and dealing directly with the people in the church. The deacons and pastors were considered equal in authority. The elders were above them and spent most of the time preparing teaching material, praying, and "revelating" (revealing) with Mark. The bishop's position was as main overseer of the whole organization.

Ron Binks was the maintenance supervisor, but he was not really considered a leader. Some of the leaders were on salary, and some were on unemployment. Originally, Jim Flood was named an elder and Rusty Evans was named pastor. However, a few weeks later, Rusty was promoted to elder and Jim was demoted to pastor. At this time, Rusty was reporting more visions and words from the Lord than the other leaders.

So, to summarize the current leadership situation:

Bishop: Mark
Elders: Mick Ahrens, Rusty Evans, and Bill Norten
Pastors: Jeff Bechtel, Jim Flood, and Greg Curry
Deacons: Larry Barrett, Phil Bechtel, and Bill Riggenbacher

Wednesday, June 4, 1975

Yesterday, a young woman died who used to come to J.U. regularly. She was trusting God to heal her of diabetes. The name "J.U." is buzzing around the hospital, because she said that we were her church. I thank God for the revelators. Mick Ahrens was caught up yesterday, and the Lord told him about this girl. She was moving away from the shadow of God, and God let Satan kill her so she would go to heaven and not die spiritually. She was torn between two worlds. God saw that her heart was pure, but failing, so He really had mercy on her.

This very pleasant young woman was not a regular attendee of J.U. at the time of her death. She and her parents came for a while, but then started going to the Glory Barn after the Man-Child Revelation came forth. We were not as adamant about trusting God for healing as they taught at the Glory Barn. Several people who attended the Glory Barn, including children, died over the years due to either not taking medicine or not following a doctor's advice. As far as I know, the Glory Barn is no longer in existence.

Wednesday, June 4, 1975 (continued)

It seems that with all the revelation that is coming forth, the written Word is losing its power with us. I really don't know, but I'll keep a watch. Now that I'm a deacon, I don't really know what to do. I'm confused on the definition. I'm getting over the shock of separation from Mark, although I still feel funny about being led by Jim Flood!

Tuesday, June 17, 1975

Last week, Mick Ahrens had a vision of a man and God holding hands. Then God pulled back, and the man groped for God's hand and found it. God told Mick that He must do this to us because He has extended His hand long enough and now we must seek and extend our hand. When we find His hand again, we will have entered into another realm. I believe this vision includes finances.

Friday, June 20, 1975

Last month, Ron Binks was taken off maintenance and Bill Riggenbacher was put in his place. Then Bill got called to go back to work. After consulting Rusty, along with other leaders, we put a different brother on maintenance. Then Bill decided not to go back to his former work. God said Bill's decision was a mistake, because it messed up His perfect will for Bill and others.

Wednesday, June 25, 1975

I just wrote a letter to Terry pleading with him to come back.

Terry and Cary left J.U. a month or so earlier, and I think they did the right thing. They spoke their version of the truth to the leadership, and then they left quietly.

Tuesday, July 1, 1975

Mark just came in and told me that Rusty talked to God last night. Jesus had a bag of jewels tied to his belt, and He reached in and gave Rusty two of them. One was for special discernment for the mentally impaired and one was for casting out Devils.

The Lord said that this week we would be entering into our next step and that things would begin to flow. I just read about our good times at the beginning of J.U., and I feel that joy will soon return. Hallelujah!

The grinding feeling that I've been experiencing since just before I got married is getting more intense when it comes on me. Perhaps I'm just getting more Spirit conscious? I remember distinctly that this grinding began when I was filled with the Holy Spirit. The Lord recently told the elders to let others begin to exercise their inward witness.

When I heard Rusty was caught up to the throne of God, I started to get jealous. This is something that I must still fight, but I refuse to let it dominate me! I will put positive thoughts into action. I will continue to seek God for a personal relationship. I love you, Jesus!

I suppose that the reason I feel jealous when God exalts others is simply because I have a lack of faith and assurance in my own personal relationship with Him. I also forget about what God has already said about me and what He's already done for me. I confess: *God is with me and will soon give me an extra touch.* I believe that! I must continue to seek Him. Praise God!

Monday, July 7, 1975

The supernatural is here! Rusty fell out today and saw Christ as plain as day. The day Jesus gave Rusty his jewels (July 1), he also interceded for some prisoners of Russia. That was a "number one" vision, but the vision he had today was on level number two: a trance.

It might be good at this point to explain my definitions of the levels of visions (they are "my definitions" because they are not found in the dictionary). I have assigned level numbers in order to separate what I perceive to be distinctly different types of vision experiences.

I call the lowest type a "level one" vision. This is when a person perceives or sees something in his spirit, similar to a daydream, but somewhat clearer. The "level two" type is a higher level vision—a trance—which is what Peter experienced in Acts 10:9–16 when he saw the sheet let down from heaven. It was quite real to him, and quite a profound experience.

The "level three" level vision is the highest type. This is when God allows people to actually see spiritual things with their physical eyes, and they are aware of themselves and their own physical attributes and earthly surroundings. This is what happened to the apostles after the resurrection of Jesus. Jesus appeared to them while they were in a locked room. They saw Him, touched Him, and heard Him with their physical senses.

Having someone in our midst reporting that they experienced a number two level vision was a significant "wow!" to me back then. It still *is* a big deal to me, except now I feel better about pressing the issue as to the validity of the reported experience. As you can tell from the following journal entries, I was pretty excited about Rusty's visions. All of Rusty's opinions carried much more weight for me from that time on.

Monday, July 7, 1975 (continued)

On July 1, Jesus told Rusty about a new spiritual ministry for us that involved three Soviet prisoners. He said the J.U. leaders would actually teach them and minister to them in order to spearhead the Man-Child and revival in all Asia. He said that if we or someone else don't minister to these three, all Asia will be lost, because it will miss the revival. Jesus said that these three men are the only ones capable of receiving the deep things of the Spirit.

The other day, Rusty saw two of the prisoners in a number one vision. One is Spirit-filled and the other is not. We will teach the Spirit-filled man. He will get the other started, who will be the main spearhead of revival. The reason we can't deal directly with this man now is because he doesn't have the faith or knowledge to ask for outside help. In fact, today when Rusty was with Christ, Rusty could *only* give the man a drink of water because he asked *only* for water. Jesus told Rusty, *I would give him meat, if he would ask. But in the meantime, I'm bound. He must ask.*

Rusty ministered today to the Spirit-filled prisoner who is now being tortured in an upright box at a concentration camp. Rusty made it cooler in the box and also commanded the blood in the man's his lower legs to circulate. He also ministered to the non-Spirit filled man who is being dehydrated to death in the back of a courthouse-type building. When Rusty asked Jesus if they could see him, Jesus said, *Not yet.* Rusty commented that it was *so* real when he was at the concentration camp that he felt as if the guards and other prisoners could see him.

Jesus said to Rusty that Mark has the gift of diversities of tongues, which involves him exhorting others of a different language in their own tongue. Mark will also understand what he will be speaking. This brought an inspiration to me: Is it possible that "diversities of tongues" and "interpretation of tongues" are two unrelated gifts?

Jesus said that we will not have a fleet of planes or jets. He said we will be translated! He said that the world's economic crisis will halt most trans-continental travel. This will result in mass starvation. Jesus said that this will be a time of great miracles of feeding.

Jesus told Rusty that Mark is *the* spearhead of the Man-Child and that the growth of the Man-Child is pretty much going to grow at J.U.'s pace. We are on the front lines and others are following, but they are by no means passing us by or gaining on us. We will lead the world to sonship and then to revival! Heavy! He said that Mark will soon be translated to other countries to teach them of the spiritual ways of God. The Spirit-filled prisoners have seen visions of Mark talking with Bill Norten about J.U. teaching lessons.

Jesus said that we in America do not appreciate our blessings and that we take too much for granted.

As you can see, the supernatural certainly had gone to a whole different level as far as I could tell. I had no reason to believe that anyone would lie about visions or words from the Lord, so I assumed that God was moving mightily among us indeed.

I understood that inspirations might get garbled or perceptions of words from the Lord could get distorted. I even understood that people might think they had a word from God, but it was just their own imagination. But I never considered that anyone could say they saw Christ with their own eyes or say they heard God in a literal voice unless they literally *did* see or hear Him. None of the past J.U. leaders have ever confessed to me that they were lying. Without a confession, or without a clear supernatural word to me from the Holy Spirit, I simply cannot say that they were lying about these visions.

However, I suspect that Rusty didn't really have the high level vision in the above journal entry. I even suspect that on many occasions, he and

Mick Ahrens were receiving "revelations from God" that were coming from their own imagination. And, I suspect that both Mick and Rusty were making up revelations, especially toward the end of J.U. So, if that were true, why was I at all open to this deception? It's because I saw no reason to disrespect Rusty or Mick at this time, and I believed then (and now) that these types of supernatural things *do* happen in the Church. I expect to see them happen more as I go on in my life and ministry.

We were spiritual kids at this time, and God winked at our exaggerations and lying for a brief period of time. How could He do this? The Father is most holy and doesn't wink at just anything, but He looks at us through Jesus. I *do* believe Jesus winks at a lot of things based on our maturity or lack of it. There are many things we allow a baby to do that we don't tolerate when the child is older. I think God acts the same toward us. Acts 17:30 states, *And the times of this ignorance God winked at; but now commandeth all men every where to repent.*

But I believe that I will see the day when knowingly lying and selfishly deceiving the flock—thereby hurting trusting young Christians—will bring about swift action from God, similar to what happened to Ananias and Sapphira in the book of Acts. They died instantly.

To be fair, I must say that some of the revelations and visions were truly from God and brought some truth and deliverance to my life and others. But it's confusing when truths and deceptions come at the same time. Some people don't believe that a true prophet of God can say right *and* wrong things in the same sermon.

So, *does* God allow this to happen in our churches today? When we hear someone share a "message from God," do we *have* to accept all of it or none of it? Is it either/or? Can we decide which statements are true and which are false? If so, *how* can we decide what is true and what is false? The answers to these questions (if answered correctly) could save you from a world of hurt and confusion. Hopefully, by the end of this book you will know the answers to these questions.

The prayer shack, nestled in the woods, deep in the Binks' property.

The inside of the prayer shack with pieces of carpet spread over the dirt floor.

Thursday, July 10, 1975

Two nights ago, Mark called a meeting of the elders, deacons, and pastors. When we prayed, the Lord told Mick Ahrens that the leaders were on the edge of a hedge. The supernatural was on the other side of the hedge, and we were just reasoning out circumstances why we couldn't step over. We didn't realize our legs were longer than the small hedge. The Lord said, *Tonight, you must step over.*

At 12:30 A.M., we met at the prayer shack that Ron Binks had built behind his parents' house. Bill Norten read a Scripture that God revealed to him some time ago: *Thus saith the LORD of hosts; In those days it shall come to pass, that* ten men *shall take hold out of all languages of the nations, even shall take hold of the skirt of him that is a Jew, saying, "We will go with you: for we have heard that God is with you"* (Zechariah 8:23). This Scripture bore witness with me that this night we were to fulfill Bible prophecy.

When we had feet washing, Mark felt impressed to wash my feet, and I got choked up. I broke down afterwards and cried for longer than I have in many years. It felt good! Then I felt faith rise up. After we symbolically took hold of Jesus' skirt, Mick fell out, and then reported that Jesus said our prayers were heard and accepted! Jesus also said that because we have accepted part of Himself, He will show us His fullness! I believe it!

My confession is this: I dwell in heavenly places, far above all principality, power, might, and dominion. I have stepped over the hedge, and I walk in the supernatural! I suspect that I will be tried (as the other nine also) for a season on this confession, but I believe it and *expect* the results! *Now!*

Tuesday, July 15, 1975

Hallelujah! I have never walked in *so* much victory as I have lately! The reason for this is that I have begun to understand and put into action the Law of the Spirit.

Mark spoke on this subject one night, basing his teaching on Romans 8:2: *For the law of the Spirit of life in Christ Jesus hath made me free from the law of sin and death.* He defined the law and taught on how to use it.

Tuesday, July 15, 1975 (continued)

I'm being set free. From now on, when circumstances appear bleak, I'll just keep faith, patience, and love in operation. I will not grieve or fret because these are negative forces.

When a person puts on negative forces, he *hinders* God from helping the situation. God wants to help, but the circumstances cannot be helped when negative forces are harbored. Up to this point, most of J.U. (including myself) have not been able to keep victory when circumstances look bad.

I have really been getting set free by the teaching that has come forth from Mark. I expect a total understanding of the most sought-after question I've had since being saved: What is grace and the mystery of salvation? I believe this understanding will be the main motivation in helping me minister to others effectively.

Wednesday, July 23, 1975

Lately, I have felt "the Lord on my head." Mark mentioned yesterday that when he was doing jobs as an overseer, the Lord would seem to massage his head. Mick talked to the Lord, and He said it was His assurance that Mark was doing his job. Yesterday, I was rebuking and chastising my teenage cousin who was visiting us, and I felt that I might be beating him down too far. But then I felt the Lord massage my scalp. That manifestation gave me a peace that what I was doing was right.

Thursday, August 7, 1975

Lately, Rusty has fallen out and had visions quite regularly. I believe that all the leaders should become this way soon in order to be effective. I keep reminding the Lord that the supernatural is now and I believe it!

I believe the grinding I have been feeling is definitely fear or anxiety. When I concentrate on trust, this sometimes defeats the grinding.

Last week Mark preached on Revelation. He opened it right up. Hallelujah! It really isn't so complicated. It fits in perfectly! The Lord said He was going to go through all of Revelation with us.

Wednesday, August 13, 1975

Last week, the Lord told us about David Wilkerson. He said that David was called as a prophet to America and not as a street youth worker. Since his deviation from God's will (staying in youth work), familiar spirits have fed his organization money so that he would stay out of God's will. He was sent to New York specifically for Nicki Cruz.

Both David and Nicki are called into the Man-Child. We prayed for them last week and also for other organizations. I feel someone should call or write David Wilkerson so that he has a chance to repent. The Lord said that David Wilkerson was going to have a vision from Satan that will point at groups such as J.U. as the Devil's working. We asked the Lord three times for some way to stop it, but He wouldn't answer.

The demon of exclusiveness was now coming on us in full force. One by one, we began to cut off respect for any other organizations or Christian leaders. These "revelations" *may* have touched on a little truth, but this truth was used to totally destroy our respect for other Christian leaders and organizations. Destroying the respect of outside influences is one of the cornerstones of exclusiveness. *It wasn't long before we respected no one outside our group.* There is a fear that accompanies this demon of exclusiveness. It causes you to stop judging your immediate leaders and excessively judge leaders outside your own group.

By the way, I think we were sadly mistaken—David Wilkerson has one of the best and most credible ministries in the world.

153

Wednesday, August 20, 1975

During the past few days, I have been going through a trial like never before. After being told by Mark to move my office out of his house, I set up an office at the Front Street building, only to have the setup completely taken apart and moved again by the leadership to another part of the building.

Also during this time, rebellion would rise up within me, and I would immediately quench it and put it under. When I would rebuke it, it would leave. But as soon as another change came forth and Mark would administer it, it would rise up again.

Tuesday night, I went out to the prayer shack to get hold of God, to get rid of the rebellion, and to make things straight about the issues that were rising up in me. These were the thoughts that were going through my head: *God is unhappy with me because of the rebellion and selfishness that is rising up out of me . . . Rebellion is serious . . . We must be led by the Spirit . . . I must not have been led . . . I've messed up . . . What if God demotes me from responsibility? . . . What if I get taken off full-time ministry, like my sister and Bill Riggenbacher?*

After praying for an hour at the shack, I realized that I needed help from the brothers. I was being tormented too much and felt I couldn't take the pressure much longer. I needed help! I went to Mark's and told him the story. He called Mick and asked him to go to the Lord about it.

Mick seemed to be able to fall out in the Spirit at will when Mark needed information from God.

I felt a peace that God would minister to me in my time of need. And He did! This is what God said:

You're going through a time of purging for removal of negative forces in your soul. Up to this time, they have been hidden in your job, but God says it is time to let them be brought to the top so you can see yourself and defeat them by faith. He's creating situations and conditions for this to take place. After you get purged of these forces, you will be ready to move into a greater spiritual ministry that God sees ahead.

Afterwards, I praised God that He had mercy on me. I was greatly relieved that I didn't have to go back to punching holes in the wrong place at the factory.

Thursday, August 21, 1975

Rusty fell out after the meeting last Saturday night, after which he told us that the Lord was angry! The Lord said that the leaders had to change in the following areas:

1. We need to quit leaning on Mark to supply the word of exhortation at the meetings.
2. We haven't made ourselves available to preach. Only to prophesy, lay on hands, and so forth.
3. We haven't gotten down in prayer during the week and asked for something to give to the body.
4. We like the status of being leaders, but we don't take on the responsibility of leadership.
5. We kid around and don't exhort each other seriously about the needs of the body.
6. We look at ourselves as being above the body.

I am determined to pray and get those things changed.

Friday, August 22, 1975

Today I had an appointment with Rusty for personal revelation on my walk. First, the Lord set my priorities. They are as follows:

1. My relationship with God.
2. Distribution of Training Center material [lessons Mark and the elders put together to be the foundation of J.U.'s training and teaching].
3. Audiotape ministry head and technician, music included.
4. Purchasing of major equipment.

It surprised me that the Lord didn't mention anything about firing up (encouraging) the sheep. Mick Ahrens suggested that if I do my job and fulfill those priorities, I will naturally assume the firing up part.

Next, the Lord exposed some basic negative forces that have been motivating me and the respective negative forces I use to cover them up. These include:

1. Fear of rejection, pride and introversion.
2. Fear of man and false humility.

The Lord said that I should use the Word against these forces when they rise up. Also—and I feel this is very important—I should begin to trust God. All this revelation bore witness with my Spirit.

Thursday, August 28, 1975

After an early leaders meeting at 6:00 A.M., the Lord ministered to Rusty and Mick that I was soul possessed (mentally obsessed, not physically possessed) with inferiority. We rebuked the spirit together, and I was instructed to live out and confess my deliverance from this *past* bondage.

Monday, September 1, 1975

After a leader's meeting, the elders informed me of a few changes that God wanted me to make in my life:

1. I should type the teaching material labels myself or have Val do it.
2. I should stop meddling in other J.U. ministries.
3. Val is to use the car only one day a week, including errands and groceries.
4. I should return the 10-speed bike I have to Jeff Bechtel.

The Lord also said:

1. I make little jobs big.
2. I am to hand in to the elders an hour-by-hour report regarding the work of the ministry.

As you can see, personal revelation and direction from the leaders at J.U. was now commonplace. This set the stage for blind following and disaster. Remember, the strength of this type of revelation is that an element of truth is usually present. Adding to the Word of God, or adding to a revelation from God, is damaging to the hearers. Unfortunately, it happens a lot.

CHAPTER 13

THE BLACK HORSE

GOD MOURNING FOR THE BODY OF CHRIST

Wednesday, September 3, 1975

At a leaders' meeting last Wednesday, the Lord informed us that He was mourning for the body of Christ and also Jesus Unlimited. He said the "Black Horse" was going through J.U.

*I*n the previous chapter, I wrote that Mark had preached on the book of Revelation and explained about the meanings of the seals being opened. The third seal was about "The Black Horse":

And when he had opened the third seal, I heard the third beast say, "Come and see." And I beheld, and lo a black horse; and he that sat on him had a pair of balances in his hand. And I heard a voice in the midst of the four beasts say, "A measure of wheat for a penny, and three measures of barley for a penny; and see thou hurt not the oil and the wine."

(Revelation 6:5–6)

Mark said the Scripture meant the judgment of God on the body of Christ, including the people of J.U. He said that God was now beginning to judge all Christians, and giving them a last chance to repent. God

159

would then cut off all those who had not laid down their lives for the cause of Christ or those who had held back anything from Him. The penny referred to in the Scripture was considered to mean a person's full commitment to following Christ.

Wednesday, September 3, 1975 (continued)

The leaders studied the list of the J.U. people and put them in categories of "walking in light," "those not drawn," and so forth. Then the Lord ministered to us individually. This is what He said about me:

1. I have light to walk in that I haven't walked in.
2. Val also has light to walk in. She's almost to the point of not trying. It is serious. She's like a strong-willed bronco that must be broken.

This took me by surprise. Nothing came to me immediately about any light that I had not walked in, but the revelation bore witness with my spirit. My first suspicions are that I haven't clamped down on Val. It has been hard to put a finger on the problem without any doubts.

"Bore witness with my spirit." Really? How about tempering that thought with this analogy: I was walking through a canyon with rocks falling down all around me. When one finally hit me, I said, "I *thought* one of those rocks was going to hit me." In other words, I was continuously feeling that I wasn't measuring up to the leadership's expectations. When they brought their disappointment to my attention, *of course* it would be expected.

Thursday, September 4, 1975

At a leader's meeting last night, God said the Black Horse has already gone forth and that many are not walking in the light. Many will turn back when faced with a decision. God gave the statistics of J.U: about half are not walking in the light that has been given to them. A quarter of the people are walking in all light, and another quarter is not being drawn.

Concerning the leaders, I know that Phil and I were pegged as having not walked in the light, and I suspect that the pastors got the same word. I have no idea about the elders.

Yesterday, I felt the Lord "on my head" for the first time in a few weeks. I can feel the Spirit there now. I don't understand. The Lord expressed terrible disappointment in the body for not walking in the light. I'm in the same category, but the Lord is comforting me with His Spirit. My confession is that I want to change and do God's will, *not my own!*

I have no idea about what light I haven't walked in. Last night I wrote six possible areas, in order of probability:

1. I have not clamped down on my wife.
2. I have not done a study on negative forces.
3. I have not spoken during the meetings.
4. I have harbored negative forces.
5. I have meddled in other ministries.
6. I have not walked out and confessed my freedom from inferiority.

When I got up this morning, I felt that none of the things listed were really it, although I felt I should do them. I thought this morning that it probably has something to do with the Black Horse. But I'm still not sure what God wants done. Maybe God wants me to give away my stereo, my car, my bed. I don't know!

I've made all things common, and I can honestly say that I would get rid of them today without feeling mistreated. It would be easier to do this than to clamp down on Val, although I don't even know where to clamp down. Lord, I ask You to show me. My first suspicions are now:

1. I have not made all things common. I should give my stereo to Bill Riggenbacher
2. I have not taken a burden at the meetings to speak.
3. I have not clamped down on Val.

The Lord said that Val hasn't walked in the light and that she is almost at the point of giving up. Also, the Lord is almost to the point of not drawing her.

At this time, there were about 200 people coming to the open meetings. Around eighty people were coming to the teaching nights, including the leaders and their wives. The open meetings consisted mainly of worship and an evangelistic message. The teaching nights were only for those who felt called to Jesus Unlimited. Mark separated the teaching nights as follows:

- Monday: For those who were (in his opinion) not "walking in the light" and those who were "not being drawn."
- Tuesday: For those who were "walking in the light."

The leadership was now making judgments on the condition of people's hearts, which is a very dangerous practice. The Holy Spirit *does* sometimes reveal the intents and condition of people's hearts, but it doesn't happen often and it is *not* to be entered into lightly. The Lord is merciful to babes and adolescents who don't know what they're doing. Woe to anyone who would *knowingly* add anything for selfish reasons!

Monday September 8, 1975

We've been going through quite a time here at J.U.—probably the most important step since we began. According to God, the Black Horse is riding through J.U. and the demons are waiting for permission to deceive any of God's people who won't lay their will down and walk in the light they have received. God has been mourning for about seven days and will continue to do so for another week. All the meetings have been canceled.

All efforts to go forward have been postponed while God mourns. When Phil, Bill Riggenbacher, and I were about to pray all night concerning the deacon's ministry, the Lord said to Mick that we shouldn't pray about it but instead mourn and pray for the body. It is strange, but God hasn't let me do anything for a few days, even here at work. Yet it is OK to relax and do leisure stuff. Right now, the elders are playing pool, ping pong, and working on cars. Strange! But God's ways are not our ways.

I feel in my spirit that as soon as God is through mourning, He will move like lightning. This will be the beginning of the sword in the world. God will move and all who were not willing to change and "give their penny" will be deceived. As it says in 2 Thessalonians 2:11: *And for this cause God shall send them strong delusion, that they should believe a lie.*

Thursday, September 11, 1975

At a Thursday morning meeting, the Lord spoke to Mark and one of the elders. Mark then charged that God had said:

1. Cut the silliness.
2. Act like men of God.
3. There will be no games at the leader's meetings or regular meetings. We can come back later to play.

This revelation was not surprising, and bore witness. About this time, the ten leaders went on a retreat campout on a deserted Lake Michigan beach at South Haven.

Saturday, September 13, 1975

On the second night of the campout at South Haven, the Lord ministered through Rusty about my life and past. He said:

1. I am competitive toward Mark and his image. He is my goal. I use him as my standard of going forward or attainment.
2. I have a fear that I have been going backwards spiritually. I started close spiritually to Mark at the beginning, and now I'm feeling left behind the front lines because I'm not number two anymore.
3. These perceptions are wrong, and I must seek to purge my conscience from them.
4. I am in God's will where I am and should seek Him to go forward.

This revelation was not a surprise, and bore witness in my spirit.

Friday, October 4, 1975

God was mourning for about four weeks, so I haven't written much. He said we could mourn with Him or just "be there," ready when He came out of mourning. It really made me miss talking to God, and it really made me realize that my God is a Being with feelings. God mourned from about August 27 until September 26 at 12:00 noon.

Sunday, October 5, 1975

Last Wednesday, there were two pieces in a local newspaper about J.U. The first piece, a letter to the editor, was rather blasphemous. The second was an article by the editor. God told us not to do anything about this, because the editor wasn't trying to be blasphemous. When I read the article, I felt bad toward the people who blasphemed, but after a while I realized that this stuff must happen to fulfill prophecy. God said it would happen.

This past week, the elders were prevailing for several days to seek the "face of God we don't know about." After they prayed, they reported to me that it involved faith and the supernatural walk.

Thursday, October 9, 1975

This week, the Lord gave us some pointers on new perspectives:

- It takes no more faith for revival or miracles (or anything else!) than for salvation. Just ask and trust.
- Three areas that we must physically grow in as we grow in numbers:

    1. Pastors
    2. Deacons
    3. Chairs

If we hadn't received this revelation, we would have experienced frustration, carried an unnecessary burden (worry), and used a wider variety of unnecessary teaching. Our minds and all our ideas we've ever had about God must be renewed. God told us three steps to take to get out of this rut:

1. Establish in your heart that I will lead you out. Trust in Me.
2. Start to walk in the "true faith walk." Walk with Me, and then just ask.
3. Never come to the place in which you can't take a day off at the spur of the moment to get alone with Me.

When a person looks to the natural, he tends to become natural and carnally minded. So three ways to further our relationship is (1) Get alone with God; (2) Walk in light; and (3) Share God with others.

Every once in a while, a revelation would come forth like the one above and it would strengthen us like a breath of fresh air. That is one of the Church's biggest challenges: discerning the good from the bad. Weeds are always mixed in with the wheat (see Matthew 13:25). For some reason, God has chosen to allow this to be the prevalent mode of life. Bad mixed in with the good all the time.

Tuesday, October 14, 1975

All last week, I felt that something was wrong in the tape room, and I even mentioned this to Rusty and Mick. I also had a feeling that I was spending too much time on the tape ministry. I thought I had begun to change that situation, but Rusty told me that God said I am getting into the electronic work too much and that to purge me of this the following steps must be taken:

1. The Front Street building and office keys must be confiscated.
2. I am not allowed to touch anything electronic without first asking the elders.
3. I need to begin to work more with the brothers in the work of the ministry.

This revelation took me by surprise, because I thought I was doing something about this problem already. However, the revelation definitely bore witness with my spirit, even though it really *hurt* to have my building key taken away.

Wednesday, October 15, 1975

The past few weeks, I have felt that prayer is needed to pull us forward. I really felt an urge for us all to pray, because I *understand* that there is a lack and that prayer would correct this problem.

While we were praying last night, Mark casually mentioned that I should fire up the people tonight, because it is the deacon's job. Immediately, I felt fear, but later I exhorted and reminded myself that this was the reason I was out all last week praying. I felt that J.U. was at a standstill, that the deacons aren't really firing up, and that I couldn't do it myself. *I need fire from above!* So I exhorted myself:

- I should have faith because I have asked for the ability to fire up the people.
- I *am* available.
- I couldn't just *do* it. I need God's help. [After all, this was before Nikes were invented.]
- I had to trust in God.
- I had to be open to His leading.

I have a clear conscience. I have been obedient to the Spirit when He moves on me. I can't remember one time that I quenched a time of anointing. I am open and available!

Last night, the elders called a meeting of all of J.U. We are going to pray for twelve hours every night from 7:00 P.M. to 7:00 A.M. for as long as it takes for us to break through. I'm sure that the deacon's ministry will be greatly affected by this surge forward. We also believe that this breakthrough involves the fairly unknown faces of God (according to Ezekiel 1:10).

166

Lately, I've commented concerning my deacon's ministry, "I feel like a revelator without ever having a vision or word of wisdom." It is clear to me that I *must* have God-given help to be effective in my ministry—help that has not *yet* been tapped. Yet my fears are short-lived when people talk to me about the weak deacon ministry, because I realize *I* can't do my ministry as a deacon with what I've got now anymore than a revelator could do without visions or a revelations from God. That is how I have felt lately.

While we were praying last night, Mark had a vision, and Mick interpreted it. Mark saw a whirlwind with a clear white center, with debris being scattered from near the center. Mick said the whirlwind was power generated by our prayers. The clear white in the middle was the fullness, the ideal church body. The debris that was being scattered was the carnality, demons, and anything else that has been stopping us.

CHAPTER 14

PERSONAL
REVELATIONS
MARRIAGES UNDER ATTACK

*A*round this time, Mark confirmed Rusty as a prophet in addition to his position as an elder. It wasn't a big deal to me back then (or now for that matter), because many churches do this, and the Bible is clear that the prophet's ministry is still valid and operational.

As revelations from God through Rusty and Mick became more and more personal, the ability to harm individuals became greater. At first, the revelations were rather general and somewhat helpful. But soon they seemed to take the form of retaliation against people who had bumped into the pet peeves of the elders and Mark.

As people began to judge and question the validity of some revelations, the revelators and Mark seemed to come back with hurtful revelations directed towards them. Often it was the wives who spoke up, and many men were reprimanded for not keeping their wives "in line." During this time, some wives (along with some single persons) were declared "unsaved." Unfortunately, Val and I were no exception to this rule.

Sunday, October 19, 1975

At the beginning of the leader's meeting, God revealed the following:

- We have hardened our hearts toward God in certain areas, and we are now being judged for it.
- When a word is brought forth, we mentally accept it but don't really receive it or walk in the light of it.
- Many times, we exaggerate and bring in unbelief. We don't believe each other.
- We don't truly receive God's words from leadership. When we are told that God changes His mind, we inwardly disbelieve these words from leadership.
- When Mark or elders tell us of a problem with a person in the congregation, we tend to smooth it over when dealing with that person. This makes the leadership appear deceitful, foolish, and exaggerating.

All of this has served to spread disrespect to the body, allowed demons to run and influence part of our lives, and caused spirits to come into the body and confuse it.

Rusty then reported a vision that he had when he was riding around town doing his prophet's ministry. God told him to drive by the Front Street building. As he paused in front of the building, he saw a huge sword with a black cape over the handle stuck down the center of the building. The Lord told him:

Judgment and a sword has come to J.U. because it is not exempt from judgment anymore than other churches. It will be a judgment unto death. Many people will be judged for doubting Rusty's prophetic ministry simply because results have not yet begun. Judgment will come and also come to them that doubt. Then they will see judgment come to themselves.

Many people, including yourselves, disrespect the words spoken even out of your own mouths. But those words are respect, cause respect, and are power in themselves. Respect is the ultimate and inevitable result every time.

You haven't been looking to the salvation and restoration of the world because you don't want to.

Mark then took each one of us aside and charged us with what had been revealed earlier in the day. The following is a condensed version of what the revelators said about me:

- I need to see Val as she really is.
- Val will repent when I speak to her about this, but she will rise up in pride a few days later. I must stand firm. [There were thirteen other points mentioned, but I left them out because they were about Val and were not very nice.]

After this revelation came forth, I went into an office and began to meditate on what I was to do. Because the Lord said we were hard-hearted and slow to receive His Word on these subjects, I was moved to force myself to accept these words. Yet it *was* hard for me to grasp, so I cried out for mercy that my heart would be opened to see myself.

After a few minutes of meditation, the elders received an unexpected revelation for me, which was:

- After receiving the revelation, I had lost respect for myself. I felt demeaned for thinking Val was spiritual when she wasn't.
- Before the revelation, I rated both Val and myself high on the spiritual ladder. After the revelation, I rated both Val and myself low on the spiritual ladder. But I should rate Val low and myself high.
- When I continue to demean myself, I demean my calling and actually demean Christ (not speaking necessarily of righteousness, but *calling*).
- If I don't stop and repent about demeaning myself, I will receive the same judgment that any other person who demeans me would receive.
- I have been called and chosen. It is Christ who has called me, chosen me, and made me somebody. He has said it. I must therefore not demean the Lord's chosen.

After everyone was taken care of and we had gathered again at the front seats, Mick said that if we don't take heed to the seriousness of the hour, the J.U. leaders, the body, and all creation will not be delivered, and the faith of all concerned would be confused and scattered.

Then Mark caught a revelation and said, "We don't really believe this could happen. We have hardened our hearts, so we can't receive this

171

truth." As I write this (4:30 A.M.) I am beginning to *really* feel the change and realization of what was told to me.

Monday, October 20, 1975

After praying all night, I went to talk to Mark at the Front Street building. Mick revealed what he had received concerning Val:

1. Val's spirituality is demons.
2. Val isn't saved. She needs a good born-again experience.
3. Val is a wretch, is spiritually possessed with pride, and needs to be humbled.
4. Val waits on me to be seen and accepted—a "soulish" motive.
5. Val constantly demeans me.
6. If I stand firm, she'll be saved. My presence will convict her.

God also said, *Last night you went into demeaning yourself again and if you continue, you'll reap a demeanor's damnation. Think of your father and his father and all of the generations back to Adam. Then know you were called and chosen even then.* While we were talking, God also said that confusing spirits were trying to bring in anxiety, unbelief, and hardness of heart.

After the meeting, Val went out to the shack. God told Mark to talk to Val about her condition. Then about 10:00 P.M., Mark called me over to his house to explain Val's state to me. He said that Val has not been saved for about four months, and that she didn't get saved when she went to the altar tonight. He said that Val is evil. She has served God only for her own benefit. God said: *If you would get alone with Me, you would feel closer than ever before.*

Rusty saw a vision about me and reported it: He saw me standing before God, with Satan beside me. God reached inside me and took out my heart. He held it up and admired it out loud, exclaiming its intent to serve Him. There was a pile of armor and a sword beside me. God pointed them out to Satan, explaining that I desired to serve God and to pick up the armor and sword and slay Satan. Satan blew up at these words and exclaimed it wasn't true. He said I didn't really love

172

God. Satan accused me of not being able to rise above my inferiorities. God gave Satan permission to try me. Rusty said this is my test. Satan is using this situation with my wife to test me.

I then asked about Al Fletcher, my old pastor. The answer: I fear him but shouldn't. He is evil and needs a good born-again experience.

When it came to judging others, the elders went into high gear. No one was exempt. Your best bet to stay off the "hit list" was to do and say exactly what the elders and Mark wanted. These revelations were serious, and the leadership had fully entered into making judgments that I know now were outrageous.

Tuesday, October 21, 1975

After praying most of the night, I dozed off at the Front Street building. When I woke up, the realization hit me: *I'm not dreaming. Val isn't saved.*

Wednesday, October 22, 1975

After last night's ordeal, I made Val feel convicted this morning, and then I left the house. I wrote down some questions to ask the Lord. I was in very high spirits. I could noticeably see and feel a change in me. I could look people in the eyes. I could walk downtown without feeling inferior. I felt powerful—majestic. I could feel God in me. My hand was anointed much of the day. I felt I could really tell people where they stood without feeling fear.

I talked to Rusty about what I did the night before. I asked God if I did all right and if there was anything else I should do. God said that I was doing pretty well, but that I was still giving Val too much leeway. I shouldn't be giving her an ounce of encouragement.

I tracked Val down at the grocery store, informed her of the Word from God, told her she couldn't drive anymore, and then sent her home. Then I left and went to Mark's house to see what had happened to Val.

God said (through Mick Ahrens): that Val isn't ready to be saved and that she would go back to pride as soon as the opportunity came.

I was really hurting from all this. I wanted to have Val saved, and when this revelation came, it *really* hurt. I asked God if there was anything I could do to speed up the process. He said: *Don't make one mistake with your mouth. Don't give her any exhortation or indication that things would be all right. She needs to be humbled. Right now, she has no pride, but she would return to it if she could. Your hand is anointed to set her free.*

I went home feeling bad.

Looking back, I feel *horribly* ashamed about many of my actions during this time. I should *never* have allowed this to happen to Val. To think that I actually believed I needed to hear from God through these leaders is painful enough, but it is even more painful to think that I trusted them with personal information that was none of their business. I wish I could do it over again. I'd cover my wife as I should have. Val has forgiven me for what happened during this period of our marriage. Thank you, Val, for your forgiveness.

Thursday, October 23, 1975

I woke up with the clock radio playing a few super-convicting songs. I wept, because I felt badly about Val not being saved. She wept too. I felt so miserable and lost.

I remember turning over in bed, looking out the window, and screaming in my heart to God, *Why are you doing this to me!* I felt God say, *Just hang in there, just hang in there.* I sensed that God wasn't happy and that it really wasn't Him that was doing it to me. I also sensed that I should just hang on. Someday, I would be set free from this situation.

Thursday, October 23, 1975 (continued)

After seeking God during the morning, I went out for coffee with Rusty and asked God some questions about how I was feeling. The answers were:

- I was feeling condemnation (not conviction) over last night's ordeal with Val. What I did was OK.
- The reason that I was feeling terrible this morning was because I was feeling what Val felt.
- God said I was doing all right.

After this revelation, I was overjoyed and went out and sang unto my Lord! Then I came home and worked on the back porch with Phil and Bill Norten. That day, I remember writing, "Even in the midst of tribulation and soul torment, God is well able to bind up the broken hearted."

W*ow*, what a fault! I let some guys verbally trash my wife, but then thought it was OK because *they* said God said I was doing all right. I must have been insane. The point I'm trying to make here (somewhat sarcastically) is that I was *too* dependent on the approval of the leadership for my sense of wellbeing. My joy was not based on a true relationship with God but on the approval of the leadership.

Thursday, October 23, 1975 (continued)

Before dinner, Val was rather disrespectful to me about the cats. After talking to the Lord and the brothers, I decided to give her 500 sentences. I went to Mark's house after dinner. Mick revealed:

1. Val is to come off Monday nights [the teaching night for those "not walking in the light"].
2. I am to tell Val: "No more counseling. You still want your pride. Quit being deceitful."

Friday, October 24, 1975

Just before leaving to go to work, Val asked if I thought she'd ever leave me. It really set me back to think that she was even considering it. I had few words, then went to work and asked Mick Ahrens to fall out and revelate (ask God) about the situation. God said that Val was trying to motivate me. She saw fear in me when she asked that question. He said that she *will* bring it up again, and that I need to establish in my heart what to say. *Val won't leave!* She has no idea of where she would go.

During the day, I found out that Christi was telling people about Val. It really bugged me, so I went to Rusty to ask some questions. Rusty told me that the grind I had been feeling lately before meetings and when I go home was inferiority. The bad feelings I was getting when I think about people knowing about Val's pride were pride and inferiority.

Val told my mother about what had happened to her. At the meeting, God said to Rusty that demons were using people, including my parents, to influence Val back into false salvation. God also said that we're to announce Val's condition on Monday and Tuesday nights.

Saturday, October 25, 1975

I have been confused by my feelings the past few days. I have felt like shaking my fist and asking God why He was doing this to me. I hoped I could find Rusty, because I had a bunch of questions. Ironically, when Jim Flood and I were at the Donut House taking a break, Rusty came in. I asked him questions.

Rusty said that I should not pile sentences so high anymore, because they lose effectiveness that way. From now on, I shouldn't assign more than 25 sentences per offense for minor rebellion. He also said it will still be a while before Val comes around. She's got to be humbled.

I think the leadership was thinking more about humiliating people, not helping them to become more humble.

Saturday, October 25, 1975 (continued)

For almost a week, I had been making Val feel bad when I left or when I went to sleep. It seemed as though I was continually changing moods. I asked God if I should continue putting conviction on her, bearing in mind that I was getting weary of the constant lost feeling. God answered these questions with only a short answer: *It depends on her mood.*

I assumed this meant to watch and maintain in Val a constant "lost" awareness. If she's down when I leave, I shouldn't say anything. If she's up, I should put her down.

I talked to Rusty about some of the things that I felt God was dealing with me about, but he didn't say anything. I felt God was growing weary of me not pulling out of my original depression about Val's spiritual condition. Rusty felt this was not so.

I also felt I should now begin to plunge into my deacon's ministry and go on with God, even in the midst of all this tribulation. Rusty agreed wholeheartedly.

Sunday, October 26, 1975

Mark told us about some changes that would soon go into effect: three new young brothers would come on as deacons, and I would be an elder. God said that I'll be an elder if I pass this present trial. Then Mark charged us on a few points:

1. We must change! We must take correction better.
2. Spirits are driving us toward wrong motives for the anointing.
3. We must desire to have the sheep raised up, even to the point that one of them might become our leader.
4. The leaders *will* move in either pride or in God, not inferiority.
5. If we have fear, we must face it! If our eyes are on *God*, all fears are *no* problem.
6. Know: A mighty anointing may mean death to you (due to wrong attitudes).

Mark went on to say that we had wrong attitudes toward the elders and him, because we did not desire to be among them or learn from them. God then told Rusty: *Your eyes still look at positions of the body with wrong attitudes. Think of what you thought when Mark announced the changes in leadership. What were your thoughts?* Then God said: *You have great error.*

After everybody left, I noticed I had a feeling that was significant. I no longer could look the others in their eyes. I felt sheepish. But I couldn't take my mind off of being an elder. I kept wondering what I did to deserve that position. I no longer felt as I had that day downtown when I walked in God's glory all day. I felt as if I did something right to attain the eldership position, but I didn't know what. I asked Rusty why I felt dumb and why I couldn't look the other leaders in the face. He said it was my inferiority rising up.

Monday, October 27, 1975

I went to work at 9:00 A.M. Nothing special happened during the day. Before the meeting, I informed Val that they were going to announce her condition. She commented that she always feared she would bring me shame. I told her that it had truly come to pass.

CHAPTER 15

"THE AX"

THE WORST DAY OF MY LIFE

*T*uesday, October 28, 1975, was the day of "The Ax." It began as any normal day, but late in the afternoon I got a call from one of the elders letting me know that God had cancelled the regular church body meeting. He said to show up at the Front Street building for a special leader's meeting.

When I arrived at the building, Rusty and Mark met me at the door. There were no smiles or greetings, just a serious command to go up front, sit down, and be quiet and reverent. At the front of the meeting area was a semi-circle of eight chairs, with a chopping block in front of them. An ax was lying on the floor a few feet from the block. (Because of this bad experience, even to this day when I am notified about any meeting, I insist on knowing what the meeting is about before I show up, especially if it was scheduled at the last minute.)

Mark and Rusty waited until all of the leaders were seated before coming to the front. We were wondering what the chopping block and ax meant, and there was a considerable amount of squirming in the seats.

Rusty began by raising his voice and loudly rebuking the leaders. "The leaders have changed!" he cried. "There is inner rebellion in our midst! The ax is laid to the root!" As Rusty screamed out this rebuke, he reached over for the ax handle, pulled the metal ax head across the smooth cement floor towards him and—whack!—struck it into the chopping block. (I can still hear the metallic scraping sound of that ax being dragged across the floor.) Rusty screamed a few more rebukes and then concluded with, "The rebellious and hard-hearted will be cut off, and the honest-hearted will stay! Every great man's fall is pride!"

Mark then told about a vision in which he saw himself driving a stagecoach, pulling the brake and then steering off the bad road we were on. He continued, "You're all off as leaders. You have one week to write a paper on what you see in yourself, what your downfall is, and what change you've made to correct the problem. Don't look to your own strength. God will evaluate where your heart has been. And there had better be a heart change!"

Mark then brought forth what Rusty had earlier revealed. Each leader received a rebuke except Mark and Rusty. My rebuke was:

> You go forth among men and brag of God's great wisdom He's given you for the complications you can put on this body. God said your wisdom would come, and then God would come and He would crush that carnality and that fleshliness. And then He would show you a way to rise up, but even *then* you'd walk in pride, as soon as that wisdom comes upon you.

Mark and Rusty were saying that God said I went around bragging that God had given me wisdom to run the business of J.U., and that this "wisdom" was fleshliness and carnality that only brought complications to J.U. We also were given the following written instructions:

> This paper is to instruct the leadership in their own personal discipleship, but not those they disciple.

> We, as leaders, have great error within our ranks on discipleship, and it *will* change. The problem will be eliminated either by a heart change

or by being taken off. The rules set on removal will go into action. Almost every leader is off in the area of discipleship.

After this paper is handed out, God gives the leadership one week to get their eyes on Him according to the divine plan of discipleship. If their eyes are on God, they will not judge according to the flesh, but realize that their leaders will be given wisdom (that they don't naturally have) by God to further their walk and relationship.

Now read the above sentence again and receive its full meaning. Because of the above truth, the disciple (if his eye is on God) will begin to have a great zeal to be with his leader. Why? Because the disciple will know that being with his leader and receiving instruction from his leader will thrust him forward into a higher walk. If this does not happen, it shows his eye is not on God. Look at Christ and His disciples.

For too long, we've looked to each other on an eye-to-eye level. This has caused a loss of respect, has broken ranks, has brought in pride, and has stopped J.U. from going on with God. This is sick, abominable, and will definitely change. I would have you look at your salvation experience and how you humbled yourself before man and God. You respected your leaders and would go to them, believing their words, and you grew in the Spirit. There was freedom, but freedom has been lost through *pride* and rebellion. Most of us couldn't get saved now with our attitude and our great lofty positions.

When all this happened, it really confused me. After I sought God for a while, Rusty and Mark came back to the building, where I was alone. I asked Rusty to ask God if this pride came on me before, during, or since Val was pronounced "unsaved." Rusty told me that God said, *If you want to see yourself, seek Me and you will find out and see yourself.* That night, I asked God for a revelation on humility, pride, inferiority, and demeaning oneself. I wrote down the following revelations that God gave me:

1. It doesn't have to take a week to receive this revelation.
2. *God* must give me the revelation, or I'll never get it.

After Mark told me to leave the building, I drove around for a while, and then crawled into bed around midnight. I really didn't know what was happening. I found out later that Mark was angry because he thought I had left and come back to the building, using a key. (I was disciplined earlier in the month by having my keys taken away.) I don't think that he ever realized that I didn't "rebel" against his direction.

A week later, we handed in our papers with the hope that we would be reinstated into leadership. The following entry is the paper that I handed in:

Tuesday, November 4, 1975

This is the account of what God has shown me this past week. After God led me to read the fourth chapter of Daniel, He showed me myself, and then I realized that it is *God* who raises a man up and *God* who upholds him and *God* that can lower him to the dust again. It is all God!

While I was praying and walking around in the basement, I cried out to God, "Can't I take *any* credit? What about what Mark wrote in that paper? We *grew* in the Spirit. If we can *grow* in the Spirit, doesn't that mean that some are farther along than others? Haven't *I* progressed farther than some people? Haven't *I* gone through more and attained more wisdom and experience than the recent new believers?"

Then waves of the Spirit massaged my head. It seemed as if Jesus stood before me and jangled some keys and said, *I hold the keys to spiritual growth! You can't go forward unless I unlock the doors. You go forward as I want you to. I can open the doors fast or slow. I arrange the members of the body as I see fit, when I see fit. I hold the keys to spiritual growth.*

I truly realized then that positions in the body are not earned or attained, but that God sets each person in place as it pleases *Him!* There is nothing I can do to move into the bishop's position if it isn't in

God's plan for my life. If it is God's plan for a two-month old Christian to be a deacon or even my leader, God can open the doors, raise him up quickly, and supply him with everything he needs to fulfill that ministry. A person's position depends simply on God's *plan* for his life, not on the experience and wisdom a person has stacked up. I realized that I was just a willing vessel, nothing more.

After God showed me these things, I could see myself. I really *did* think too highly of myself, which was my downfall (pride). I really thought I did something right to get where I was in leadership. When I was told I would become an elder, my pride really rose up. I didn't know what I did to deserve that position, but I said to myself, "I must have done something right." Then I felt I had stacked up enough wisdom through trials and experience to be a good elder. I wasn't looking to God but at myself. I had felt that the present leadership had attained their position over me because of something *they* did. So, naturally, when I learned I was to become an elder, I felt the same way about myself.

God showed me I have inwardly felt that the leadership's wisdom came from experience, rather than being freely given from God through grace. I inwardly believed in spiritual seniority. Because I held to this misconception, this made me feel I had to prove my leadership to others. I also always felt threatened when I saw another leader or sheep rising up or being anointed.

God also showed me that my past "wisdom" in many areas really was carnality and fleshliness. When God showed me how to rise up by looking to Him to cover my inferiority, I chose to look back to myself and to my pride to make me a good leader. I have been wrong.

I now have a different attitude toward leadership positions in the body and a new realization of my weak self. God brought about the change when *He* showed me myself.

By God's grace in showing me these things and by *His* reminding me, I can take my place in the body wherever it pleases God. I also won't feel threatened when other brothers are rising up, even to be my leader. My desire is to have pride put away forever in my life after this week—to maintain a constant realization that I'm nothing and that God is everything in my life. But even to do that depends on my God. It all boils down to looking *to God*, not myself.

At the leader's meeting that afternoon (we handed in our papers in the morning), everyone was put back into leadership positions. I was reinstated as a deacon, not as an elder. *But, I went through a traumatic experience at that meeting!* During the exhortation from Mark, he said, "You all get a second chance; you're all on as leaders," but I heard, "You *don't* get a second chance; you're all *off* as leaders."

When I heard Mark's words, I was paralyzed with disbelief. I just stared at the floor as some of the others started crying (I didn't know that they were crying from relief). After a few minutes, I realized that I had misunderstood what Mark said, but the damage to my mind had already been done.

I must emphasize that this experience greatly damaged my confidence and strength of mind. When I erroneously heard that we were all off as leaders, it was as if something in my brain had been physically damaged. I didn't feel a physical pain, but I definitely felt something snap in my brain area. I have read accounts where people described having a mental breakdown, and I think I can relate. I didn't have a full mental breakdown, but something definitely broke.

I plunged into the deepest pit of fear and confusion that I have ever experienced in my life. God brought me out of it, but only after many, many months of *torment*. I feared God rejecting me, and I feared becoming an outcast and a sinner. I had no increased fear of any other type.

Mark and Rusty reported that a few days before this, God told them to drive around to the different leaders' houses late at night and make a tape entitled, "The Holy Spirit Speaks." As Rusty and Mark sat in the car outside each house, Rusty prophesied a message about that leader. I can barely remember the exhortation to Phil and me. It was something about how sad God felt that these two men were not yet able to rise up into the fullness due to pride (in Phil) and inferiority (in me).

What I remember well was the message to Mark. It surprised me to hear any kind of rebuke aimed toward him:

> I called this man to rise up and lead an end-time army of believers who would go forth and defeat the Devil and his angels. There was a time when My Spirit led this man. But when the gifts came, he began to be led by them instead of My inward witness. If this man continues to be led by the gifts instead of My inward witness, he will lose his calling and that end-time army.

I didn't think much of this revelation to Mark at the time, but later I realized that this word was a real problem for him. He constantly asked Mick or Rusty to search and find out what God wanted. He also continually asked them to ask God for wisdom about anything he didn't understand at the moment.

I was too fearful of being rebuked by God to notice Mark's error or to question his leadership. I just assumed that Mark knew what he was doing. I didn't feel that it was my place to question him anymore. After all, he was God's man, so who was I to question him? I felt that I was just a nobody, filled of pride and inferiority, constantly being rebuked for my reasoning and worldly wisdom. I just needed to blindly submit to my elders, because God gave wisdom to them that they didn't naturally have. Right? (I hope your answer is, "Wrong!")

Of course, Mark's constant requests put enormous pressure on the revelators to come up with a revelation. Yet God often takes His time to answer in *any* manner. So here's a good question: What happens when revelators are pressured to give an answer, but God isn't talking? Hmm.

Tuesday, November 4, 1975 (continued)

Mark said I'm to work daily with maintenance. I'm to work with tapes only when directed by leadership and to do the other work as a fired-up deacon. I'm to write another paper to God, due in two weeks, about my motivations, what I felt tonight, what I feel when I'm in situations in front people, my progress, what I see in myself, and so forth.

This was the beginning of the two-week journal assignment that I was to hand in to the elders:

Wednesday, November 5, 1975

First of all, I'm not even going to try to put the pieces together. I'm going to let God do it. I feel as if my whole foundation has been smashed and I have nothing to stand on. All the absolutes I've set up in the past are shattered. I don't know what was God and what was fake. I look back to see if any of the past experiences I had with God were real and which ones I could use now for stepping stones. I just don't know. I'll not worry or even think about it. I'll let God rebuild my foundation on a personal relationship.

Right now, I have no idea what a relationship with God is. No idea. I don't have a burning desire to know God—at least I don't feel it. Maybe I do, but I don't understand where. I know that I have been wrong in the past, but I don't know what to shoot for in the future. I have no *vision* of having a relationship with God.

All I know is that God is right, wanting a relationship with Him is right, pursuing a relationship is right, and that I haven't fulfilled those things, but I want to. I don't even know whether I want to out of fear or love. I just don't know.

I now feel a great lack of fulfillment. It could be that I no longer have pride or look to pride and that, like Val, I find no fulfillment. But I pray this is just a test as to whether I'll look to God or go back into pride. I ask God right now to show me the love, joy, peace, and fulfillment in knowing Him! I put my will against pride. I'll look to God and wait for Him to answer. David said, *In thy presence is fulness of joy* (Psalm 16:11). I believe that, but I have no vision of it and can see no fulfillment in it. All I can do is pray that God will give me a taste of His love.

I am afraid to think, because my thinking has been off many times. I cannot comprehend how a person can exist without thinking things through, however. God, please show me.

God, I wrote the first part of this paper to anyone, and then I realized I was supposed to write it to You. When I went back to change the words as if I was talking to You, I felt a change, but I don't know what it was. I'm worried that I'll fall back as Val did. She saw no fulfillment in humility, so she turned back to pride. I don't even really *know* what pride is. Please show me so that when it tries to come in, I'll know it is pride and I'll look to You. I don't want pride. Like I said before, I don't know whether it is because of fear or love, but I ask for mercy.

It seems, God, I'm falling back into the same grievous torment I had when I first became saved. The paper handed out to us last Tuesday said we had great freedom. It said that freedom was lost through pride and rebellion. I remember, Lord, early in my Christian life, I *never* had freedom and seldom felt your love. I don't know why. I remember I always had great condemnation and torment. It was only recently that I *thought* I felt your love. It wasn't until the past six months that the super condemnation left. I was so happy to see it go, Lord. But now it is back and *much* worse than before. I feel as if You are casting me off. I feel as if You are sick and tired of me. *I wonder at times if I'm even saved.*

Lord, I haven't felt these feelings in a long time, and it hurts bad. *Bad!* It is pure torment. I ask for a bit of wisdom from You that I may crush this torment. I ask for mercy, Lord, that You'll help me defeat this fear. I know You've called me. But since this shake up, I have lost confidence that I'm honest-hearted, and now I question whether or not I even want to go on. *But I know you're right on, Lord.* I want to go on with You.

I remember, God, that I came to You out of a fear of going to hell. Right now, I tremble and almost lose my mind to think of spending eternity in hell. I ask You show me (let me feel) Your love and freedom that You give to others.

Lord, I need You to show me and make me feel Your love. I know I have many walls, but your Word says that the anointing breaks every yoke (see Isaiah 10:27). I believe that You, Lord, can break those walls down so that I may feel love. I plead with You, God, to have mercy on me! You hold the key. I trust in You! Help me out of this torment.

Wednesday, November 5, 1975 (Morning Leader's Meeting)

God's instructions to me from leadership were:

1. Do not help the maintenance supervisor in *any* organization.
2. Do not do any work in the tape ministry.
3. I'm on probation. God is going to watch me closely.

CHAPTER 16

RECOVERING FROM "THE AX"

TRYING TO MAKE SENSE OF IT ALL

Wednesday, November 5, 1975 (continued)

We received the following instruction at the morning leaders meeting:

1. If God doesn't give you something to speak, be humble before men. Don't worry about miracles, just care about people knowing God.
2. Be open to different types of physical discernment.
3. You didn't know about pride before. You were ignorant children.

I should establish my heart on the following: I do *not* have fear. I trust in God! My eyes are on God. God is my strength! God *is* big enough to get past my faults and self. I believe God loves me and is *not* forcing me to go crazy! (If I believed He were *not* a God of love, I would get what I confessed.)

*I*n the leader's meeting mentioned above, Mark wanted us to be open to different types of discernment. The term "discernment" will be used often from now on in my journal. Although this term is usually associated with "the discerning of spirits," we began to also use this term at J.U. to describe an interesting physical feeling.

I remember first noticing this feeling during the summer of 1975, a few months before this leader's meeting. I was confronting my young cousin who was living with us at that time. I began to rebuke him for something and was being rather forceful. I felt something on the top of my head. It felt like something prickly moving on my head, but underneath the hair, as if it was rising up or was an isolated chill. The more confronting I became, the stronger the discernment.

Mark began reporting it first. One day he said, "I felt an angel putting its hand on the side of my face" to turn him in another direction. Mark began to describe these events more and more. I came to the conclusion that I was experiencing the same thing.

Sometimes the discernment would be all over the side of my face. Sometimes it would be all over the top of my head, while at other times it would be just a three-inch diameter spot on the top back part of my head. Occasionally I felt a continuous little tickle on the scalp, as if someone were moving a toothpick around in a small circle.

This discernment still happens to me on a regular basis. I am curious to know if this happens to many people. Maybe they just don't report it because they don't consider it to be of any significance. Although I don't know what this phenomenon is, I'm convinced it is something spiritual.

The reason I believe this is because one day I while I was reading in my car, I felt this discernment on the back left part of my head. I felt a strong urge to look behind me, and I saw one of the brothers walking toward the restaurant. But he was too far away for me to hear him coming. It was clear to me that my discernment and this man walking up was not a coincidence. The windows were up, and I could not have possibly heard him coming. Yet I felt this urge to look in the direction that the discernment touched me.

Over the years, I've noticed some patterns and consistencies regarding this discernment:

1. It happens more often when I am praying a lot, when I am in a spiritual battle, or when I am ministering to people or counseling.
2. It can happen when I feel far away from God and haven't been praying or seeking God much at all.
3. It often happens when I act aggressively or when I meditate on being overly (wrongfully) aggressive. It's like a warning. It works.
4. It always gives me comfort, because it reminds me that *God is!*
5. It causes me to pray. Usually, I have no strong impression as to what to pray about. I just pray for whatever comes to mind.
6. It seems that once it begins to happen, it often happens for a day or so and then goes away for days, weeks, or even months.

Wednesday, November 5, 1975 (Evening at McDonald's)

Question to God (through Rusty): Why have so many spiritual happenings been blinded to me?

Answer: Because I look too much to the physical and expect too much. As a deacon, God will speak to me spiritually. I'll think it is myself sometimes, for I have not yet learned to discern the voice of my spirit. Many of my past "revelations" have been soul. I'll make mistakes, but begin to step out.

Revelation in car coming back from McDonald's: I try to formulate a relationship.

Question to God (through Rusty): Why do I have tormenting thoughts of rejection by God?

Answer: I am soul possessed with religion, and outside oppression is coming against me from a demon. We cast away that oppressive spirit, and God said that I must establish my heart to trust Him. I must establish my heart to help me move out of the tormenting thoughts of rejection. Mark said it was the Devil tormenting me. Rusty said to rebuke it when it comes on me, to trust in God's mercy and love, and to know I've been called and accepted by God.

Here is a case in which God worked through imperfect men to help me grow closer to Him. We used the phrase "soul possessed" at J.U. to describe a type of demonic oppression. Looking back, we should have used the phrase "soul *oppressed*." Christians cannot be "possessed" with an evil spirit, but we *can* be oppressed to the place that we are continually dealing with that spirit and constantly living it out.

Deliverance comes primarily by being exposed to the truth through biblical counseling and then by being surrounded with truthful input from friends, sermons, and books. Taking the proper authority and rebuking the oppression can speed up the deliverance.

Rusty and I prayed, renounced that spirit, and then asked God to lead me out of that wrong thinking.

Saturday, November 8, 1975

Revelation at the shack, middle of the night from the elders: *Evil spirits have caused some in the body to believe that a person working a secular job cannot go forward or operate in the Spirit. God has directed three deacons, including me, to find part-time jobs to help break this conscience in the body.*

God said that we leaders are under the law toward the body, thinking we owe them something. We must establish in our hearts that our calling is to God and *not* man. *God* supports us, not the body.

Phil Bechtel and I both got jobs at the Open Pantry, a little grocery store just a block away from where we were living. It was a perfect part-time job for me because I had worked at a large grocery store just before Val and I were married. Looking back now I wonder if it was the lack of finances at the church that sparked the above revelation.

Wednesday, November 12, 1975

After a leader's meeting, God said to me through Rusty: *You think I am down on you, but I'm not.*

All during this period at J.U., I constantly fought feelings of being rejected by God. I seriously doubted my salvation at times, and the torment was often overwhelming. I called Mark or Rusty frequently to get their encouragement and support. The following is a pitiful account of my condition and my unreasonable dependence on direction and acceptance from leadership.

Thursday, November 13, 1975

After feeling I wasn't ever saved, I went to Mark and Rusty and found out that I really was saved. They revealed to me that I had never felt God's love at Boulder's Chapel because I had a fear of not being accepted by the older, established people. That was pride. Then things got better at J.U., but as others began to rise up (and I saw it), pride again rose up, again quenching God's love. The only way I had communion with the brothers was when God used me, and that's a poor foundation. Now I should forget everything, even my commission. I should just want to know God.

This evening while taking a bath, I thought to myself, *Maybe I don't want to see myself.* I fought back, confessing that I *did* want to see myself. Then I thought, *In order to see myself, I might have to accept the fact that I don't want to see myself.* When these thoughts came to me, I was extremely tormented that I was lost for eternity. I just confessed that I want to see myself.

Whew! How about that for a batch of condemnation and confusion! In the journal account below, Jeff Bechtel and I had just had a minor disagreement about the operation of a tape recorder. I helped him through a problem and "won" an argument. This account is significant because it documents the first time in my life that I recognized the feeling of pride in me.

Thursday, November 13, 1976 (continued)

This morning when Mark pointed out my pride regarding electronics, I really felt fear because I didn't see it. I even thought I handled the situation with Jeff Bechtel pretty well. But I'm starting to see myself tonight. I notice many times that my inner thoughts are: *I knew that was right* or *This is what I should act like* or *I thought I handled the situation pretty well.* There is a queer feeling when I think back and meditate on these thoughts. I believe it is pride. Pride came in when I heard about wrong faith teachings. I thought, *I was right after all.*

Making a judgment that I "was right" or that I "handled a situation well" was not pride. But pride *was* involved here because I was associating those thoughts with feelings of superiority along with some type of weird pleasure. Concerning my references to pride in my journal, I am still convinced that most of them really *are* about genuine pride—the bad kind that irritates people and hindered me from really serving and loving others.

I am thankful for this learning experience, even though it came with so many things that were not good. Maybe you can also catch this pattern in your life and be set free from the tendency to unreasonably and unwisely compare yourself to others. *But they measuring themselves by themselves, and comparing themselves among themselves, are not wise* (2 Corinthians 10:12).

Friday, November 14, 1975

2:00 P.M.: Bill Riggenbacher and Ron Binks pulled up at the shack. I felt fear and *pride.* They're going to pass me spiritually. I look to God.

9:00 P.M. (at a meeting): Many times I catch myself wondering if Mark and Rusty are looking at me when I'm exhorting people. I usually wonder like that when I catch myself or realize suddenly that I *am* firing people up. Then I look to see if anyone sees me. I don't know how to act, so I just confess it to God and will trust Him to bring me out of it.

You'll have to bear with me on the following journal entries. What I'm allowing you to see are the things that were going through my mind pertaining to pride and other motivations. I came to the conclusion that I was just jam-packed full of pride. Most of it actually *was* bad pride, and I'm sorry for it.

Saturday, November 15, 1975

At a morning leaders' meeting, Mark informed us that God said He is breaking us down to our basic negative forces. We must submit and yield. After the meeting, God said that no matter what we think, none of us knows what a relationship is.

8:30 A.M.: Phil was singing. I felt pride that I could sing better.

9:03 A.M.: People were talking about my family. I felt pride.

9:05 A.M.: As Phil was talking about a revelation of the Word and Mark disagreed, I felt pride because I felt the same as Mark earlier in the day.

10:00 A.M.: I realize now that my fear of people rejecting me is only a result of a very basic negative force—fear of rejection from God. I realize I must let my pride down, submit to God, and trust Him. But I don't know how. All I can say is that I want to know God and that I desire to trust Him so I can know Him better. I don't want to resist purging. I want to see myself and change.

12:20 P.M.: I whistled. Felt it sounded pretty good. Pride.

1:05 P.M.: There's strife between brothers at maintenance. I have no idea how to patch things up. I ask God for the answer.

5:25 P.M.: As we left to go to South Bend (to watch a movie as a leadership training time), I switched from the front seat to back seat. I felt pride when I caught Rusty's eyes as I switched.

5:30 P.M.: I feel fearful that I'm going to be like the people in Charles Bronson's movie *Hard Times*. I want to see myself.

5:40 P.M.: I looked at one of the newer brothers whom Mark feels will soon be a leader. I saw the love of God and contentment in them. I feared that I wouldn't grow in it more.

6:00 P.M.: I felt pride in the fact that we, the sons of God, are together. I looked at us from the outside as "something."

Movie: I wanted to see the girl who was in bed. I moved up in my seat, but Mark's head was in the way. I wanted to see her, yet I didn't. *I realized that I really want pride, yet I don't.*

Movie: I told Greg how I thought the movie would end. I either said it from pride or to set up pride for the end of the show.

Movie: I felt pride that I knew about oysters.

Movie: I felt pride over the fact that I don't really want pride.

8:30 P.M.: I felt pride in being a leader.

8:35 P.M.: I was reading this part of my journal that I'm going to hand in and got pride over it. I thought it was pretty good, looking from the outside as if Mark would read it.

9:10 P.M.: I felt pride that I didn't have the problems that the others had with certain trust situations.

9:15 P.M.: Mark mentioned King Saul. My fear of rejection from God rose up.

9:25 P.M.: I felt pride over telling the story of Naaman the Syrian. Or was I just glad and fulfilled?

After the movie, Mark said, "You must admit that you have fear and then confess it is no longer part of you."

Sunday, November 16, 1975

Mark said that I had a wrong attitude toward my deacon ministry in maintenance. He said this had something to do with a statement I made about being off for two days.

2:00 P.M.: I felt good that Val and I put more into the apostle's fund than everyone else. Pride.

3:05 P.M.: I fixed Mick's stereo and felt pride.

3:10 P.M.: I praised my dad for finding good deals. Pride.

7:05 P.M.: I felt pride in the way I spoke in tongues.

Monday, November 17, 1975

11:25 A.M.: I felt pride when I whistled like a quail.

1:55 P.M.: I felt pride over being a son of God.

2:10 P.M.: I felt pride over playing with pool balls in front of one of the brothers.

2:25 P.M.: I felt pride over knowing about petty cash procedures.

Tuesday, November 18, 1975

Well, Lord, You have been with me close during these past few weeks. I look back and remember the grievous torment I went through a couple of times. Yet I have noticed a trend that has brought me out of those moments of torment: There was no regular thing that I went through to get out of it. I can only say that Your grace brought me out of those times. I just trusted You and not what those tormenting thoughts said You were. I'm even afraid to take credit for looking to You.

I really feel a change in me during these past two weeks. I realize now that I'm full of pride and that I can hardly say anything without being motivated by pride. I don't want it, Lord. I don't want it! I thank You that You are showing me what pride is and getting through my hard heart. I thank You for leading me into simplicity and just knowing You. I'm even beginning to feel joy in walking with You.

Right now, Lord, I'm afraid of operating in spiritual gifts and miracles, because I might get filled up with pride. I don't care about going to work part time or even full time, as long as I'm walking closer to You in doing it. I just want that relationship.

197

Right now, Lord, I feel pride over this paper, but I know—or at least I think I know—that these are my true feelings. I can only confess the pride and be open to You for rebuke and correction. I do want to change.

At a leaders' meeting, the following revelation came: *Don't use your relationship [with God] to further your ministry; use your ministry to further your relationship.* When these words came forth, they made no sense to me. I marvel at that because it seems so right to me today. I can't even fathom how it could be any other way.

Tuesday, November 18 (continued)

Lord, I know the reason for spiritual gifts in my life is to help others and even help my relationship with You. I don't really understand exactly how I can use my ministry to further my relationship, but You said it, and I believe it. I hope You'll give me understanding before You manifest the gifts. After all, what good is a gift without a relationship? I ask You to not give me any gifts until You perfect my relationship with You. I'll not look to the gifts for justification when they manifest, and I'll use them as You teach me to. All things have become new. Do not fear! Trust.

Friday, November 21, 1975

Mark challenged me about the thermostat work I did on the Ford. I tried to cover my broken off bolt mistake by blaming it on his brother Jeff's advice. After I did that, great condemnation came on me. King Saul blamed his mistake on others, too.

Around midnight, I read about an evil spirit being sent to Saul. There is fear on me so bad that I am shaking uncontrollably. I fear God has left me for my mistake in pride and has sent me a tormenting spirit.

I shook in bed so violently that I thought it would wake up Val.

Thursday, November 27, 1975

Today we had Thanksgiving dinner at the Smiths. When I walked in, I felt *very* self-conscious. When people would ask, "How're ya doing?" I would get really flustered. I had no words to explain what was happening to me or about Val's condition about not being saved. But I *did* feel God with me, and I looked to Him.

My lousy mistake was at grace time. Val's dad asked her to say the blessing. She immediately whispered a refusal and tried to tell her dad she couldn't. I spontaneously whispered to Val (no one understood me, even Val), "Just go ahead and do it." Val's mom kicked her husband to help him understand the situation. All this happened at the same time. Then Val's dad caught on and said the blessing. No one at the table even appeared to notice a problem. I realized afterwards that I feared the people and wanted to avoid a scene, so I compromised.

Even though I made that mistake, I felt God was not down on me and understood I didn't want to say it. I chuckle in shame when I realize that God covered me in the midst of my mistake. It was almost as if a space of time was removed and nobody saw a thing. I look to You, God, to bring me out of fear of man.

At the leader's meeting, God said that the greatest danger is that the leaders may *try* to do things to become leaders or want to be anointed more than they want the sheep to be anointed. After the meeting as the leaders met around the pool table, Phil began to talk about my mistake at the Smiths. I felt ashamed and did my best to gracefully change the conversation. I can't express the shame I felt.

Right now, I can't express the shame I feel for not being a better husband.

Friday, November 28, 1975

At the leader's meeting, God said through one of the revelators that my relationship with Him is based on circumstances or when He uses me. Even discernment makes me feel closer to God. This is wrong,

199

because I should base my relationship with God on faith, not physical manifestations that happen to me. It is why God has held back so many things from me.

While Mark was preaching, I noticed my attention wandering to some people who came. I realized I always used to do that, even back at Boulder's Chapel when someone new would come in. When Mark says something, I take that and mentally imagine what the religious people think about it. I think it is pride in what Mark is saying and also fear of man and my eyes set on the hardhearted. I look to You, God, to remove this from me.

Friday, December 5, 1975

I heard that Paul the paperboy had a vision of hell. Envy rose up in me.

Sometime in mid-December, Val was pronounced "saved" by the leadership. I don't remember the exact day or the way it happened. Poor Val. I would like to add some of her comments on this issue, but it is still too painful for her to talk about it.

Thursday, December 11, 1975

Mark brought forth the following at the leader's meeting:

1. All of the leaders have had a wrong foundation regarding the things of God, the anointing, and regarding working long hours for God and the body.
2. Because of this, we have false justification (pride). In our self-justification, we actually feel closer to God. Paul said: *Watch your foundation.* Study 1 Corinthians 3:10–15, Matthew 16:16–20.
3. Our foundation has not stood on a relationship, but on the things mentioned above. We must establish our hearts if we're going to be led out by God.
4. The honest heart will hear God's voice and will not be deceived.

Monday, December 15, 1975

I notice I'm getting prideful toward Mark and Rusty, saying things like, "It should be done this way" and "Rusty should be helping out more." I'm not dwelling on it, but it is rising up. I look to You, Lord. It will lead to rebellion if You don't take it out of me. Terry and Cary did the same thing. I ask You to humble me, Lord, before it is too late.

When I think about this period of time I call "The Ax," I look back on it with some fear and considerable sadness. This type of bondage has happened numerous times throughout history, and it is happening even now in many parts of our country and the world.

We must remember that our faith in God is personal. He loves us and is always with us. He testifies to our hearts what is true, even though we might have leaders adding to that truth or contradicting it and causing us to live in bondage. If we continue seeking God, and do not give up, He will eventually deliver us, one concept at a time.

CHAPTER 17

ALL THINGS COMMON

LEARNING TO LIVE IN PEACE WITH OTHERS

*D*uring the summer of 1975, we tried to live out what the Early Church did in its beginning. They made all things common, which meant that they shared many of their possessions with each other (see Acts 4:32–34).

Many of the single people started living together in "set-up household" groups that the leadership "ordained." These houses were quite large and were usually rented by one of the single leaders. There were at least two women's homes and two men's homes filled with single people who were invited to live there. These set-up households had strict rules, and everyone participated in making "all things common" just as the leadership did. The leadership closely monitored these households and strongly advised the residents on how to manage their lives and money. Overall, the set-up households were a positive experience for those who participated.

Being totally dedicated to the J.U. vision and organization was the norm. Early on, people gave significant portions of their income, and the trend grew to total commitment for the average attendee. The leadership sold extra possessions and donated the money to the apostle's fund. For example, I cashed in my life insurance policy for $660.00 and donated the entire amount.

Although there was a great deal of dedication and giving, we started running out of money that summer. It seemed that when a person gave his all to J.U., Mark saw it and made him a leader. However, because these were the people who were giving most of the money, when they quit their jobs, they were unable to give. As a result, the funds to support the ministry dwindled. Money hadn't been a problem for almost a year until just before "The Ax."

Mark became our first full-time minister in the spring of 1974, and I went full time shortly after that. The following January, we added Bill Norten, Mick Ahrens, and Jim Flood. In April, Rusty Evans and "Furry Curry" came on board. By mid-summer of 1975, we added Bill Riggenbacher and Mark's two older brothers, Phil and Jeff Bechtel. So within six months, we added eight full-time people to the payroll in addition to Mark and me. Our money had dwindled to the point that we had to tighten our belts and find some way to make ends meet.

Mark told us that God said love wasn't flowing between the leaders and that was stopping the Spirit from moving in the meetings. God said we should move in together according to our inward witness. Although Mark said the motive was to get the love flowing, I think it was the lack of funds that brought about this direction.

I felt impressed to move in with Phil and Sandy Bechtel. Mark confirmed it. I wrote in my journal, "I don't really want to move in with Phil because we are opposites, but that may be *the* reason God wants us together. I'm looking forward to being freer in the Spirit as a result." That freedom did come. Unfortunately, it came many years later after a lot of reflection on the problems we all experienced.

Val and I moved in with Phil and Sandy in September, just before "The Ax." All of the other leaders and their wives doubled up as well. The single leaders lived in the "set up" homes.

Around this time, Phil and Sandy had a baby girl. We were all living in a little single story, two-bedroom house. That's two *little* 10' x 12'

Two families packed into this little house,
trying to make "all things common."

bedrooms, a kitchen, combined living and dining room, and a typical Michigan (dirty) basement. On the weekends, Phil's kids from a previous marriage would also come and live with us. So we had four adults, two kids, one baby, two cats, and a dog all crammed into that little house.

Phil suggested that either they or Val and I move into the basement. I *hate* basements, but I had to admit that it was better for Val and me to move down there. So we cleaned up one end of the basement, put up cardboard walls and painted everything. I ended up using duct tape to make it almost airtight, because I hated the thought of sharing our bedroom with spiders, bugs, and other basement critters.

Doubling up helped our financial situation for a while. But soon the money got tight again, so we put on a huge rummage sale. Because Val and I had moved into Phil's house, most of our things were in storage. So guess whose stuff went to the sale? We sold our silverware and many other items at rummage sale prices.

Val and I had truly given up all for Jesus. We both felt that it was the right thing to do and that this was necessary to fulfill our ministry. Neither Val nor I have any regrets, although it does still hurt when we think about all the nice wedding gifts that we gave up at bargain prices. We can look back, though, and say without a doubt that we gave it our best. We gave it our all.

During the events of "The Ax," we didn't notice the little things in our households that bugged us. However, when the effects of that situation began to wear off, we all started noticing one another's faults around the home, and the sparks began to fly. The following journal entries provide some examples of this.

Wednesday, December 17, 1975

Sandy seemed unhappy that the grill wasn't cleaned off immediately after we used it. This set it all off, and Phil picked it up from there. He was disgusted because there wasn't much butter left in the dish. He felt Val should have replenished it.

Sandy is doing dishes, and I sense she is angry. So is Phil. He thinks Val is not helping enough. Val fixed batter for pancakes and thoughtfully left it for Phil and Sandy. Then she sat down to knit until all the dishes were dirty, but Sandy went right from eating to dishes. Phil now feels strife toward Val and me because of it.

Oh, the joys of living with two families jammed into one house! I have struggled with trying to decide how much of the household strife should be left in this story. I certainly do not want to leave the impression that I'm just complaining about Phil and Sandy. I think that I have exposed enough of my own poor behavior to show that the most important issue is the lessons learned. I do want to make one thing clear: I believe Phil and Sandy were (and still are) dedicated Christians. They are endeavoring to do God's will and are glorifying God in many ways.

For the most part, I enjoy Phil's company. But I doubt if we could go back and live together again without the same problems rising up. As I ponder this, I can't help but feeling sad as I wonder what the good of all this was back then. Neither Phil nor I have changed enough to tolerate each other in close proximity for any long period of time. Did we go through all that for nothing?

One day I was discussing this with a friend, and we came up with an explanation. There was one good thing that happened: *Our sin was exposed!* The situation forced our poor motivations, selfishness and inferiority to the top of our consciences. At least we now *know* that we are sinners and that we need Jesus to forgive us.

I know that I have a tendency to react to conflict by doing nothing and stewing about it. I know that I can't live or work too closely with persons who react to conflict in an opposite way. The faster opposites can forgive each other for all the things that rise up in a household, the more likely it is that they can live together.

So I concluded that stewing (thinking about the situation, getting angry inside, and doing nothing about it) is sin and that taking your frustrations out on other people is sin. I think that stewing is a better way to handle conflict than throwing the cat across the room. Phil (probably) thinks that stewing is childish. One thing we *do* have in common is that we have a need for Jesus to fix us.

Saturday, December 20, 1975

I notice Phil has acted the same since we moved in, but he didn't bother me for the first few months. Now I'm constantly motivated to please Phil and keep unity. My attitude is, *I'll do anything, Phil. Just don't get mad.* It has come to the point where I can't stand to be around Phil, except when we're just talking about God.

To work on things with Phil is such a strain, as he mostly gets upset or cranky when things don't go his way. It's almost impossible to solve a disagreement by my decision and still be unified. It seems clear that there is a problem here with my inferiority and his superiority—and that there is pride on both sides.

Tuesday, December 23, 1975

What do I do when Phil's temper flares up? I used to enjoy being home and being around Phil. Phil's temper flares and my inferiority seldom caused strife among us, and the love flowed. I feel that what we did then was not so much look to God, but we just held these negative forces inside. Now, after continually putting it under on both sides, we cannot hold it down anymore. It is rising up and must be purged. Lifestyle conflicts are not the problem here. It is a case of suppressed inferiority and superiority being forced into the open for purging.

Tuesday, December 30, 1975

At a leader's meeting, Mark stated that when God leads us to fear and inferiority, we must not resist being humbled and seeing and experiencing our wretchedness.

Thursday, January 15, 1976

All day, I noticed real fear and walls within me concerning Phil working at Open Pantry. I feel motivated to compete with Phil for the boss's approval. I feel real fear that Phil will gain more approval than me. I look to You, Lord, to show me why I do this. I *will* put forth an effort to help Phil learn the grocery business, even at the expense of him passing me up. Later, I felt all sorts of pride while working with Phil (I know how to use the cart, stock, and other tricks of the trade).

I was somewhat familiar with store practices and was skilled in stocking groceries because of my past experience. Phil was a department manager of a Montgomery Ward store before going full time at J.U.

Saturday, January 17, 1976

8:45 A.M.: Phil turned on the television too loud when Val, and maybe Sandy, were still sleeping. It seems as long as Phil missed sleep because of the kids, everyone else should get up. I feel a great urge to introvert and just let this situation slide, but I don't feel this is right. I don't know if I'm wrong or not, but the strife is real. I must step out and motivate (step out and do what I think is right) even if I must be rebuked and am wrong.

10:00 A.M.: After walking to the store with Phil and feeling the love flowing, I don't feel I'll open up the problem today. But I look to You, God, to give me strength and wisdom if You prompt me to say anything.

10:30 A.M.: The store manager called and said Phil would work three nights, me just two. I felt shot, and it hurt my pride.

Tuesday, January 20, 1976

I notice two different attitudes I could have: I believe Phil was wrong yesterday when he made noise. *Or*, it really does bother me when Phil makes noise in the morning.

Saturday, January 24, 1976

Mark brought forth the following at the leader's meeting:

1. When purging comes and you feel weak and shot, *know* that it is ordered of the Lord. You're being broken down to see the real motivations, not joy and feelings.
2. You *must* be able to bow down before a little child, if he speaks God's words.

Mark and the elders decided to buy a couple of vans with the apostles' fund money. The vans were put in the names of Mark or Rusty and were to be used for ministry-related endeavors along with daily transportation. They were also supposed to be available to other leaders as needed. We bought one about this time, a pretty red short-bed van. We converted it ourselves into a nice luxury van, with carpeted walls and ceiling. Then, a few months later, we got a light brown long-bed van.

Thursday, January 29, 1976

Today, I noticed a fear and jealousy of not being able to use the van.

I don't remember ever driving the vans. Mark usually drove the red van, and Rusty drove the brown one.

Monday, February 16, 1976

Phil told me about the wives not walking in love. When I would think about the situation, I felt real bitterness rise up in me.

Tuesday, February 17, 1976

Direction from Mark: It is hard for me to work with other brothers (especially leaders) without strife arising. At the leader's meeting, the following was discussed:

1. No longer will God tolerate disobedience to His leading concerning purging.
2. We should realize our errors and begin to see where we don't have a love for the truth in our lives.

Sunday, February 22, 1976

Phil disciplined his baby daughter. I felt fear and hatred rise up toward him. It seemed he did it out of wrath.

Thursday, March 4, 1976

Lately, I've noticed that I seem to be changing for the worse concerning my dealings with people, especially at home. I seem to be beginning to act just like Phil when he handles things harshly. I see it in myself and don't like what I see, but I seem to be powerless to come out of it. I look to You, Lord.

Wednesday, March 17, 1976

I felt God wanted me to talk to Phil about a wrong attitude he has. However, it seems that the words go right over his head. I get confused. I become so discouraged and frustrated when this happens. I feel like maybe I smoothed it over or was wishy-washy with words.

Saturday, March 20, 1976

Phil and Sandy left without asking if we'd take care of their baby. This didn't really bother me too much, nor do other things as they used to. But it *would* bother me if I dwelt on whether it was right or not. Inside I feel a leading to just forget what was done and overlook it. "Let it slide."

I pray that I'm beginning to walk in love—laying aside set courteous standards—and not just avoiding a hassle.

Tuesday, March 30, 1976

Phil *violently* threw Timmy the cat off the chair, for no good reason. I felt immediate disgust over the act and defended Timmy, saying, "Phil, he didn't know Sandy was to sit there!" I said it with noticeable disagreement. As I thought about the incident, discernment was all over my head. I realize I felt *very* threatened by Phil's action. Great fear rose up, and fear makes me unable to talk without strife. As I think about these incidents continuing, I feel I can't go on living with Phil. I can't stand it much longer.

Sunday, April 4, 1976

I used to be able to approach people and straighten our problems out. But now I have a terrible time. I suspect that this situation was covered in pride before.

8:00 A.M.: I've felt my love for the truth fading lately, because every time I step out, I feel pride, mess up, or I'm out of the Spirit—especially at home with the situation with Phil, right and wrong, conscience, and selfish love. I often feel like just doing nothing, but now I remember what God said through Mark and Rusty: "Do not fail to motivate," (that is, do not fail to step out and do what you think is right), and "Satan said I couldn't rise above my inferiorities." Tonight I will again move in what I feel is the truth and remain open for rebuke.

11:30 P.M.: Tried to talk with Phil about what I feel God showed me. Again, I couldn't speak because of three things:

1. Confusing, contradicting thoughts
2. Fear of Phil
3. Belief that strife would rise up as I thought of his faults

I feel pressure from God to motivate (move in what I feel is right) and to tell Phil what I feel God has shown me. But if I have strife, I don't feel I should speak. I am at a dead end! The strife must be taken out of me or I won't feel the direction will help Phil. It will just cause him to put up walls!

12:00 A.M.: I'm praying for understanding on how to warn and speak without strife. Yet there is a question in my mind: Am I out praying to loose the bonds of iniquity or to learn for my pride's sake how to chastise without strife? Again, I'm having a nullifying thought against an action to move. But I feel *God* wants me to seek Him tonight.

12:30 A.M.: Answer to getting rid of strife: Simply look to God and *trust* Him to take it out of me. Anything else results in pride.

12:35 A.M.: God really ministered, and it felt so good. The revelation was so definite, and I really believed I was in His care as I drove home. I still feel it was God's will for me to pray. Not works or merit. I can't help but feel good and fulfilled.

Thursday, April 8, 1976

All day, I'm clearly seeing my self-love motivations around people. Sometimes I think, *What's the use? I can't love them truly so why even try?* But I know that's wrong and that as I continue to motivate, God will change me.

Friday, April 9, 1976

7:45 P.M.: I'm sitting here at the Front Street building looking at people. I feel so empty. Yet I see the need they have to be fed. Tonight I see more worthlessness, emptiness, and selfishness in me.

9:20 P.M.: We had a meeting on unity and serving each other. I looked out among the people and felt such a lack. I could see my selfishness and how I lack true love and concern for the body that comes from the heart. I felt fear because I knew I should have fervent love for them, and I also remembered my recent realization of my selfish motivations. But faith also arose as I recognized that only God can put the love there for them. All I have to do is want it and trust God to put it there.

Monday, April 12, 1976

At the leader's meeting, we discussed the following:

1. We must have *daily* discipline toward the Spirit.
2. We should never judge revelation on set consciences of emotions (anger, for example).
3. The voice of God is the inward witness *only*. Revelation is not God's voice until it has gone through the inward witness.
4. Word is not light until the words hit the heart, not the head.

In other words:

1. We should take up our cross daily (see Luke 9:23).
2. Just because a person has a wrong attitude about what they are saying or how they are saying it doesn't mean that *what* they are saying is not correct. For example, just because a person brings forth a word in anger doesn't mean the words are not true. The anger may be out of line, but the word may be true.

3 and 4. You should judge all input by your inward witness, including someone's interpretation of a Scripture passage. You should never believe a word or vision from anyone unless it makes sense to you, based on your knowledge of the Bible and your own relationship with God. *You* should feel that it is a word from the Lord. If you're being hammered by an overbearing preacher, sometimes spending time in prayer will bring you to a peaceful understanding of a Scripture passage. Sometimes an issue comes up and you won't find the specific answer in the Bible. Then you have to pray and depend on the Spirit's guidance, your inward witness. You should be open to being wrong, but humbly call it as you see it. And remember this: if you are not open to being wrong, then you are wide open to deception.

Who could argue with the above teachings? In the midst of Devilish attitudes and tainted doctrine, little bits of truth still were coming through.

Tuesday, April 13, 1976

Talked to Devin Stockbay about two faults, and it went *very* well. God's love was there. I thank You, Lord.

Saturday, May 15, 1976

When Phil comes to me about Val, I feel his bitterness toward her, his lack of love and concern for *her* as a person, and his selfishness in coming to me about Val—not concern for her. How can I receive a *legitimate* gripe against Val when his motivation to do it is so clearly wrong?

Tuesday, May 18, 1976

I received the following direction from Mark:

1. I need to have a *trust in God* over the tight situations that arise in our household. *He* will correct and solve the problems. *He* will give me peace in my heart.
2. I need to overlook Phil and Sandy's faults. Let God judge and speak to their hearts in *His* time, not the time *I* want it done.
3. I need to repay evil with love and try to understand the reasons Phil and Sandy do not walk in love at certain times. We must seek God for this ability to love.

Sunday, May 24, 1976

I feel God ministering that I should remember that He lives in Phil. I need to believe Phil is honest-hearted and really *does* want to do God's will. I should not rail at him where he's off.

Tuesday, May 26, 1976

5:30 A.M.: this morning, Phil was stomping on the hardwood floor above us as he played with the puppy. I felt strife and couldn't understand why they make so much noise.

It got pretty loud. I couldn't understand why they didn't think about our need to sleep and be a little more considerate.

Tuesday, May 16, 1976 (continued)

12:30 P.M.: I heard about Bill Riggenbacher's snow tires being given away out from under him. I felt strife toward Devin Stockbay and Bill Norten for not walking in love.

I remember us all joking about each other's things as *our* car or *our* stereo or *our* snow tires. The problem was that after a while, many things were not taken care of because everything was everybody's. There was a lack of respect for all the stuff that was "ours." In the above case, Bill Norten and Devin decided that Bill Riggenbacher didn't need his snow tires as much as someone else, and so they gave them away.

Tuesday, May 16, 1976 (continued)

1:45 P.M.: I need help and a change in my attitude in situations where I feel others don't walk in love. I develop strife rather than concern. I see it and know it is wrong. I ask You, dear God, to take it out of me. In the meantime, I don't see how I can function as a leader. This problem doesn't seem to come up with the congregation, but it is constant in the household and with other leadership. Only a love for God and for knowing Him will be the ultimate answer to this problem. And I lack it.

Things in the household that bring out strife in me if I dwell on the situations:

1. Household finances: Lack of discipline in spending and no accounting for money spent.
2. Housework: Phil's set ways concerning housework.
3. Actions: When Phil snaps at his wife out of frustration, kicks or throws the cats, or acts harshly when doing something.

Wednesday, May 27, 1976

6:30 A.M.: I had breakfast with Phil to try to find some unity, and we got it. Real love. But as we were wrapping it up and leaving, I felt dead inside. Especially when Phil talked of new cars, money matters, and other leaders. I felt a voice saying inside, "Well, no unity anymore. You are off track already. You didn't say all you should have." But I believe that is Satan's voice trying to discourage me. Satan is the problem.

12:00 A.M.: I came home and heard about Phil eating the piece of steak left from dinner that had been saved for me. I felt Phil was wrong, but I am unable to speak correction to him because of strife. I trust You, Lord, to take the strife out of me, or I'll never be any good to You.

This last sentence is close to the truth. God can even use the Devil to get good things done, but what God *really* wants to do is show His love through *us*. And the more that we can be purged of frustration and strife, the more we can move with God to bless others.

I also feel that America will someday experience a severe economic disaster. This will force many Christians to move in with another family, while others will voluntarily open their homes to people in need. Although I would not like to go through that type of experience again, it taught me things about myself and about others that I couldn't have received any other way. I am thankful for that experience. The lessons that we learned during this time will be helpful in the hard times to come.

CHAPTER 18

SURVIVAL FIGHT
STRUGGLING TO MAINTAIN MOMENTUM

*B*ecause God wasn't blessing so much in the outward miracle ministries we had hoped for, we struggled to keep the momentum up and rolling in a positive direction. God could not bless us with miracle-working gifts of the Holy Spirit and deliverance because we were off base in so many areas, and we would have interpreted this type of blessing as His endorsement. In a sense, His hands were tied. God wanted to mightily deliver people through miracles and His deliverance power, but that would be bad for us (the leadership).

At this time, I believe that we had swayed too far off course and that God was no longer drawing any more people to our ministry. God desired the purging of our selfish desires and subtle hypocrisies, but He disdained our cultish practices and blind following. There was now more bad happening than good.

Yet in the midst of all the bad things, God still worked in the lives of each of the leaders, teaching and drawing us to Himself. That *can* seem very confusing, until you realize that God works that way sometimes. He will *never* leave us or forsake us (see Hebrews 13:5), and therefore we will occasionally sense God's presence and outward blessing, even when we are in sin or in bad situations. He loves us and is constantly working in our lives to bring us out of bondage and into the light of His freedom and truth. He will also use the bad things that others impose upon us to bring about good changes in our souls.

The leadership structure at J.U. was now securely in place. Most of us blindly followed, because we felt that to go against the leadership was to go against God. If Mark had been evil hearted, he could have enjoyed a lot of sin for a while. But I feel that Mark tried to do the right thing. He had no conscious intention of using our dedication for his own selfish desires. But *oh* was he driven to see us rise up into the men of God that he envisioned for us!

There were still around 100 dedicated followers that came to the body meetings and more than 200 who came to the open meetings. But God now left us to our own devices, and we found it increasingly difficult to move forward with our vision of the army.

Two good things started to happen in my life: I was learning not to be threatened by others when they rose to the occasion, and I was also beginning to help people because I loved them, not because I needed them. Up until this time in my life, my main motivations for helping people had been fear and compulsion (fear of not doing God's will and compulsion from the leadership). Gradually, a transformation began to take place. I began to feel God's love welling up within me to genuinely care for others.

All of the journal entries in this chapter took place within the time frame of the previous chapter.

Tuesday, January 13, 1976

I noticed that I always prod and try to find out what a leaders' meeting is all about before we have it. Is that fear? Or maybe me not wanting to see myself?

How about this: "Once bitten, twice shy"?

Tuesday, January 13, 1976 (continued)

Mark brought forth the following at a leaders meeting:

1. Trust God minute by minute that He's there and will show you direction for activities.
2. Determine in your heart that what you've done is God's will.
3. Wield the Sword of the Spirit when the Devil comes against you.
4. Show a desire for Mark's direction.

Mark also mentioned that we've covered the body by compulsion because we were *told* to do so, not naturally.

Saturday, January 31, 1976

Mark came in to the Front Street building and was talking seriously with Rusty. Then he told us to quit playing pool and begin to pray. I felt shot when I saw Mark's seriousness and I didn't act at first. When he told us to pray, it was hard to begin. I felt humiliated.

Thursday, February 19, 1976

While working on the car, I got all geared up and confused on what to do. I feel as if I'm not obeying the Spirit when I'm working on it.

Saturday, February 21, 1976

Direction from Jeff Bechtel: I wasn't working on the cars to help the body and sheep, but to get the job done. It seems as if whatever I feel God wants me to do, it clashes with what one of the other leaders thinks I should do. I look to You, Lord, to straighten me out so I have no strife.

Sunday, February 29, 1976

Directions from Mark from a leader's meeting:

1. If we look at a leader from a natural ability standpoint, we will have pride when we get put in a leader's position.
2. Error in leadership: Strife toward sheep who disobey our witness or don't agree.

3. Error in the body: Sheep have the attitude that all other Christians who aren't at J.U. are Antichrist.

I wonder where that attitude came from? Seriously, Mark and the revelators were constantly telling us that certain well-known ministers were Antichrist. I think it was natural for the rest of the leadership and congregation to take on the attitude that *everyone else was on the wrong road*. In the above entry, Mark was trying to tell us that there really were Christians in other places.

Monday, March 8, 1976

Mark told me that I try to please people to avoid hassle. I expect courtesy from others according to my own selfish standard.

Tuesday, March 9, 1976

9:45 P.M.: I prayed for one of the sisters and felt pride that I was the one to be there for her to be healed. When she fell out, I was surprised and felt pride a few seconds later. I feel sort of justified and excited. Is it because I'm glad to see God glorified or is it pride? I didn't feel much pride, but I trust the Lord will purge me completely.

3:00 P.M.: I talked to two honest-hearted hippies who came by the building today. When they asked about J.U., I felt shot because I couldn't relate God. Then Phil and I talked about the revival coming soon, and it seems I'm too messed up for God to use me for a long time. But I trust in You, Lord, that You'll give me everything I need to do Your will. You can raise me up in five seconds.

Wednesday, March 24, 1976

Right now, I'm not sure what God wants out of me. Should I do nothing or seek God? I can't reach out in works. But God told Mark: *Woe unto the shepherds that feed not the flock.* I can't motivate out of obligation, but the body is dying. Maybe it is time for leadership to make a decision and let Mark step back, but Mark said last night that it is *God's* turn to move. I feel a leading to get together with some people to teach, but Mark and the other leaders didn't feel that was the problem.

I asked Mark last night if I could get some groups together and teach some lessons we've learned in leadership. He said that would be OK, but he didn't see how doing that could be productive when things are so spiritually dry.

Friday, March 26, 1976

At the body meeting, I felt pressure and extreme concern for the feeding of the body. I walked around superdry with no direction or exhortation for the sheep. I looked at people sitting, waiting to be fed like newborn birds with their mouths open. I'm a called shepherd and feeder of the flock, but I haven't received anything from God to give.

I saw and felt my own worthlessness greater and greater as the night went on. When Mark got up, my feeling of worthlessness grew. When people testified under the anointing, I felt relieved that the sheep were being fed. I felt very clearly my worthless natural ability to feed the sheep, but I also felt faith that God *is* able to feed the flock when He wants to.

Saturday, March 27, 1976

At my parent's house, I couldn't think of anything to tell them when they asked, "What's new?" and "What have you been doing?" I looked for something to show or tell my parents and brother. Seems I have absolutely nothing to offer for communion with others. Not just Spirit-food, but also now I don't have anything in my soul or flesh to offer either. Even my parents and brother asked what my problem was. I just can't hide my emotions anymore.

Saturday, April 3, 1976

The following came out at the leader's meeting:

1. Satan drives evil thoughts in every person (lust, adultery, pride and so forth).

2. The fear of becoming evil is the result, and that is torment.
3. To escape torment, we will either eventually accept these thoughts as our real self or we will look to God.
4. God said these thoughts are not from us, but are evil spirits speaking.
5. When fear comes from these thoughts, rebuke the spirit.
6. Satan drives everything from fear.

Thursday, April 8, 1976

All day, I'm clearly seeing my self-love motivations around people. Sometimes I think, *What's the use? I can't love them truly so why even try?* But I know that's wrong and that as I continue to motivate, God will change me.

Monday, April 19, 1976

The deacons received directions from Mark. Jobs are not being done. We need to make a list of jobs and post them. Have the sheep do them, not us.

Saturday, April 24, 1976

Lately, I have seen one of the new young deacons working with other brothers and fulfilling the deacon's calling. I praise God that I actually feel joyous that he's rising up, not threatened.

Inward Witness: In the past, I taught the sheep to come to a high standard of responsibility for my own selfish motivations of pride, not for the sheep's benefit.

Sheep, sheep, sheep. The Lord refers to us as sheep in a loving, caring way. However, there was clearly a lack of equality at J.U. in the proper sense between the way we viewed leadership and "the sheep." How about this question: What *is* a leader? A leader *leads*. He is not so much a commander. He is not so much a boss. He leads. He serves. He *leads*.

Friday, April 30, 1976

At the leader's meeting, we were told to begin to support our own households.

Finances got worse as the leadership began to wander from God's will. Three or four months after the Man-Child revelation came, J.U. only had enough money to pay for the rent and utilities for the leaders.

While living with Phil and Sandy, our whole household was required to live on $50 per week. Although Phil and I made more than that from our part-time jobs, we put all of those paychecks into the offering. As J.U. ministers, we received a total of $50 for gas, groceries, and personal items. We had to use one-percent milk, because that was cheaper. Whole milk became a luxury back then! (And none of us were on diets, either.) It's interesting, though. I felt *very* secure about always having enough to eat and having a roof over my head. I felt that security then more than at any other time of my life.

At the leader's meeting in the above entry, we were told not to count on money from the offerings as much and begin to look for full-time jobs to support our own households. J.U. simply couldn't afford to keep us all on the payroll for much longer. This really saddened me because I loved the ministry life.

I remember walking down the road from my Briarcrest apartment shortly after starting my full-time work with J.U. I was on my way to work at my little office in Mark's home. I felt such joy and said out loud, "I wouldn't trade this life for a million dollars!" At that time, the ministry was flourishing and I was living on $100 per week with our rent and utilities paid directly from J.U. That wasn't much money, but it was enough for me. I don't think Val was as happy about it, however. In any case, that lifestyle was quickly coming to a close.

Monday, May 3, 1976

The following was discussed at the leader's meeting:

1. Get full-time jobs to support the body, not only ourselves.
2. *Don't* look at jobs as a rut.
3. The body will go through a cycle now:

   - As we begin to support the body and appear to buy worldly items, some of the sheep will try to follow out of lust and not Spirit. They will get into financial trouble and will need help.
   - We will then tell them about our lives and discipline.
   - When people with dishonest hearts question our integrity, we must not be motivated by them.

Tuesday, May 4, 1976

At a leaders' meeting, there were two questions to ask ourselves: (1) How should you handle a situation when someone comes for direction but you have none? (2) What's the best way?

Friday, May 7, 1976

During the last two days of job-hunting, I have really been shot. I haven't been close to God and I can't get my witness on *anything*. I am a wreck inside. Lord, please give me strength to look to You and do Your will about a job.

I loved the ministry life, and I did not want to go back into a secular job.

Saturday, May 8, 1976

After such a hard week, tonight I had a release of joy as God came through again. Today I felt a love well up for Lee and other brothers. It seems like this is happening more and more often. When it wells up, it is so easy to love.

Rusty and Mark said they had a witness for me to go back to work at Dayco, my old job. The previous few days, I have felt totally wrecked inside about working at a job. I have felt no inward witness in this direction. Today, however, it seems as if I have a right attitude about working in general and *why* we're going back to work as the apostle Paul did.

I have no inward witness to apply at Dayco. I am only being obedient to my leaders. I am willing to go there and work. Rusty and Mark came to me in love, freedom, and with a witness from God. I cannot deny that. So I will obey in *faith* that God will cover me as I do this.

I trust You, Lord, to settle me.

Sunday May 9, 1976

I have experienced turmoil day and night, because I have no witness to go back to Dayco.

Tuesday, May 11, 1976

The past few days have been the greatest shake-up in my life in a long time. I am so confused about going back to work. There is such a cloud in my soul. I am in a daze about it. When I meet and talk to people who don't go to J.U., I am unable to explain what I'm doing without feeling deceitful. I think it's because I'm not convinced that this is a step forward. I have been turning in applications out of submission to leadership.

I received the following direction from Mark: I need to be covered by the body at times. Sometimes, leadership has to protect people from going the wrong direction by giving them wise counsel. This is one of those times. God probably won't give me a witness on where to go, but I must trust in the leadership to cover me.

I feel faith in my leaders and I feel a peace and trust in God to cover me through them. I feel at times that this situation is probably the result of the bad attitudes I have. But as I seek You, God, all I ask is that You take the confusion and strife out of me and give me peace.

I will go back to work. I just feel I shouldn't go back with a wrong attitude. Something needs to change first. I don't know what.

I ended up going back to work at Dayco as a production worker. On the first day back, I was given the job of helping one of the more skilled men. I always liked this guy. He was a slim, good-looking muscular guy, a typical man's man who was well respected by the other workers as well as the management. Shortly after starting to drill on a frame with him, he stopped, looked at me, and said sort of sarcastically, "I thought you were gonna save the world."

I felt peace along with great sadness and true humility as I simply answered, "Things didn't work out the way I expected." He just took in my answer, gave a shrug as if he received it, and went back to drilling. I immediately gained this man's respect, and we continued to work well together for many years.

CHAPTER 19

THE NEW FREEDOM

TRUTH AND DECEPTION

About this time, Mark had a dream that he felt was from God. This dream had a huge impact on the direction of J.U. In his dream, Mark saw Father Abraham relaxing on top of a hill at sunset. Abraham was quietly sitting and smoking a pipe, watching the sunset, and just communing with God. It was a very peaceful, pleasant setting.

The main message to Mark was that smoking a pipe was not sin and not at all offensive to God. Mark and Rusty bought pipes and began to smoke them openly. It wasn't long before (it seemed) everybody was smoking a pipe. I honestly don't have any particular memories of smoking a pipe back then, but I'm sure I did.

I remember hearing about this dream and feeling that it was a breath of fresh air (no pun intended). I judged it then to be of God, and I still believe it was from the Lord. The doctrine that Mark began to teach was called the "New Freedom." This began as a biblically sound doctrine complete with grace, discipline, and moderation.

Basically, the summary of this doctrine was that the Apostle Paul said, "All things are lawful for me, but all things are not expedient: all things are lawful for me, but all things edify not, and I will not be brought under the power of any" (1 Corinthians 6:12; 10:23). There is liberty in Christ. This liberty is to be used to love and serve others. It is not to be used to fulfill lusts (see Galatians 5:13).

So, the first part of the doctrine dealt with unbiblical traditions of the Church concerning abstinence from smoking, alcohol, and other areas of legalism. I remember only pipes being mentioned at first. The second part of the doctrine was about using our liberty to love others.

The traditional argument against smoking is that it defiles or destroys the Temple of God, according to 1 Corinthians 3:17. However, this argument is weak on two counts. First (and most importantly), this passage is *not* talking about sins against ourselves or sins against our own physical bodies. It is dealing with our sins against *each other* in the body of Christ. It is saying that we are not to malign, tear down, or defile each other through factions, pride, envy, and gossip. We are to build up the body of Christ on the foundation of Jesus. This passage is not at all referring to habits that could become harmful to our physical bodies.

But for those who would still hold to that popular interpretation of this passage, there is still another reason that their argument is weak: Many other practices that they accept are actually more risky to the body than smoking. If the level of risk of smoking is said to be sin or destroying to the body, then everything else that is *as* risky should be considered sin as well.

Debated factors of similar risks include certain types of travel, sports, occupations, and many types of food. Here's my point: Taking the risk of smoking one cigarette isn't a sin any more than taking the risk of playing soccer or working a half hour in a coal mine, unless you sense that God doesn't want you to smoke. (Just for the record, I *do* see a high level of risk in smoking a lot of anything.)

One traditional view is that one can become addicted to certain substances. This is a valid concern. Paul said that we should not be brought under the power of anything, and that includes cigarettes, alcohol, sports, television, or *any* food.

So the sin should be labeled as being brought under the power of a substance, not about the risk involved. To enjoy a glass of wine or prime rib under certain circumstances is not sin in itself. However, Ephesians 5:18 says, *Be not drunk with wine, wherein is excess; but be filled with the Spirit.* This is not a command to abstain from alcohol, but a command to not solve problems or escape reality through alcohol. Gluttony could come under the same category. We should look to God for answers that will solve our problems.

Many families *have* been ruined by the abuse of alcohol and tobacco. So, while some of these desires are "lawful," they should be viewed the same as guns, punch presses, or even a surgeon's scalpel: they are dangerous in the wrong hands. As Christians, we have the Holy Spirit and the Bible to help us discern what practices are good or bad for us. We also have pastors and other sources of godly counsel to help guide us. If you have any doubts about what you should do concerning these substances, the best advice I have for you is this: Don't do it!

The second part of the "New Freedom" doctrine had to do with *using* our liberty to love others and to come out from some of the traditional thinking about what is evil. This portion of the doctrine was based on 1 Corinthians 9:19–22:

> *For though I be free from all men, yet have I made myself servant unto all, that I might gain the more. And unto the Jews I became as a Jew, that I might gain the Jews; to them that are under the law, as under the law, that I might gain them that are under the law; To them that are without law, as without law, (being not without law to God, but under the law to Christ) that I might gain them that are without law. To the weak became I as weak, that I might gain the weak: I am made all things to all men, that I might by all means save some.*

Within the bounds of the above thoughts, we can go places (like bars) and do things (like drink a glass of wine or beer) in order to have contact with and minister to persons who do not know Christ. The traditional scriptural opposition to this is 1 Thessalonians 5:22 which says, *Abstain from all appearance of evil*. But this really means to abstain from the appearance of *real* evil, not perceived evil.

Here are some examples of perceived evil with alcohol and how it would affect your behavior:

- Don't ever go into a bar, because there is alcohol being consumed there, and that is evil.
- Don't ever go into a bar, because some people in there will get drunk.
- Don't patronize a grocery store where they sell wine, because the grocery store is making money from the sale of alcohol.
- Don't have a drink of wine with your spouse at a restaurant, because people use wine to get drunk, and therefore it is the appearance of evil.

Jesus was not at all concerned with doing things that the religious people *thought* were evil. There are several examples of this in the Scriptures:

1. Jesus healed on the Sabbath day.
2. He let His disciples extract grain from the stalks on the Sabbath day.
3. He talked to the Samaritan woman at the well.
4. Jesus turned water into wine and apparently drank wine, because some people called Him a "winebibber," or drunkard.

All of these things offended the Pharisees who perceived those acts as evil, but Jesus didn't let that stop Him. Therefore, we don't have to be afraid of offending the self-righteous when doing things that they *think* are evil but really are not. We *do* have to be careful of using our liberty and causing a weaker Christian to sin (see 1 Corinthians 8:9–13).

In my research for writing this chapter, I came across a very interesting discovery. There are *no* journal entries for this time period (which was about five months). During my time at J.U., we almost always handed in written accounts of the prophecies and revelations from God. I have a complete notebook of these writings. This notebook also has *no* entries during this period. There is absolutely no written documentation of *anything* we did. Usually the old J.U. checkbook register would show a clue as to what we were doing, but it showed only the regular expenditures such as rent, utilities, and paychecks.

In September, Val and I enjoyed the freedom of moving back to Mrs. Larson's house, as Mrs. Larson was going back to California to live with her son. We invited Craig and Julie Berringer to move in with us. The Berringers were friends who had gone through most of J.U. with us up to this point.

Craig, Julie, and their toddler, Jacob, were very easy to live with. The peacefulness was wonderful compared to the difficulty of the previous year with Phil and Sandy. The contrast was so outstanding that I had to ask, "What made the difference?"

One could be tempted to say our difficulties with Phil and Sandy were caused by the terrible spiritual trials we were going through at that time. I don't think so. They were caused by personality conflicts. Phil and I were opposite in the way we handled conflict. The contrast was too great for us to enjoy each other's close company for more than a few weeks.

It isn't that I was any less sinful than Phil. When conflict came, he reacted outwardly and I reacted inwardly. The difference was so great that I just couldn't live comfortably with it. I want to emphasize again that I always had (and *still* have) a high degree of respect for Phil as a Christian brother in the Lord. We had many good times together, and I expect to have more good times in the future!

Craig and Julie's method of handling conflict was just about the same as ours. Neither Val or I *ever* felt any strife toward them or coming from them. I think a clear line of authority in the household helped keep the peace. I was the director of the property—Mrs. Larson had given me the authority. When we lived with Phil and Sandy, there was no line of authority. Therefore, the rules of conduct and confrontation were left up for constant interpretation. There's nothing like knowing the rules before entering into a situation.

It is hard for me to believe that I didn't write for five months. It's interesting that I was making 20 to 25 entries per month just before this period. It was a strange time, with things falling apart as the "New Freedom" was running awry. A lot happened during that time. Mark and many other people began to say, "God just isn't around." The New Freedom was fully embraced, and unfortunately abused. Many people—including some of the J.U. leaders—eventually went to extremes, allowing themselves to be brought under the power of some of their activities. Fortunately, I was able to stay away from the worst of it.

Another new doctrine that came out towards the end of this time period was "moving in your desires." This doctrine was based on a few Scriptures in the Bible and made some sense to me, but I was concerned about its likelihood to encourage people to sin.

The essence of this doctrine was that Jesus said, *If ye abide in me, and my words abide in you, ye shall ask what ye will, and it shall be done unto you* (John 15:7). Paul said, *For it is God which is working in you, both to will and to do of his good pleasure* (Philippians 2:13). This meant that it is God in us who gives us both the desire to do His will and the willpower to do it. If you are walking with God and wanting to do His will, He will put His desires into you. Therefore, when these desires rise up, we should follow them.

We were talking about *wholesome* desires, of course. I remember the term "peaceful desires" being used during the explanations. But with the "New Freedom" in full swing in a relatively young congregation, it was a dangerous combination. I believe this doctrine is true in its purest form, but getting to and abiding there is another thing. We will always have to acknowledge that some of our inward desires are destructively selfish and are *not* to be followed.

Has anyone come to the place where all his or her desires are totally wholesome? I don't think so. I don't think we can *ever* come to the place where we don't have to resist ungodly desires. We *can* grow in grace and we *can* grow in Christ's likeness, so the ungodly desires will diminish. I am very thankful that some of those desires have already been stripped from me.

I am totally convinced of one aspect of this subject. We are born with some type of healthy selfishness that is not sinful in itself. An example of this is Jesus in the Garden of Gethsemane. Jesus did not want to go to the cross and practically *begged* the Father to relieve him of that task. Jesus even gave the impression that the Father would accept Jesus' decision to not go through with the task. But Jesus (thankfully) decided to follow the Father's wisdom and pay the penalty for all of our sins. Jesus had selfish desires rise up, but he didn't move in them. So having these selfish desires couldn't have been sin, because Jesus was *without sin* (Hebrews 4:15).

Our congregation spent the summer moving away from some forms of legalism, testing some new waters, and moving in our desires. Unfortunately, instead of using our newly found freedom to reach out in love and help others, many began to use this freedom for selfish desires. This resulted in us turning more and more inward, and we as a group began a spiral downward toward greater deception.

The "New Freedom" began with people smoking pipes, but before the end of the summer, some people—including some of the leadership—had gone from pipes to cigars, to cigarettes, to wine, beer and liquor. I still believe that the original doctrine was from the Holy Spirit and that many people put it in proper perspective and used it for its intended purpose: to love and serve others. However, if anyone was looking for an excuse to sin, they now had one.

CHAPTER 20

"GOD'S NOT AROUND"

DEEP DECEPTION

*H*ey, let's all sit in a circle and pass around a joint as a type of communion." Deep deception doesn't just barge in like this. It sneaks in a little at a time until the bizarre and ridiculous isn't so bizarre or ridiculous any more.

People were now using the phrase "God's not around" more often. Mark said that as long as God wasn't around, it would be OK to do what we wanted until He began to move again. As the leadership began to find full-time jobs (and do less ministry), they also began to enjoy many worldly pleasures. Most of these were healthy activities, such as weight training and fishing. I remember many conversations where a leader would justify the time spent on these things by saying, "We can do these things now while we're waiting on God to move, because right now God's not around."

God can't encourage us when we're going down the wrong road, so it may *seem* like He's not around. But God has already said, *I will never leave thee, nor forsake thee.* (Hebrews 13:5). Therefore, when God seems to be scarce, we should examine the road we're on. Sometimes we're on the right road and our troubles are just attacks from the enemy.

Determining whether we are being attacked because we're on the right road or suffering consequences because we're on the wrong road can be confusing. But God is faithful and will eventually make His will known if we don't give up asking and looking for it.

Thursday, December 23, 1976

Lord, there is no money coming in to support Mark and the building. Do You want Mark to go back to work?

Sunday, December 26, 1976

We went to Mark's last night. The time there climaxed a realization that has been coming to me the past few weeks. I have felt a longing and desire that I haven't felt in years. When Mark, Jim Flood, one of the younger brothers and I prayed last night, I felt just like I did when Mark and I prayed before J.U. began. I believe this feeling is a love for the truth and a greater knowledge of God.

Several weeks before, I had been at the Front Street building praying and talking with Mark and a few other leaders. We were sitting and lying around on the platform. As we were discussing a subject, someone asked Mark a question. Mark looked thoughtful, paused, and then answered the question with "I don't know."

At that very moment, I felt a spark light up in my heart. It was a definite feeling that I hadn't felt in a long, long time—a feeling of thirsting for truth and searching for understanding coupled with an atmosphere of confidence and acceptance and God's blessing. Like a light bulb turning on, a feeling of personal responsibility and desire to know the truth filled my heart. I was familiar with that feeling but hadn't felt it in a long while. I did not realize it at the time, but *I had just come out of a state of blind following.*

Today, I look back and see that blind following had replaced my search for truth.

Friday, December 31, 1976

Since the beginning of J.U., everyone's heart began to gradually relax from seeking God. This is partly due to Mark's type of leadership and partly due to the people's corruption. I didn't realize it, but I let Mark do the seeking. After nearly three years, the same love for seeking the truth has returned but with a much greater maturity and wisdom. The greatest lesson learned is: *I can do nothing of my own. That which I hear, I do. What I see the Father do, I can do. And apart from him, I can do nothing* (John 5:19; 15:5).

I have also learned the difference between the love and strength of God to motivate from and motivation that comes from a manipulated conscience.

Lord, I believe there is a bit more refining of this lesson, and I pray that You will imbed this in my heart before You anoint the people of J.U. with power. I really feel the body beginning to have life again. I felt You witnessed to me tonight that from this night forward, this body will begin to live again.

One of the leaders told me earlier about the spirit of death being broken tonight.

About this time, Mark began to report that he was fighting the spirit of death. He said that he would have to face it. We had many leaders' meetings where we would pray about this problem. Mark was clearly in mental agony about his collapsing vision for J.U. and its apparent doom. Along with this agony, that spirit of death feeling had come on him. During this time, Mark had often become either depressed or puzzled, or just the opposite: full of burning faith and fiery exhortation.

Leadership meetings were not as frightening as they had been before. Mark seemed to be much more tolerant of our faults, and often he would just try to encourage us to keep up the faith in our commission. Although one of the elders said that the spirit of death was broken, it quickly became clear that it was not broken at all and continued to hound Mark unmercifully.

Monday, January 10, 1977

> Lord, I remember a few weeks ago, I asked You to let me share in Mark's pain. Now I'm laid off, and I thank You for that. After talking all day to Mark about the building, I feel full of drive and geared-up ambition.

When I was laid off from Dayco, I spent the day talking to Mark about all the possibilities for using the Front Street building to make money and for the Lord's use. Donations were dropping off, and Mark was looking for ways to keep the ministry going. Losing the building represented failure, so we were looking for ways to keep it.

Wednesday, January 26, 1977

> Please, Lord, deliver us. Please lead us. Mark is tormented; there is no passion. Where is the commission? Where is life with You? How do both come together? Where is the power of the Spirit? Where is the Spirit of revival?

We were still having regular leaders' meetings at the Front Street building. There, we would pray, talk about the ministry, and get direction from Mark.

Monday, February 7, 1977 (12:00 Midnight)
Direction from Mark at the leaders' meeting:

1. *We* are the strength. *We* are the ones to fight the spirit of death.
2. Our mind will fight, but we will have to believe the Word from the heart.
3. Tonight we were broken down to the basics, to the unshakable. Tonight the fullness is born. Tonight we look to the unshakable love between us. Tonight a circle is formed. Satan cannot harass any part of the circle until he goes through *all* the parts. *The fullness lies in the love between us.*

Saturday, February 19, 1977

At the leaders' meeting, we discussed how *we* are the body of Christ. *We* are the fullness. *We* are the strength to face the spirit of death.

As you can read in the above two entries, Mark was still battling this spirit. During one of these meetings, Mark reported the following dream, which he felt was related to the spirit of death:

I was on an open plain. Off in the distance was a ram. Then the ram charged. I was expecting to be brutally rammed by its horns and was understandably scared. The ram plowed into my belly—and then a funny thing happened. It didn't hurt. I was flabbergasted that there was no pain. The ram was gone. I woke up feeling puzzled.

I suspect that Mark was beginning to have suicidal thoughts, because of the urgency in his voice as he exhorted us.

During the previous few months, some of the leaders began to smoke heavily and use profanity. Occasionally, they would drink past the point of sobriety. Even though I don't believe that the act of doing all these things necessarily sentences you to hell, it *does* indicate a weakness in the spirit when you lose control of your fleshly desires and impulses. I was concerned about those very things that were happening more and more. I even began to bum cigarettes from the guys.

I used to smoke back in high school, and I loved it! However, because I wanted to be a good wrestler, I quit smoking during my junior year. I can even remember my last cigarette. Our family was on vacation, and I was sitting on a dock on the inland seaway in Sebastian, Florida, next to my brother. I took the last drag of my last cigarette and flicked it into the salt water. This was before I was a Christian, and it was *hard*

to quit. For months I wanted to smoke and struggled like most people when they try to quit. The desire to smoke finally left me, and I was glad to be free.

Then came a day of awakening for me at J.U. I remember getting into a truck with two other leaders. They both lit up a cigarette, and did that smoke ever smell good to me! They offered me a cigarette, and I was about to accept it when I recognized a feeling that had been gone for years. It was the feeling of dependency and the need to smoke. It felt like tentacles wrapping around me and binding me up with its power. I'm thankful that I had the strength to say no and to recognize the bondage that was trying to get control of me. I haven't been tempted to smoke a cigarette since that day.

About this time, Mark and the elders felt that we should not have any body meetings for one month. This was a real shocker in one way, but it also bore witness to me. The purpose of this was to show the people of the body that they didn't really need the meetings as much as they needed to be dependent upon God. Although the formal meetings were suspended, we were encouraged to continue fellowshipping with one another. It was like a vacation to me and probably to most of the other people as well.

After this four-week layoff, we came back together for a few weeks of regular body meetings at the Front Street building. But then Mark felt that it was time to just let it go. I think it was definitely the right thing to do. No more meetings felt good in one way, but it also seemed like a reminder of our failure to build that big organization we'd hoped for.

One precarious aspect of not meeting regularly was that we had a congregation of young people who were testing the "New Freedom," and they needed fellowship and guidance. Another aspect that added to the danger was our belief that all other churches were off track and headed for Antichrist. That left the people with nowhere to go. We still had each other's friendship, and most people continued to fellowship and talk about God. But that is not entirely the same as gathering together purposefully to glorify God in song, hearing the Word, and worshiping Him. Most of the congregation maintained their faith in Jesus and rode out the storm.

Friday, March 4, 1977

At the leaders' meeting, we discussed how we should not *search* for desires. When peaceful desires do rise up, we shouldn't go against them. *When* we feel free to do so, we should move in our desires.

I began to hear reports that some of the leaders were smoking dope. They were just rumors at the time, but I suspected them to be true. Then a leader told me that a few of them passed around a cigarette as a type of communion. That seemed really bizarre. (I need to clarify that the leader did not indicate that it was a replacement for Holy Communion. It was more of a camaraderie type communion.) Because I still had a very wrong concept of leadership and still considered Mark and the elders as my leaders, I understood no real way to confront them on these issues.

One night, all of the leaders got together at Bill Riggenbacher's house to pray and fellowship around a campfire. It was cold, but we enjoyed the fellowship and the warmth of the fire. Then Mark and one of the other leaders announced that we were going to pass around a cigarette as a type of communion. I immediately felt squeamish and uncomfortable, feeling it was not a right thing to do. When the cigarette came to me, I remember thinking, *Although I don't feel this is a good thing to do, I still have the freedom in Christ to go along with it.* Which is what I did. I went along with it.

I went home that night rather troubled. The next day, I shut myself in my bedroom and began to earnestly pray about what was happening. Then the Lord spoke to my heart rather clearly and profoundly. He said, *What you did the other night was not good. The guys are going down a wrong road, and it will get worse. Soon someone will suggest the same thing again, except next time it will be with dope. Be ready for it. It will happen.* It was *so good* to hear from God. His Word was a lamp to my feet and a light to my path! His Word is peace! His Word brings strength and courage!

I had to decide whom to follow: Mark and the rest of the "leaders," or what I felt God was saying to me. There was an overwhelming fear of going against Mark. Those who did so were usually pronounced unsaved and headed for hell. It was even said that they blasphemed the Holy Spirit and would never able to come back to God.

I made my firm decision next to my bed in Mrs. Larson's house. I figured that I might have to go to hell for going against Mark, but I was ready to stand up against him and the other leaders if they tried to lead anyone into more things I felt were wrong. I felt that I might possibly need to sacrifice myself for their safety. I needed to warn the leaders and stand against them for their sakes. I was ready!

Then came the day, less than three weeks after I made my decision, when all ten leaders were at the Front Street building, walking around and praying. We would often spend hours at a time praying. We might pray lying down, sitting, or kneeling on the carpeted platform, or we might just walk around the building and pray while we were walking. While I was walking, I heard one of the elders call Mark over to him. I sensed something was up, so I tightened my walking circle to hear what was being said. I clearly heard the elder say to Mark that he felt God wanted us to all smoke dope together as a type of communion.

I remember walking away and saying to myself in full resolve, *Well, this is it.* I was ready. Then I walked around the circle again and came back toward Mark and the elder. I fully expected to do what I was prepared to do, but Mark didn't go along with the suggestion from the elder.

I heard Mark say to him, "Boy, I don't know. I'm going to have to get a witness about that. I don't think so."

I walked away feeling glad that Mark had made the right decision. I didn't have to do any confronting, but something significant happened inside of me. I was ready to stand up for what I thought was right, even if the rest of the leadership disagreed. I remained full of resolve to do what I had to do if there ever was a next time. There never was a next time.

I wonder if something was broken in the spirit world when I decided to confront the leadership about the abuse going on. It was as if the demons saw they would be beaten and ran from the fight. I still embraced the "New Freedom," but now I was *truly* free because of discipline and truth in my life.

Mark and some of the other leaders continued their downward spiral of experimentation into self-indulgence. The other leaders didn't want to hang around with me any more, so I didn't get much of a chance to discuss my new thoughts about our differences. I had a few discussions with them, but I was never put into another position in which I had to strongly confront them in a tight situation.

CHAPTER 21

THE CLOSING OF J.U.
HAVE MERCY ON US

*I*n late April of 1977, Mark and I met as the executive committee of J.U. We needed to go through some of the legalities of document-ing the corporate changes that were rapidly taking place. Rusty was distancing himself from the organization and had already resigned as vice president. Mark and I decided to revoke all ministerial ordinations, close down the apostle's fund, close the bookstore, and shut down the building. Christi took over Rusty's spot on the executive committee.

It was rather painful for me to close down the building. It represented failure to me, and it was heartrending. An auctioneer was going to rent the building. He was moving in as we were dispersing all the stuff we had accumulated. Some things were given away to other churches, some things were given back to those who had donated them, and some things were sold to continue to finance what ministry was left at J.U.

On May 1, we were buildingless for the first time in almost two-and-a-half years. Although we made the decision to close down the building, we still felt that the organization and ministry would continue. All the other leaders now supported themselves except Mark. However, Mark worked hard to find a vocation that would be compatible with his ministry, and he tried several jobs (mostly in sales).

Sunday, June 26, 1977

I have been in confusion the past few months. I'm wondering where we are and where we are going as a body. Yesterday, I came to the conclusion that the people of J.U. *are* headed for destruction unless God does something.

Up to now, the thing that has kept me from this conclusion is that I always felt God would do something. I still believe this, except I realize now that God *must* do something. Until now, I haven't realized the seriousness of this time. I also have been blinded to the truth of this deadly road we've been on. *It went from pipes to cigars to beer to cigarettes to hard liquor to getting drunk to smoking dope to getting almost down to adultery—and now divorce.*

If it had happened all at once, it wouldn't have slipped in. But it happened over a long period of time. Wrecked lives and distress have overtaken some. Seeing some people turn to divorce was the tipping point for me. It seemed that most of these things didn't hurt the user for a while, but now I see people completely shaken and distressed and unhappy. And I only see worse ahead.

Father, I pray You'll deliver us. Have mercy on them and on me, too. We have sinned. We have no power to perform Your Word. Pride has overtaken all of us at times. There is no solid ground but You. Please, Lord, shorten these days and save us.

I had just found out that one of the leaders decided to divorce his wife. This was the last straw that convinced me that permanent damage was being done to us. Up to this point, I thought we were experiencing scratches, cuts, bruises, and broken bones. But now fingers and arms were being cut off. The damage was permanent.

Thursday, June 30, 1977

Yesterday I made a decision. I have decided to continue in the things of God that I have learned, to continue to do the things that have given me peace with God, and to continue to seek truth and a greater knowledge of what God is *really* like.

This was a *hard* decision because after talking with Bill Norten, Ron Binks, and Greg (among others), they say we can't search anymore. I say we should not search the same *way* anymore but continue in every thing that we have strength to do.

I realize that this decision will probably bring a division between some leaders and me. However, I can't help but feel that if I go along with them, I'll hurt them—or at least not help them at all. I see their lives being driven down, and there *is* strength to do what I feel is right.

I can remember the exact day that I wrote the above entry. Several of the leaders had come to my house and had asked to borrow some tools. While they were there, we mildly debated about which way we were headed and what we should do about it. We simply did not agree. I felt so bad, because I sensed I was losing their friendship.

I stood outside the garage and watched them walk away and get into the car with my tools. As I watched them slowly drive down the road, I just stood there staring, feeling utterly forsaken and alone as the car faded into the distance.

Saturday, July 2, 1977

It seems I have found a new strength the past few days. It is like I have something to live for now. But I wait for Your leading, Lord. Have mercy on the people of J.U.

Friday, July 22, 1977

Last June 26, I wrote that I saw worse times ahead. That has come. One of the girls here in J.U. has been raped. A suspect has been sought in the body. Unless these people see the road they're on, the next step is murder. God, please help them! And me! It hurts.

The rape was never officially solved. Unofficially, I found out later that the perpetrator was not part of our group. It was a person who came to J.U. for a while, and then left.

Friday, July 22, 1977 (continued)

Lord, I heard yesterday that the leaders who smoke don't want to be around me anymore. I don't condemn them. But why do they dislike me? Is it possible that they just don't want You anymore? Have *they* forsaken You? They say that You are not meeting them when they step out in faith. I ask You to tell me why all this has happened. I do believe that You led me out of Boulder's Chapel and that You were at J.U. But where did we err so seriously? Is there any hope for Rusty and the rest of them?

Lee said that unless You do something, we're *all* going to the pit. But I believe You won't let that happen to those who simply hold on to the sound things we have learned and to seek out the things we aren't sure about. Have mercy on us, Lord.

Friday, August 5, 1977

I have thought lately about maybe gathering together in the name of the Lord. I feel a need. I want to also strengthen my brothers. I ask You, Lord, to help me if this is Your will.

We had stopped having regular meetings several months before this, and I was beginning to feel the need to get together with other believers for the express purpose of worshiping God, studying his Word, and encouraging each other. For many years, I had gone to church and meetings because I was told to go, not so much because I felt a big desire to go. Now I felt a peaceful, natural desire to gather as believers in Jesus.

On Sunday August 21, 1977, Mark, Christi, and I met for the last time as the legal executive committee of Jesus Unlimited. It was a sad time for us all. The purpose of the meeting was to finalize the shutting down of the organization. This meeting had failure written all over it. The mood was dismal. We just did what had to be done.

I was given the responsibility of putting together the final paperwork. Two days later, I had Mark sign the official Certificate of Dissolution and sent the document in to erase the name of Jesus Unlimited off the state rolls forever. I felt like a failure. So did most of the other leaders.

CHAPTER 22

THERE'S NOTHING MORE TO LIVE FOR

DESPAIR

Friday, August 12 1977

Concerning Mark's statement, "There isn't power on earth to deliver a man's soul," maybe not, but there *is* power to *lead* us to that power. I put my trust in You, Lord, to anoint some people to be Your vessels. You can take anyone and mold him or her. I pray You'll use me too.

*M*ark was extremely discouraged and constantly complained about the lack of God's power to deliver people out of depression or sickness. In the above entry, I had just talked with Mark on the phone and wrote about what we had discussed. I had to agree that the anointing for deliverance seemed to be sparse, but I also felt that God's power *was* available—though hard to find at that time.

I suspect that Mark was going through serious depression and was venting his own frustration about not obtaining deliverance for himself. I had no idea how serious his depression was. However, even if I *had* known, I wouldn't have known what to do about it.

Saturday, August 20, 1977

I got into a little fight with Val today. After things calmed down, we drove around for a while and ended up at the camp. The gate was open, which was unusual. As we walked toward the cross, I was hoping it was still there. I was I worried that it might have been torn down. When I saw that it was still standing, I sat down on the steps and started to cry. I said to myself, *I just don't know what went wrong with the camp.* I talked to Val about our worsening relationship, and then we prayed. I didn't know if we should pray, because Mark had recently mentioned something about the lack of integrity in most of our prayers.

We were in such a horrible state! Many of the leaders were not praying anymore because they had been told by Mark that most of our prayers were in the flesh, not acceptable, and even disgusting to God. Mark and the others who didn't want to pray considered me to be full of religion. They looked at me as one who did religious things in my own strength, having a form of godliness, but not really acting in faith or out of a love relationship with God.

Their opinion of me was not entirely without merit. During the beginning and middle of J.U., I certainly *did* put too much trust in my own works to please God and my elders. That would be called pride and, yes, I was full of it. I *still* battle that spirit.

However, even though we often served God out of pride or religion, there were many instances where we did things purely out of a love for God and in faith. But because I was still influenced heavily by what Mark said, I was extremely self-conscious. I was actually worried about offending God by praying!

Saturday, August 20, 1977 (continued)

When Val and I prayed, the following happened:

1. A new strength came into me to love my wife.
2. God gave me a clear understanding on how I was to love Val.
3. I experienced renewed faith and trust in God and our relationship.
4. I gained real peace.

This peace remains until I think to myself, *This might not really be faith but Antichrist justification.* But then I realize it is praying, faith, and trust that help me do what I know is right, and it is those other thoughts that rob me of what God wants to give His people: faith, peace, and a free will.

Praying together *was* a good thing to do, and God *did* answer our prayers when we prayed. The opinion of the other leaders was not correct. We *should* pray!

In September 1977, Rusty left Penny. She was extremely upset and asked if Val and I would consider moving in with her for some much-needed support. We accepted Penny's offer to share her little rented farmhouse. Her offer came at a good time, because we needed to move out of Mrs. Larson's home. After several months, Penny moved to an apartment in town, and they soon got a divorce. Rusty moved to another state.

Mark and I were trying to figure out how to continue in the freedom and challenges of ministry and still provide for our families. We were not particularly skilled, and we were only able to get jobs at little more than minimum wage. Entrepreneurial endeavors seemed to be the only way to make a living and enjoy the freedom and challenge of the ministerial life.

Sadly, Mark had the hardest time getting back into the work force. J.U.'s failure to rise up to his expectations shattered his self-esteem. He tried working at a health spa, but he couldn't do the phony style they required of the salesmen. He also tried making and selling jewelry, but just couldn't sell with enough enthusiasm to make a living. He couldn't (with a clear conscious) sell some people expensive jewelry that they really didn't need or couldn't afford. Mark also helped out in a catering service, but the owner pushed immorality on him. He was very discouraged by the corruption that his boss was into and had to quit to get out of that situation.

Mark was very true to his own heart in these areas. He just couldn't be deceitful or put on a show of false emotions just to sell something. Mark was still a true servant in this respect.

It seemed that every job Mark tried ended up in some sort of failure. His search for a compatible job eventually led him to Colorado. During the fall of 1977, Mark and Christi moved out to Colorado Springs near Christi's dad. Mark's brother, Jeff, and his wife also moved to the same area. I don't remember what Mark tried out there, but he continued to have trouble settling into a life.

Saturday, October 1, 1977

> Today I am really confused. I got a letter from David Wilkerson about divorce and adultery. I agreed with most of it, and his attitude seemed OK. Agreeing with him scares me terribly, because of all the revelation by J.U. leaders against where he was headed.

As I was coming out of the "blind following" syndrome, other Christian leaders began to sound right and even *encouraging*. At J.U., we had been conditioned to believe that all other ministers were heading for Antichrist worship. Therefore, when other ministers sounded right, fear would hit me when I realized I agreed with them and might be headed for Antichrist worship, too. I was also tormented by this thought: *What would happen if I went against Mark, and he was right and I was wrong? What if I'm the one who's going away from truth and beginning to support Antichrist leaders?*

It took years for most of the J.U. people and me to trust leaders in other organizations. There are some who *still* feel that the past J.U. members are the only ones on the front lines of spiritual battle. As I mentioned earlier, I would say that David Wilkerson has one of the finest and most effective ministries in the world today.

October 1, 1977 (continued)

Mark has been gone for about a month now. Already I seem to be drawing away from him, and that scares me. Inside I can feel myself seeing mistakes and faults and failure in him.

I ran into Brother Al at the hospital, and he said he's going to stop by and see Val and me. This has me very upset inside. Lately, I have been afraid to run into Boulder's Chapel people. I feel a notion to give Al a chance to make peace with Val and me, which scares me because I remember a word that said he was evil.

Why am I so afraid to see him? Why do I feel guilty around him? Is it because I have judged him unjustly? I think the only reason I have no confidence before Al is that I'm not where God wants me to be spiritually. My heart condemns me. Therefore, whenever a strong-willed person condemns me and says I should be going to their church, I feel condemned.

So why do I feel condemned? One thought says it is because they're right and I should do what they say. But another thought says it is because I haven't sought and found out what God *Himself* wants me to do and where *He* wants me to be. If I get direction directly from God, then I will do it and not feel condemned.

Father, I need truth and to be in Your will for peace. Grant me a clearer picture of my direction and the strength to perform it. The only thing I can think of is that I have *forsaken the assembly of ourselves together* (Hebrews 10:25) and You want me to start meeting regularly with a group or a body of believers. I'm a bit afraid to take on the pressures of leading a gathering without clear direction from You, but I have no confidence in any other group or church. Speak to me about this, God my Father. I love You.

At this point in time, many people (including ministers) began telling me that God wanted me in their church. It is amazing to me how so many people and ministers feel comfortable telling you that God wants you in *their* church. How juvenile and spiritually childish! It *did* help me to get a grip on the fact that God wasn't really speaking to any one of them. They couldn't *all* be right. I eventually decided that I couldn't listen to anyone with that message. It was the SPIRIT OF ERROR.

I began to call together some of my friends to seek the Lord, pray together, and worship Him. We had no set day or time, and so we sporadically met in different people's homes or out in the country where we could just walk, talk, and pray.

Friday, October 28, 1977

I just went through a mighty battle. So much weakness and confusion. The will to serve God in *any* circumstances was almost gone. *But*, I hereby testify that God gave me strength. I cried for strength. I asked and He answered. I felt an establishment rise in me to go on into *anything*. I write this to remind myself in the future that God will give strength to me if I'll ask for it. I realize now that I can't *fight* the doubt and weakness. I *must* look to God for strength.

Friday, November 18, 1977

I've been walking pretty strong the last few weeks. I don't think I should dedicate myself to any organization. The only leading I get is that God wants me to continue to meet with my brothers and pray with them. I look to You, Lord, to cover me.

I talked to Phil last week, and he feels that the J.U. people (other than leadership) are "left behind" because they didn't "sell out" enough. I can't believe that.

Phil meant that these individuals would not be part of the Man-Child and wouldn't partake of the activities that God was going to do with that group just before the rapture. He also believed that they wouldn't be caught up in the rapture. The J.U. Man-Child doctrine included the thought that the non-Man-Child Christians would be left behind as part of the Antichrist or be saved through martyrdom.

Friday, November 18, 1977 (continued)

Weren't we (J.U. leadership) just given the ability to sell out? Were the sheep called to do what we did? Look at leadership now—they're the most screwed up mess in the whole lot. Would You want everyone to go through this torment? Remember all the *extra* exhortation that leadership received from Mark? How can the others be judged as harshly as the leadership? I pray that You will have mercy on the remnant of J.U., the sheep *and* the leadership. Thanks, Lord, for this feeling of being close to You. You know this is where I love to be.

Late in the fall, Val and I trucked some of Mrs. Larson's furniture out to California for her and then flew back home via Colorado. We stayed a few days near Colorado Springs in a motel near Mark and Christi's place. We all went sightseeing at Pike's Peak one day, and as I talked with Mark, it was obvious that he was not feeling confident and happy with his new life.

My friend always loved the outdoors. He was a good trapper and hunter, so he figured Colorado would be the best place to move. I think he was happy with the surroundings, but his heart was yearning for some type of wisdom from God that he was not finding in the Colorado wilderness. The most lush, beautiful setting becomes a barren desert when you can't sense the presence of God in your life. Val and I left Mark to his search and returned home to Michigan.

November 27, 1977

Lord, I'm praying and asking You to show me where You are in my life and in the life of the rest of the J.U. people. I'm sensing this: We are to still seek a relationship with our Creator and pray with our brothers about the things that burden us. We are to believe that God has *not* totally forsaken us, but that He has let these things (the failure of J.U. and the overall confusion) happen to turn our eyes and hearts toward Him. It is not yet time for God to raise us up.

Father, I pray that You would stop all of Your manifestations of power that would cause us pride and thereby draw us away from a relationship and a true walk with You. At this point, Lord, it seems that Phil and Mark have yet to return to this; instead, their eyes are on the commission.

December 4, 1977

Father, I ask You for discernment about Mark. Did You plunder him, or did he simply get his eyes off You? Or both? This is what I get:

1. At this time in his life, Mark judges You by the emotions he feels, not by what he believes. Therefore, he is unstable.
2. Mark says there was always a tint of corruption in every move of the Spirit in the past. But I think there *were* times when the move *was* pure, free, easy, powerful, and undeniable.

December 10, 1977

I just prayed for Mark, and God was really there. I also felt that the shaking time I preached about (May 27, 1975) is yet to come and that we (me, Mark, and other former J.U. members) should prepare for it. Back then, I spoke that in order to get through this time, we should hold to the Word and things unseen. I believe these are still true:

1. To hold to what relationship is left and to seek God for a purer relationship.
2. To believe the written Word over the sight of the eyes.

December 27, 1977

I asked God tonight if He would give me the strength to pray and seek His face for several things: What happened to Mark? What happened to the J.U. organization and mission? What is the spiritual condition of the people who dedicated themselves to that mission? I trust You, Lord, to bring this to pass.

January 1, 1978

Mark called this morning, and we talked for quite a while. It's the first time in a long time that I didn't get depressed after talking with him. Lately, I've felt like fasting for the situation concerning Mark and the body, but I had no strength. After talking with Mark, I now have the strength! Praise You, Father.

Be it known:

1. I fast to loose the bonds of depression and lack of faith that hold Mark (especially) and others in the body.
2. I fast to understand what happened to Mark and the body. Was it failure or did God plunder us?
3. I fast for Penny and Rusty.

January 12, 1978

I talked to Mark two nights ago. My heart began to burn again, just like the last time we talked and just like during the time before J.U. I was fired up and feeling closer to God than I have in a long time. Tonight I got away from that closeness, but I am aware of a faith that God *will* bring me close to Him again.

Mark was splitting wood with his father-in-law and somehow got a couple fingers caught in the splitter as it was moving through the wood. I don't remember for sure which finger was cut off, but I think he lost one knuckle on his third finger. In the following entry, I reported that Mark felt a greater awareness of God ever since the accident. I can relate to that, because when I look back to the times that I have been hit with very bad news, or hurt badly, I can remember sensing God's presence and his comfort even in the midst of the trouble.

Romans 8:28 that says, *All things work together for good to them that love God.* I think this was one of the things that God allowed to happen to Mark to show him:

1. He was not forsaken.
2. God still loved him.
3. That he should continue to look to God for comfort and deliverance from depression and discouragement.

January 22, 1978

Mark called this morning and said he had a dream about us getting together again. He said that ever since his finger was cut off, he's had a constant awareness of God. He is beginning to get fired up. Faith is beginning to control him and give him life. I felt generally good and fired up when we were talking.

Sometime in January, Mark started talking to Lee Funt about possibly moving to Florida. He was miserable in Colorado and was still looking for a peaceful life with meaning. Lee was making good money driving a dump truck for a construction company there and seemed happy with the new life he had chosen. Florida was booming with jobs and entrepreneurial opportunities. The weather was great, too!

So Mark and Christi decided to move their family to Vero Beach, where Lee and Ruth Ann were living. Mark and Lee decided to go into an informal business of hauling away debris from construction sites. I say "informal" because they didn't incorporate or form a partnership. They just went around and secured work almost day by day.

I was tempted to move, too, because so many of the past J.U. members were leaving town. If I had left, however, it would have been an attempt to escape instead of facing truth in my life. I'm sure that many people left town with God's blessing, but it just didn't seem right for me.

January 29, 1978 (The Blizzard of '78)

This past week, things got dry spiritually. I couldn't seem to pull away from the tube. Then I was snowed in for three days.

After praying for a while and sensing a need for a change in my life, I thought I heard very clearly in my spirit, *Move to Florida.* But when I thought about the possibility of Mark moving back here shortly—instead of staying in Florida—I felt doubt and deadness.

Father, do You want me to move down there? I will. I will. Please confirm it. The only thing that keeps me here are the few friends I meet with regularly to pray with and to seek You. They need me, but they are growing stronger. I would like to move and cut the roots from this present living atmosphere: house, good job, and good security.

Inside I feel as if I could be jumping wild, just to get out of a rut—a change in surroundings to get away from what You really want out of me, which is a change in the spirit. Inside I suspect deceit when I talk of going to Florida. I look to You, Father, to keep me and lead me.

Actually, I *really* just wanted to get away from my job. I hated it! I was used to the freedom of the ministerial life, and it was hard to be back in a 7:00 A.M.– 3:30 P.M. lifestyle. My biological clock has a natural wake up time that gets me to work at 8:00 A.M.

My sister, Penny, Val, and I flew to Florida for a vacation to see Lee, Ruth Ann, Mark, and Christi. Lee and Mark were still working together, and Christi worked as a waitress at a nice restaurant. When Lee and Mark found construction sites to clean up, they made very good money, but it was not steady work. Sometimes they would go a week without a job. The lack of financial stability was tough on them. Mark, Christi, and their toddler Abraham were living in a rented house trailer.

I had a good time talking with Mark about God, J.U., and the future as we saw it. In general, Mark was frustrated and not happy with his situation. He was having serious trouble finding God's place for him and Christi. He still felt his calling to minister, but the failure of the J.U. organization still plagued him. The struggles were beginning to take their toll on Mark and Christi's marriage.

While in Florida, I came across a small house trailer for sale in Vero Beach. It was located in a trailer park right next to the Los Angeles Dodgers' winter training camp. A good arm could throw a ball into the park from the trailer's porch. It was the most beautiful trailer park setting I have ever seen. The trailers were set in the midst of five acres of lush green grass and tall pine trees, full of shade, with the trailer fairly secluded. Because I was considering moving to Florida, this one bedroom trailer looked mighty good at that time. The price was right, too!

At a fast food restaurant in Florida, Mark and I try
to make sense of our situations.

Tuesday, March 14, 1978

I just got back from Florida. I started feeling strife and unrest when the airplane was nearing home. I ask You, God, what do You want me to do? All I get is *Seek My face.* But I feel so *ugh* inside when I hear that. I ask You now for the strength to seek Your face and to know Your will for me. I'll seek You for this:

1. Your will for me
2. Mark's depression to be healed and for his search for direction
3. Your will for the body of J.U. that is left.

March 18, 1978

Lord, I believe You want me to buy that trailer in Florida. But I am so fearful of three things:

1. The drastic nature of the move
2. The revelation not to leave Niles
3. Going against the revelation that we should be out of debt

Father, I pray You'll cover me if I have made a wrong decision. I feel You will. I commit this situation to You. I also ask that You'll help me pay off the trailer very soon—maybe within three months so we can move down there as soon as possible.

I decided to buy the small house trailer in Vero Beach. I borrowed the money and continued to work at the factory to pay it off in a hurry.

The revelation of not departing from Niles referred to something that one of the J.U. leaders revealed a year earlier. God said the people of J.U. were not to leave Niles, and that Niles was going to be the hub of revival for the world and the base of our operations. Since then, I can't even remember how many people have said that about their town or organization. The revelation of getting out of debt has been reported from just about every prophet with whom I've come in contact.

At this time, Mark was still in Florida, and I was looking for any excuse to run away from Niles. What I didn't know was the seriousness of Mark's depression. I also didn't know how badly he and Christi were getting along. They were reaching the point of separation.

April 9, 1978

> I felt discernment on the side of my head, but no inward witness other than to pray. As I prayed, I felt that maybe I should continue in prayer until I heard from You. But that is so hard to do, Lord. As I waited, I felt You say a few things:
>
> 1. I am called, chosen, and ordained to bear fruit that will remain.
> 2. I shouldn't put stock in long range visions. (It seems that You're softening me to take a disappointment here.)
> 3. I shouldn't turn my heart away from serving my brothers and sisters.
>
> I ask You, Lord, to let Your will be done. But please hurry! Get me out of Dayco! I feel like I'm dying there! Please deliver me.

About this time, Mark came back to Niles by himself and told me that he and Christi were going through serious marriage troubles. He showed dangerous signs of deep depression and started seeing a counselor. This counselor prescribed some drugs for Mark in an effort to help him through this difficult time.

Mark continued to pour out to me more of his frustrations with God. He often would go into a blubbering ramble about how there was so much pain in the world and about how God's power was not available for deliverance. I don't mean "blubbering" as a derogatory term. I mean that Mark would try to express his feelings and anguish and talk in a half-pleading, half-crying mode: "Larry, you just don't understand! You just don't understand!"

I remember walking away from one conversation saying to myself, *That's right, Mark, I don't understand. If I accepted the things you are saying, I'd be crazy just like you.* However, if I was truly firm in this belief, I would have done more to help Mark out of his depression. But many people still looked at him as the "Leader of the Man-Child," and

I still had some fear of going against him in *any* way. If I said he were "off" or sick or heretical in his statements, I might be touching God's anointed.

Mark never questioned God's existence or power, but he *did* question God's ways. And even though Mark was angrily questioning God's ways toward him and our J.U. situation, he often put forth a type of righteous indignation toward God, similar to prophets and other men of the Bible like Habakkuk, Job, and Jonah. This was the main reason that I did not openly say that Mark was heretical in his reasoning.

I was still not firm in my belief that it was right to humbly question leaders and men of God. In my early Christian life at Boulder's Chapel, I was taught that if we said anything against the pastor, we were in danger of hell fire.

Mark was in Niles by himself for only a few weeks, staying with his sister Melody and her husband Jim. After that, he felt encouraged enough to go back down to Florida and try to heal his relationship with Christi. They were not able to work out their problems, however, and soon Mark was back in Niles. He was even more depressed than before.

I wish that I'd had enough experience and understanding to help Mark out of his state of mind. I could not get him to stop believing lies about God and other things. In one of my last conversations with Mark, he ended our talk with, "God has left me. My wife has left me. There's nothing more to live for."

CHAPTER 23

NOT A TRACE
THE SEARCH FOR MARK

*I*t was mid-afternoon on a spring-like day in April when I received a call from Mark's brother-in-law, Jim, with some unsettling news. Our conversation went something like this:

"Larry? Mark is missing. He left all his identification in his room at our house."

"When did this happen?" I asked.

"Sometime early this afternoon," Jim continued. "He filled a double prescription of his depression medicine, and we're afraid that he committed suicide somewhere in Mickey's Woods." (This was a wooded area not too far from where J.U. first started.)

I quickly joined Jim and four of our friends at Mickey's Woods. We searched all day and part of the next day for Mark. We were not frantic or desperate; in fact, our mood was more like, *He said he'd do it, but we still don't believe it. We should search the woods just in case he really did what he said he would do.*

Mark had been fighting depression for a long time, and we were all weary from the struggle, similar to a cancer victim's family. This disappearance resembled the possibility of resolve and some relief. At the same time, we certainly did *not* want to find him dead.

No trace of Mark was found. We couldn't file a missing person's report because we had no proof of wrongdoing, so the police couldn't help us. After talking to many friends and relatives, I pieced together some facts:

1. Mark was depressed. There were reasons for his depression that were understandable. He was going to a counselor who believed that Mark was clinically depressed enough to prescribe drugs for him.
2. Mark had talked about suicide to several friends. When in Florida, he told Lee that he was going to commit suicide and he would do it at a place in Mickey's Woods. Mark told Lee that he knew of some bluffs that he could crawl up into and that no one would ever find him.
3. Mark left his identification in his room.
4. Mark was wearing a blue jean jacket and pants.
5. Mark filled a double prescription of drugs just before disappearing.
6. At least one can of a beverage was missing from the refrigerator.

Mark was last seen walking downtown by the karate gym toward Mickey's Woods by our friend, Vicki Seller. Mark smiled and waved to Vicki as he walked by the gym window. Mark disappeared that day, and there hasn't been a confirmed sighting of him since then.

Mark's dad and mom, Brother and Sister Bechtel, firmly believe that Mark is still alive. Shortly after Mark disappeared, Brother Bechtel said he had a tremendous burden to pray for Mark. He said, "You just don't get a burden to pray for people who have died."

To add credibility to Brother Bechtel's belief, a similar thing happened to one of my friends. She never met Mark and only knew bits and pieces of the story that Val and I shared with her over the years of our friendship. One day she was thinking about Mark and a spirit of prayer came on her at a level that she wasn't used to. She felt an extreme burden to pray for Mark and did so, but she felt quite strange about it because she thought he was dead.

Val's younger sister swears that she saw Mark come into the place where she was working in Niles just a few years after Mark disappeared. When she said, "You're Mark Bechtel, aren't you!" the man just got up and walked away without saying a word.

Maybe he *is* still alive.

So what happened to Mark anyway? Here are five possible scenarios:

SCENARIO #1

Mark decided to commit suicide. He purposefully left without his identification, walked the three blocks to the pharmacy on Main Street, and got the double prescription filled. He then went 10 short blocks through downtown Niles toward Mickey's Woods. Our mutual friend, Vicki Seller, was in the karate studio on the corner of Front and Main. She looked up and saw Mark walking past the large front windows and waved hello to him. Mark smiled and waved back. Vicki didn't see whether Mark turned right or went straight across Front Street. Both directions led to Mickey's Woods, but I think Mark turned right onto Front Street. He would have walked by the old J.U. building and then taken the railroad trestle across the river. At that point, he could have entered Mickey's Woods immediately to the right, but I think he continued on to the side road past his old house, the place where J.U. first started. Then he went north into Mickey's Woods, found the hiding spot in the bluffs, and took the overdose of drugs. The bluffs covered him up, just as he said would happen.

SCENARIO #2

This scenario is the same as the above, except as Mark was crossing the river on the railroad trestle, he slipped and hit his head on the railroad tracks and got amnesia. Mark then continued walking down the tracks in a dazed state on into Michigan City or even Chicago. He has yet to discover who he really is because he had no identification. Mark was reasonably educated, a very likable and capable person. He could have begun a new productive life and may come back someday when he reads this.

SCENARIO #3

Mark decided to leave town and leave everything behind. He made it seem like he was going to commit suicide, but just planned on going west to start a new life. Maybe someday he'll come back and make things right.

SCENARIO #4

Mark really was the Man-Child leader, and God took him directly to heaven like Enoch and Elijah the prophet.

SCENARIO #5

Mark just lost touch with reality for a while. Because he left without any identification, law enforcement offices and mental institutions could not find out who he really was and send him home. This happened to the King of Babylon in the Bible (see Daniel 4:28–37). Because of pride, God caused a spirit of insanity to come upon King Nebuchadnezzar, and he lost control of the kingdom, wandering the fields for "seven times," meaning either seven months or seven years. The King eventually repented of the pride and called out to God. Then God restored the kingdom to him. Mark may just be insane somewhere in the world and may come back to his senses sometime in the future.

What do I think? I think it is scenario number one, but I hope it is number two. I don't think it is number three or four; it might be number five. I wish I knew back then what I know now about

Mark was last seen by Vicki Seller as he walked by
this corner building and waved to her.

The train trestle Mark may have walked across.
Mickey's Woods is on the far side of the train tracks.

depression and suicide. I know now that Mark displayed classic symptoms of dangerous suicidal thinking. If I knew then what I know now, I would have watched him more closely. I just didn't believe he would go through with it, and so I more or less ignored it.

I don't think that Mark ever was dangerous like Jim Jones or other religious mass suicide cases. He was *never* physically threatening to anyone and *never* even hinted that anyone else should follow him in suicide. Even in his depressed state, he seemed to be genuinely glad about other people's prosperity and happiness. He was just in so much emotional pain about his own situation and couldn't seem to climb out of that dark hole in his mind.

I often wonder why God allowed Mark to vanish when so many people's lives centered on him. Finding Mark's body would quickly answer a lot of questions. It would have immediately caused us to fix our eyes on Jesus and search out the answers to questions like, "Why?" But his fading away—but not *entirely*—leaves such a temptation to consider scenario number 4, as some still *do* believe.

Mark's wife, child, parents, friends, and so many others that Mark truly helped in life were left with no solid explanation of what happened to him. There has never been a funeral, no memorial service, no mourning for a permanent loss, and no real closure for all of the people involved. I felt so sorry for young Christi, who suddenly was a single mom with a toddler. She eventually remarried and raised their son to adulthood.

After Mark disappeared, my dreams at night continued to include him for years. Mark was in my dreams weekly, then monthly, then occasionally; and now, almost never. Mark was my best friend in my early adult life, and I miss him. I do regularly pray for his family.

I find it amazing that there is so little in my journal about Mark during this time. I suppose it was too hectic—and the situation too uncertain—for me to write about it. I think I was waiting for some closure to the situation first and then I would write it all down. That conclusion has been a long time in coming, and we're still waiting.

CHAPTER 24

REBUILDING

WHO AM I?

*A*fter Mark disappeared, we were left to sort out the details and try to find direction for our lives. Many people wondered about the camp and what had happened there. From our initial prayer meetings, we felt that God wanted us to take it over and use it for His glory. There were many times when people prophesied that we would get it, and I really believed that God wanted us to have it.

So what happened? Concerning those prophecies, I'm sure some of them were just from young Christians' imaginations. But I'll go out on a limb and say that the Holy Spirit inspired some of them.

An easy out concerning those prophecies is that almost all of them had a condition attached to them, as do many of God's promises found in the Bible. For example, in my journal entry on September 23, 1973, I refer to the reports that God said we would get the camp "if all were obedient." I think that we were not only disobedient, but God out of His love for us kept the camp from us for our own good.

God does all things out of love. If He had given us the camp when we wanted it, it might have been bad for us. We could have been too much in the spotlight in the community and hurt the kingdom of God by so many people seeing our gross mistakes. We were not mature enough to handle the responsibility and so, out of love, God let it go to another organization.

Thursday, May 25, 1978

> I feel tonight that I should be open to a change of heart to stay at Dayco and not run away from it. I trust You, Father, to help me lay my will down. I ask in *Jesus'* name.

I remember working at a big machine press and praying, *Lord, please deliver me from Dayco.* I remember hearing rather profoundly from God that night that I should be open to being delivered *within* Dayco, not necessarily delivered *out* of it. I felt God said I needed to flat out accept the situation that He had put me in and not fight it anymore. I was to work hard at doing the best I could wherever He put me, and at this time Dayco was it.

What was the bottom line? Stop complaining, buckle down, and serve Dayco with all my heart as a service to God.

May 28, 1978

> I felt today that I must gather more often with other believers to pray, study the Bible, and worship God. I must either gather with my close brothers more regularly, or dedicate myself to an established church. I believe You want me to begin to gather regularly with what is left of J.U.

I called several friends from J.U. and we started meeting every week to pray and study the Bible.

August 18, 1978

> Lord, tonight we're going to ask You for direction on our personal lives and direction about our group:
>
> 1. Do You want me to move to Florida? Or just go for a visit? How long and when?
> 2. Do You want me to stay at Dayco or try to start a business?
> 3. What is Your will for our gathering of believers?

We decided to regularly gather on Friday nights to pray and study the Bible. "We" consisted of myself and five or six other guys. Eventually, our wives joined us as well. It was a typical home church gathering: rather informal, with a light agenda of some singing, praying, and Bible study.

October 27, 1978

I felt bad about some things when Devin Stockbay, Ray Lander, another brother, and I got together to pray without Barry Lasma:

1. I felt their judgment toward Barry lacked compassion with traces of selfish frustration and impatience.
2. As we talked about leadership positions in our little home church, I felt pride coming from them. Not so much haughty pride, but inner, subtle pride from an unpurged soul. It is pride that they can't see or feel, and they don't recognize the feeling as pride.

This pride is the subtlest of all, because it is the pride of our society. It is so much a part of our society that it is almost impossible not to fall into it when a person moves into a leadership position.

This pride will take much experience to discern when it is rising up. They should feel a peculiar feeling when they move in it. When they move in humility, they should feel an assurance without defensiveness or fear of opposite views.

This pride covers up the fear of failing and blocks off trust in God for success. It is a false confidence in oneself; an assurance based on position, seniority, and experience, not trust in God. I need to find out:

1. Should Barry Lasma come to the meetings? Why or why not?
2. Should I speak to the guys about what I felt?

A few of the guys began to ostracize Barry because they felt he wasn't dedicated enough or acting spiritual enough in their eyes to warrant admission into our newly formed prayer group. Barry loved sports and spent a lot of time tending to this passion. He was quite light and fun loving, but he enjoyed praying with us, and I felt his company was beneficial to all.

Oh boy, here we go again. The SPIRIT OF ERROR was again trying to work its way into our midst.

October 31, 1978

No doubt about it. I have been motivated by fear too much lately. Fear of rejection of the guys, especially one in particular. I ask You, Lord, to bring me out of this and let me judge accurately.

November 5, 1978

What does it mean to go forward in God? What is real progress in a body of believers? What does God consider as progress?

1. Broken and contrite hearts
2. Fruits of the Spirit
3. Servanthood

I listened to a body meeting tape (I had missed a meeting). I was very pleased to hear a well-rounded exhortation by the other four guys. Thank You, Lord.

November 12, 1978

I asked God if trying to follow my inward witness all the time was of Him, and if it is why haven't I been able to keep up with it? He replied, *Because you are at war! You are being warred against. There **is** a battle. A Christian's life is not a road void of attacks.*

November 18, 1978

I've been fasting for about a week. I felt it was time to get back into God's *perfect* will. I finally received strength to seek God. Thank You, Father! I truly am happier when I am close to You. This is what I feel You want me to do:

1. Exercise regularly.
2. Discipline my life.
3. Don't do things in a hurry to get done so I can then get close to God, do *all* things as unto the Lord.

I believe my third point is absolutely true. There are many who believe that we must have a set time every day to seek God in order for Him to be truly pleased with us. I believe that those set times are only to be used as the law or a schoolmaster for a while. I believe that we can move on to a place where we do everything with God and also be alone with Him often to commune intimately and seek Him for guidance and strength. There are times when even those who have "graduated" need to put themselves back under the law when they get a little out of touch with God.

December 8, 1978

I just had a good home church meeting. We've not met for a while. We went into a bondage that wasn't from God. I began to be afraid of one of the other guys. Several of the others did too. This brother began to push us to conform to his views ("This is God." "That isn't." "Don't go there or do this," and so forth). He began to "lead" us quite outwardly, almost as if he felt called to lead us. This is a very important lesson. It is the SPIRIT OF ERROR.

Barry Lasma was the first to be hit, and then me, and then Devin Stockbay and Ray Lander. We all agreed that there was a problem. We prayed and now, four weeks later, the situation is much better, although there was still a twinge of the problem tonight at the meeting. I almost succumbed to it. The other three also felt it.

Tonight when we didn't succumb to that spirit, we had the best time in the Lord in a long time. I am now more convinced than ever that we are on the right track.

Be it known: The wisdom from above is first pure, peaceable, and so forth—*not pushy!* The Lord says to me: *That spirit will try to come back again soon. Stand firm. Do not succumb to it. It is not from Me. Look to love, not faults. Be motivated by love, not frustration, when you help people out of their faults.*

Thanks, Lord. Larry

That was then, this is now, and I still agree wholeheartedly. In all fairness to the "other brother," I need to point out that our *reaction* to this brother was just as bad as his problem. Yes, being overbearing and purposely intimidating is not good. But running away from conflict and cowering in the face of intimidation is not good either. Both of these actions are acts of selfishness and cowardice. I obviously feel that my sin is not as bad because "it is the way I am." The other brother likewise feels that his sin is not as bad as mine for the same reason. We all do these things because of our individual sin.

Monday, January 1, 1979

Well, that spirit of error is back again. At least, it is *trying* to come back. Father, I pray You'll deliver me and keep me established in Your peace.

"It" will never go away totally, because there is a battle. We are at war. We have an enemy that works overtime to keep us fighting against each other. The enemy capitalizes on our individual sins and causes us to fight each other. Hopefully, this book will help bring some of these sins to light so that maybe we can see more of ourselves. Then we can ask God to help us move away from this type of selfishness and into His way of dealing with conflict.

Each time we find ourselves fighting against each other, we must stop and pray and seek God together. We must pray until God answers with wisdom and peace. This is what we will have to do until the end. We *must* get used to it.

In early January, Val and I decided to go to Florida and move into our one bedroom trailer to decide if this was the place we wanted to permanently live. I told my boss at Dayco, "I am going to Florida to live for seven weeks and I'm considering moving there. Will you hire me back when and if I return?"

He said, "Don't quit, Larry, but take a leave of absence. Then you won't lose your benefits or seniority."

I took his advice. Val and I loaded up the car and headed down to sunny Florida, pulling a trailer loaded with my motorcycle and other things. We had about $700 saved up for the trip, and I was really looking forward to that sabbatical. Lot rent was only $10 per week, and that left almost $90 per week to spend for food and other things.

We spent a lot of time on the beach surf fishing. I have wonderful memories of Val and me in our lawn chairs on the beach: our backs to the wind, drinking hot black coffee and eating little pecan pies, looking out over the ocean, and watching for my fishing pole to start wagging away with fish. Sounds like a great retirement, doesn't it?

Lee had landed a job in a local fire department, and I thought it was also a perfect job for me to pursue. A typical firefighter would work one day on, then get two days off, one day on, two days off, etc. I thought it would be a perfect way for me to make a good living, yet have time to minister on the side. (At that time, I had no idea that a firefighter's job was so dangerous or stressful.)

February 8, 1979

Last week, I prayed for direction about my life. I felt God say, *Don't get hung up on a fireman's job, but seek Me for an opportunity.* For five weeks here in Florida I really haven't received anything but that. I'm still a full-time factory worker and a part time pastor, but I'm not doing either of them very well.

You said to seek You for a opportunity. So that is what I'll do. I believe You want me out of Dayco and into a job that doesn't rob me of victory or time to be a good pastor. I pray for this job. I can't see any job better than a firefighter, but You know what is best. Thank You, Lord. I believe.

I came to the conclusion that Florida was not the place where God wanted me to permanently reside. I didn't hear a strong word from God, but I just felt that I was to go back to Michigan and continue to serve Dayco until an opportunity came to me. Right! Just what I wanted to hear. Not! Val agreed, so we sold our trailer for $800 more than we paid for it and made plans to return to Niles. We weren't able to get the money from the trailer sale right away, so we ended up running out of cash near the end of our Florida sabbatical. But the Lord did a miracle to help us raise some money.

We went down to the ocean and began catching lots of pompano fish when *no one else* was catching them. Pompano are my favorite fish to eat, but they were selling for over $3 per pound uncleaned. To make $100, all we had to do was catch about 30 pounds of pompano, stop at the fish house on the way home, plop our fish on the counter, and get paid.

When we went back to the same beach the next day, an old man took our spot before we got there, so we took the spot where he was the day before. I wasn't fishing five minutes before my line was tugging with pompano. While I was reeling in one of the fish, that old man walked over to us. For a while, he just stood and stared at me.

While I was taking care of the fish I had just caught, he finally spoke, "How come you're the only one catching anything these two days? You're using the same bait as every one else on the beach, so what's your secret?"

I answered boldly, "I need money, and the Lord is helping me."

The old man just stared at me for a few moments, in deep thought. Then he grabbed my slimy hands (I had just taken a fish off the line).

He rubbed his hands all over my slimy hands, and without another word he walked back to his own fishing spot. On his first cast, he began to catch pompano too. We saw no one else on the beach catch a pompano for those two days. We caught more than enough to get us home comfortably.

February 24, 1979

Lately, I've been considering (for the past year) whether or not my next job will be to pastor this body full time. Father, I need a few more witnesses from others and also a direct communion with You on this. Please speak to me clearly so I can have faith.

I was so happy to see one of the new brothers getting strengthened and growing. Is this where You want me? Wouldn't a good part-time job be better? Or better yet, an easy full-time job so that I'll have energy to pastor? Lord, I feel so unworthy of a salary. All I need is for You (and some brothers) to speak to me for the body's sake.

And I wonder. Mark felt the exact same way. Was this the beginning of his striving to be "worthy"? Would I be obligated to prepare and preach every week? I don't think I could keep that up. The way I see it now, we would continue exactly the same (all sharing the load and burden of speaking). I would simply spend more time in prayer and helping others and visiting more. I pray You'll clarify this. Thanks.

Whoa! I think I was on to something in the above entry. We need to come to the place in which we feel the call of God to pastor and just do it. We should be open to being wrong about a vocation and consider the advice of our friends and elders. But the burden of final responsibility rests on us, not others. To *need* the benediction of others is to have a weak foundation. It is OK to want the support and blessing of others and to enjoy it if it comes, but we must not *need* it. It is definitely a distraction and weakness that should eventually be purged if a person goes into a ministry.

March 17, 1979

Larry, if you want to see the Kingdom, begin to do the things of the King-
dom—prayer, helping people, and so forth. You could begin by visiting
people more and getting involved in their problems and their needs. Not
to the point of taxing yourself to the brink of exhaustion, but as a ministry
to others and as an avenue to know Me.

When a person continues to walk in these things, and stays in the Spirit,
he will grow and commune with Me greatly. Hobbies, relaxation, and
privacy are all part of My plan for My end-time ministers.

I think many "sinners" and immature Christians feel that some ministers' lives are so religious that it's no use to even *try* to follow them, because their piety seems unattainable. Paul did some tent making. Jesus once suggested to His disciples to get away and relax awhile. I see hobbies and relaxation as a means of relating to and getting to know people in order to more effectively share the gospel with them. We can enjoy many types of hobbies with others such as hunting, boating, quilt making, and so forth. However, our motivation should be out of a love for people, not a selfish over-indulgence in a pleasurable hobby.

About this time we got some encouraging news. Almost two years after Rusty left Penny, he came back to see his parents and ran into Penny. They struck up a conversation, one thing led to another, and they ended up getting remarried. Penny moved where Rusty lived, and they have lived happily ever after. Rusty rededicated his life to Jesus, and both he and Penny are busy serving the Lord in their local church.

Late June, 1979

Fast and pray for:

1. God to reveal a ministry or me to seek a secular job?
2. Val and I have a baby?
3. The answer to *who am I?*

284

I believe in a supernatural God who gives supernatural power to his ministers to do their job. I seem to have no supernatural power. Am I really called as a minister? Now? Later? Never?

If now, I will have to have power by the end of the week. If no power is given by the end of the week, I will assume that I'm not called to minister now, but that I should seek a secular career and serve the church.

If never, I must be told clearly.

At this point, I am reasonably questioning my calling as a minister. I did not receive the amount of power I was looking for by the end of the week, nor did I hear from God that I was not called to eventually minister full time. I decided to use the gifts that God had already given me to serve the church, look for a secular career that would be compatible with part-time ministry, and be open for any leading from God to go into a full-time ministry.

August 22, 1979

Meetings are going very well lately. It seems more people are taking on an active concern for fellowship. Just what we prayed for.

We were still meeting informally in different people's homes, usually once a week. A typical gathering included ten to sixteen people, all remnants of J.U. We never met on Sunday. Friday night was the time we usually got together.

One of the good things we learned at J.U. was that Sunday was just another day of the week and not the Old Testament Sabbath day. In order to break our Sunday habit (in J.U.), we started having our formal meetings on any day *but* Sunday. We really had nothing against Sunday. We just wanted to emphasize Paul's exhortation in his letter to the Romans: *One man esteems one day above another: another esteems every day alike. Let every man be fully persuaded in his own mind. He that regards the day, regards it unto the Lord; and he that regards not the day, to the Lord he does not regard it* (Romans 14:5–6). We should do good things and walk with God *seven* days a week. We should not be more holy on Sunday than the other days.

As long as we're on the subject, now would be a good time for me to share a little about the Sunday versus Sabbath debate. In the letter to the Hebrews, the writer makes the case that Jesus is our rest. *Jesus* is the Sabbath. *There remaineth therefore a rest to the people of God* (Hebrews 4:9).

Of all the Ten Commandments, the most misunderstood is: *Remember the sabbath day, to keep it holy* (Exodus 20:8). The Old Testament Sabbath day was a *symbol* of Christ, a *type* of Jesus. It was a *symbol* of something to come. They rested one day a week physically. *We spiritually rest each day from our works.*

Adding good works to our salvation as a means of righteousness is profaning the Sabbath. It is like doing work on the Sabbath day in the Old Testament times. We do good works today because God has placed in us a desire to do them, not in order to attain righteousness.

Jesus paid the price for our sins. *He* has made us righteous. *He* has forgiven us by His shed blood and His death on the cross. *He* is our Sabbath! Remember the Sabbath day, to keep it holy. Remember Jesus' work on the cross, to keep it holy. Do not add anything to it.

I'm not against setting Sunday aside as a day of rest and a day of worship. I think it is a wonderful thing, and that is what I have been doing for more than twenty years. But I don't do it because of the fourth commandment. I do it because it is practical and good for me, and I do it to worship Jesus. Although the Bible doesn't specifically say which day or how often we should meet, it *does* say we should *not forsake the assembling of ourselves together, as the manner of some is* (Hebrews 10:25).

In these New Testament times, Sunday is holy only because *we* make it holy. We make it holy by deciding to set aside that day to worship and seek Jesus. Any day of the week could be chosen to do this and it would accomplish the same thing.

October 22, 1979

Devin Stockbay and Cary White played and sang at Wilt's church last night. A couple of the other brothers also went. They said they had a great time, and Wilt was all choked up and could hardly talk. He said he was so happy to see them. But I am concerned about the "behind the scenes" reasons for Wilt's happiness.

Will he now subtly insinuate to these brothers that last night was only the beginning of a fulfillment of his belief? Was he really happy only to see them and be blessed by the communion? Will this trigger a new wave of false hope in him? I feel that Val and I will one day be able to visit Wilt freely without bondage or commitment to his organization. But first there must be a change in him and his belief that:

1. His church is called and chosen to be *the* leader in the area.
2. We at J. U. are not walking in light simply because we are not attending his church.
3. In order to be a part of this revival, we must formally affiliate ourselves with his church.

Father, I pray for these problems. I pray for Wilt's peace of mind. I pray for a revealing of the truth of J.U., and the real fate of Mark. I pray for unity among the brethren (Wilt and us). Thank You, Father. Let Wilt see that I'm not against him. Amen.

During the time of J.U., I remember Brother Wilt saying that the J.U. people should be attending his church. I'm not certain where he got this, but I think it is related to a prophecy that took place in his church around the beginning of J.U. Occasionally, Brother Wilt would look me in the eye, raise his voice, and forcefully try to convince me that I should be going to his church.

To this day, I think Wilt still believes that we should be back in his church and that Mark is alive and will someday come back to his church along with all the other J.U. people that are around. I don't see it happening that way, but I *do* see it within the range of God's power.

In fairness to Brother Wilt, I must say that he has always been a faithful pastor, and I think he was genuinely concerned for our welfare. Near the beginning of J.U., he must have sensed our lack of depth and some youthful recklessness (not to mention some genuine mistakes). I'm sure he had a reasonable desire to see us attend his church, where we would have been less likely to get off into troublesome areas. Brother Wilt, you have been a faithful pastor for all these years, and I salute you!

January 13, 1980

> I have been concerned that there has been little preaching or teaching from the Bible, and no one seems to have a burden to do it. Since the regular Friday night meetings were started, I lost my burden to teach.
>
> Gene, Devin Stockbay, and I have joined together as a singing group. It is time to share these songs and Your message of love and peace. But Father, where do You want me to have my home base? I feel very insecure not knowing where You want me to be dedicated to.
>
> I question now whether I'm called to lead a body as I have been doing. Please make Your will known to me. I've been fellowshipping and visiting many brothers from First Baptist Church in Niles. Although I very much enjoy their fellowship and Bible studies, I feel their Sunday worship is not my style, and I disagree with some of their doctrines about the Holy Spirit.

Our friend Devin Stockbay wrote over 20 songs during and after J.U. He invited Gene Michaels to join him in forming a contemporary Christian band. Gene suggested to Devin that he invite me to sing with them also. Devin agreed, and after praying for a name, we decided to call the group *Charis*, (kare´ iss) the Greek word for grace. After J.U., Gene eventually started going to First Baptist Church, and Val and I began to attend some of their Bible studies. Devin and I continued to meet informally with the J.U. remnant in our homes.

January 25, 1980

I just finished praying. I haven't felt this close to God in months. While praying, it became clear: I felt my eyesight directed away from Wilt's church and a peaceful but *definite* impression of the word "no." It was like a gentle breeze blowing against a desire to look toward Wilt's church. I could almost feel the breeze on my cheek keeping me from looking to the right toward it. Almost immediately, I perceived the word "continue" as I pondered the alternative of not going to Wilt's church.

I felt I should visit them shortly to calm their fears of possible competition and try to explain that we are *partners* in the end time move. I also felt Val and I should continue our fellowship with the people at First Baptist. We need to be pioneers in *truly* breaking down church barriers and center our attention on God's total plan, not being prejudiced and selfish with our own group and expectations.

I felt very peaceful about stepping to the background concerning our body. It can be best explained by stating: I will no longer make controlling decisions concerning our body, but I will counsel and advise the people who do.

Father, I praise and thank You for answering my prayer about direction and getting close to You. Thank You. Thank You.

April 1, 1980

I was rather depressed back at work today. The Florida vacation was great, but the thought of continuing work at Dayco is not uplifting. I felt God ask me to write down exactly what I would like to do with my time. So, this is it:

1. Visit people
2. Pray
3. Study
4. Help friends physically.

June 12, 1980

Well, God has answered prayer! I was selected at Dayco to learn to program the new computer machine. Since starting about a month ago, I have not felt bad about work. It is no longer a burden to go in to work. I praise You for that, Lord, and thank You for delivering me *within* Dayco.

This was the opportunity that thrust me into the world of engineering. I eventually learned how to do all aspects of the sheet metal manufacturing industry. I enjoyed engineering, and I remember saying to my friends, "I now get paid to play." I ended up loving my job.

CHAPTER 25

A FAMILIAR ROAD
NEW BEGINNINGS,
OLD QUESTIONS

*T*here were now singles and couples coming to our meetings, and the group averaged 20 to 25 people including children. We all pitched in and helped Devin Stockbay as we enclosed his garage, insulated it, finished the walls, and carpeted the floor. We turned it into our church meeting place, and it wasn't long before we began gathering there every week.

Devin and several of the other guys felt that our little home church lacked "credibility," so they wanted to meet on Sunday to help change the community's perception of us. Although I was opposed to the change—I felt it was not a critical matter—I went along with it. Changing your style and perception has merit, if the motive is born out of love and concern for the people of that community. We called our group the "Hickory Street Fellowship."

I felt a desire to be a part of this little home church, but I wasn't getting much inspiration to prepare a message every week. My style was (and still is) to see a need, then prepare a message directed to that need. I'm sure that there were many things to talk about, but at this time I wasn't getting the inspiration from God to talk about them.

I was also still plagued by a fear of getting up in front of people. I have always been able to stand up and speak under the anointing of the gift of prophecy because that helps to remove the paralyzing fear. But without that prophetic gift and inspiration manifesting, I usually felt too much fear to comfortably speak in front of a crowd.

Sunday, July 27, 1980

Oh, Father, have mercy on me and help me to seek Your face. Give me a concern for Your children. Give me a concern for the lost. Our church body is dead, except Devin is feeling led now to prepare the Word for Sunday meetings.

I have felt for the past few months that I should support activities of the body, but not initiate them. I pray I'll soon move into my next step as a minister. I love You, Jesus.

Wednesday, September 10, 1980

I've been very scattered in the past few months. No direction for the body or me. The other brothers feel we need to set up a tangible church government. They feel a breakthrough is very close. I feel nothing.

I question whether or not I am really called into ministry. God has not really met me. I feel His Church should be (and is) covered supernaturally. But I have no unction, no real power to cover the body. "Father, I pray You'll show me who I am. I need to be covered, and I am looking for a church to work with. I can't go on beating my head against the wall. Am I doing more than I have been given? Please show me my calling and who I am."

Here again I question my calling to be a leader in the body of Christ. Interestingly, I think that I was doing one of the best things a pastor can do concerning the above situations. A pastor can let the flock start doing ministry as they feel led, and then he can do some *real* pastoring. (Most pastors are forced to spend most of their time as administrators.) A pastor is to guide those with less experience into the safe havens of

God's way of doing things. He should let people start leading in the areas of their gifts or talents and if they run into trouble, he can guide them out of it.

In our little home church, the gifts, talents, and activities were similar to most. Some would speak, others would lead worship or sing, some were gifted in benevolence, others enjoyed serving by keeping things clean and neat. In all of these ministries, there are pitfalls of pride and selfishness. Here's where a pastor has real work to do.

A pastor also can try to teach people some of the "ropes" before they venture into ministry. I suppose that depends on how critical or possibly dangerous that area of ministry would be without some advance instruction. Still, I would go out on a limb by saying that the vast majority of pastors are (to a fault) afraid to let their flock venture out by themselves into the waters of ministry, especially preaching from the pulpit. This keeps the church quiet, safe, and neat, but the growth of congregational fruit is also kept to a minimum.

Monday, October 13, 1980

I just finished watching *The Other Side of the Mountain* about a girl who had a ski accident and became paralyzed. I saw many who were handicapped. I suppose the Father let some of them become handicapped for some good purpose. But it seems that some were just ripped off by the Devil. Even the others shouldn't have to stay crippled.

Father, I pray for the anointing to free people who are crippled. I ask that You freely give me this anointing so that I can freely give what You've given me. I look to these verses that support my prayer:

That we might know the things that are freely given to us of God . . . .

(1 Corinthians 2:12)

He that spared not his own Son, but delivered him up for us all, how shall he not with him also freely give us all things?

(Romans 8:32)

Freely ye have received, freely give.

(Matthew 10:8)

I look to You, Lord, to bring it to pass.

Yes, I know that God uses pain and suffering to hone character. I also know that He uses the courage and love of those who are handicapped to bless others and to show that there is more to life than a perfect body. But He also uses His power to deliver and to glorify Himself. I can't apologize for the burden he's given me to pray for Jesus to live through His body of believers on earth. Jesus always healed everyone who came in faith to Him and asked for healing or deliverance. He is still alive and wants to do the exact same thing today through His body on earth. That was then, this is now, and Jesus is *the same yesterday, today, and forever* (Hebrews 13:8).

Tuesday, February 3, 1981

I have many questions that need to be answered. They need to be answered so I can go forward in faith:

1. Where am I called to fellowship or go to church?
2. Are the Hickory Street Fellowship "elders" really elders, or are we all just novices? I feel uncovered with no respect for anyone. I have a feeling that I should go to Bible school or something.
3. Am I called as an evangelist or preacher? Why can't I get over my nervousness?

Notice number two above. I said I had no respect for anyone. What I *meant* was that I could find no one whom I could follow and totally respect as my leader. The key word here is totally. I had this problem all of my Christian life up to this point. For some reason, I felt I should be able to find a flawless leader to follow and have 100 percent respect and belief in everything that he has to say. I attached myself to leaders, then was let down every time because that leader displayed a fault or clearly failed in some way or another.

We need a general respect for leaders, but we should also be able to respectfully disagree with them and realize that all leaders have faults and shortcomings. They need to be respected for the positions they hold, but they are not to be blindly followed. We should always have the freedom to humbly question a leader's actions, and refrain from following them when we think they are wrong on a critical issue of faith.

You will never find the perfect leader. You have to find leadership that you can respect enough to work with peacefully, cutting them slack in the areas of their weaknesses. You either work with them peacefully, or you go somewhere else.

You'll never come to the place where you're off the hook in the area of judging right and wrong for yourself. You are responsible for what you do. You can get input from many sources, and *it is good* to get outside input on tough issues. Most importantly, you need to know what God has *already said* in the Bible about what's right or wrong. But in the end, the responsibility of deciding what is right or wrong comes back to you and you alone.

Monday, April 22, 1981

I thank You, Lord, for my job—the best job at Dayco.

Getting paid to play! Does the Lord answer prayer or what? I also enjoyed the respect of the management and my fellow factory workers for being a good engineer. Did not the Lord answer my prayer for deliverance from a job I hated? Be patient and trust the Lord, and He will eventually deliver!

March 1, 1982

At Grace Christian Assembly, I feel I'm called to be a general overseer of the spiritual welfare of that church, mainly concerning general direction, attitudes, and motives.

Concerning our music group *Charis*: I should at this time mostly *sing* and do very little speaking. Later, I will *speak* more, and sing much less.

So what was Grace Christian Assembly? Notice the date. It is almost a year later than the last entry. Our little Hickory Street Fellowship grew to the point that Devin Stockbay's garage was too small, so we found a little old white school house out in the country that seemed to be perfect for us. It had a cloakroom, a nursery, a larger meeting room, and two smaller rooms that could be used for Sunday school. We wanted a name that reflected our ministry, so we picked a name that had grace in it. Most of us felt that gracefulness had been scarce in our early Christian lives, and we wanted to swing away from legalism, but not into lawlessness.

Most of the people attending were from J.U. I felt that I was to help keep the general spirit of the church from getting off into the areas where J.U. got into trouble. We formed a church government, opened a church bank account, and set off on the normal road that startup churches usually go down.

I had been a Christian longer than the other elders, but I was only 11 years old in the Lord, a twenty nine year old "elder." I began to feel uncomfortable with the term elder because I was noticing that I wasn't so old, and because I had failed recently at J.U. Compared to most other leaders of church ministries, I certainly was not their elder. But I was an elder at this small church for a couple reasons: I really was older than most of the people and had been on the front lines during the battle of J.U.

Our music group *Charis* was going strong, singing at churches and coffee houses all around southern Michigan and northern Indiana. We even recorded an album consisting mostly of Devin's songs, one from Gene, and even a song by Ray Boltz. I remember recording Ray's song "Other Times" and seeing him on the other side of the recording studio window, watching us record his song. Ray was relatively unknown then, but he since has enjoyed the honor of being a top male Christian singer for many years.

Wednesday, July 7, 1982

CHURCH ELDERS' MEETING

1. Song book is ready to print.
2. Finances are good.
3. Contact a realtor about a new building.

I can remember hashing out the church government with the elders as we traveled down the typical new church road. This was my second experience doing this, and I began to see a trend. There was such a clamor over titles and who controls what and who has control or authority over whom. And what *was* an elder, deacon, apostle, prophet, evangelist, pastor, or teacher? And concerning our newly forming church body, where did we fit in as individuals into these categories? Did we fit into them at all?

America is a nation with a huge number of independent churches. Many of these churches started the same way this one and J.U. did. A group of lay people had a heart to gather together in the name of Jesus, and then had the courage to make that group their church base. It is not easy to start a church this way because usually none of those who gather have been formally ordained into the ministry, and many Christians in America do not look upon that favorably.

These churches happen naturally all over the world. Believers gather together for a while. The group gets bigger and they decide that God wants them to start a church. (Did I miss something? Weren't they *already* a church?) They form a governing board, write a constitution and bylaws, incorporate under the supervision of the Federal Government, buy or rent a building, hire a pastor, then tell him how they want the church to be run. Although this is typical, there are many variations to this pattern. We were going down that same road again, having learned a few things from our J.U. experience.

About this time, *Charis* was also going through a leadership crisis. We decided to add a couple musicians, and there soon arose a disagreement as to the proper approach to our concert presentations. One of the guys thought our typical presentation was too soft and began pushing us to change it to include some new tactics. He felt that we were disgustingly traditional in some ways and that it was an abomination to God.

I felt uncomfortable with these proposed changes, but our direction was up for grabs to the loudest bidder because we had no set leader in the group. This went on for several weeks until I spent an evening down in my basement praying about it. From this prayer time came one of those memorable moments with God speaking clearly and profoundly to me.

I was walking around, kneeling and sitting while I prayed to the Lord. I remember sitting on the basement steps when the Lord spoke to my heart. This is what He said to me:

> *I call men. Men use organizations as a vehicle to fulfill the vision that I have placed within their hearts. The structure of the organization is not critical. It is the men that are important. You could have a perfectly formed organization with bad men, and you would have a bad organization. If you have a poorly formed organization with good men, then you would have a good organization. Traditions are not a problem with Me. I work within traditions. The structures of the organizations are not important to me.*

It was *so* good to hear from God! When God speaks and shares His wisdom, it answers questions and solves problems. I gathered the whole group together and said, "There are many ways to present the gospel. We all do it according to who we are and what we have experienced. We testify of the life within us, according to what we have experienced and believe."

Then I said flatly, "This is *my* organization and it is *my* vehicle to share the gospel. I don't feel comfortable with the proposed changes.

Therefore, I won't do it. *Charis* is the vehicle to share my vision of Christ, and if it isn't your vision, then you'll have to start your own organization and do it your own way. If you want to minister with *Charis*, then you'll have to do it my way."

I knew that at least one of the other two original guys agreed with me, so I wasn't just speaking for myself. There was no significant objection to my speech. We continued to minister together for a few more months and are still close friends today.

Monday, July 12, 1982

I had a tough meeting with Ray Lander and Devin Stockbay. Ray and Devin want Barry Lasma *off* the board, period! I am very concerned. There is a spirit of judgment toward Barry that is familiar. I can't put my finger on it, but it is there. This afternoon Ray softened, but Devin seems hard and prideful. This is what I recommended for this situation:

1. Ray and Devin need to see the bad part of their action toward Barry and apologize.
2. We should have a minimum of two prayer/discussion sessions to help Barry see his error.
3. Let Barry know that if an agreement cannot be reached, then we'll have to take a vote as to whether or not he should stay on the board.

Barry had missed a Sunday morning service due to a sports event. I agreed that Barry should either accept the responsibility of an elder by being at church meetings or leave the board. But I sensed a bad spirit in Ray and Devin's dealings with Barry. Their attitude toward Barry was ungodly. My recommendations were never followed, and eventually, Barry left the board.

In the above entry, I mentioned that "I couldn't put my finger on it." I can now, and it is the SPIRIT OF ERROR. I agreed that we needed to deal with Barry about this problem, but the motivation from the guys was mingled with the SPIRIT OF ERROR. This type of error usually rears its head during the formation and development of a new church. It should serve as a warning sign that the leadership is off when they begin to do things from frustration and anger, rather than from the love and resolve that comes from a good time of prayer.

Wednesday, July 21, 1982

Barry Lasma didn't show up for our early morning board meeting. When we sat down, I brought up the question (wondering where Barry was). One of the elders knew Barry wasn't going to be there and responded to me in an offensive manner that I believe everyone saw. His attitude and reaction to my question was forceful, in an attempt to intimidate me and motivate me to be against Barry, and that was irritating.

Yes, Barry should have been there, but the elder knew about it and should have told us sooner. We all were concerned about Barry, and were all watching out the window and waiting for him. Lord, please give us wisdom!

This was the type of immaturity that was wearing me down. That elder was and still is a great friend and strong follower of Jesus, but I was constantly dealing with these types of problems on the board. I continued to question the wisdom of our being elders and began to lean heavily toward going back into the layman's position. I felt that I needed to learn more about God before trying to lead a congregation of believers.

Tuesday, September 21, 1982

I have been praying about direction for my life and the ministries in which I'm involved. What are my goals?

1. To help people physically and spiritually through fellowship
2. To be hospitable
3. To be freely given:

    A. Mercy
    B. Wisdom and insight into salvation

C. Wisdom and insight into future events
D. Be able to freely give lots of money away

Freely give. Hmmm. How many of us daydream of getting rich quickly and then sharing it with our friends and loved ones? One day I felt God clearly say to me: *Larry, if I gave you all the money you wanted, you would destroy men's lives with it.*

Obviously, I was seriously lacking wisdom on distributing wealth to others. You can actually hurt people if you don't do it right. I think God wants to give us all the wealth we can handle. That's the problem. Most of us just can't handle that much.

October, 1982

Charis broke up.

It is easy to be involved in an organization with no leader, but only if the group is small. As the group grows, the need for a leader grows with it. With the additions of our bass player and drummer, the sound was nice, but it also required a lot more work to get tight on all the songs.

The song arrangement task also became harder. Now there were five people who came from five different perspectives, and all needed to end up feeling good about the final arrangement. We worked hard together to get there. But without a mutually respected leader, it was just too much work. Gene was the first to decide to back out, and I immediately felt it was the right thing for me to do as well.

The remaining guys in the group found replacements for Gene and me, and they continued to minister for at least a year or two and then disbanded.

Friday, November 27, 1982

Well, Charis is now done. You have answered our prayer for direction in that ministry. Now I pray for new direction for Val and me. It amazes me. You have moved so swiftly. Thanks again, Lord.

Lord, I pray for direction concerning where I should go to church. I feel I am Grace Christian Assembly's "elder elder" but seem to be pushed into submitting to Ray Lander. The peaceful feeling is that I need more preparation from older men of God. But when I think of Grace Christian Assembly, I seem to be more concerned about losing out on the big move. That sounds so shaky and dangerous.

But truly they need to be covered by one who has had experience in these matters. If I left, wouldn't I be deserting them and not fulfilling my responsibility? They are still close to my basic doctrine. Or are they? The lack of wisdom and fruits of the Spirit are so great in many areas. It is very uncomfortable for me to see bad things respected (like unnecessary harshness, excess emphasis on title definitions, and types of deceitful communication). Father, I commit my way to Your leading.

I mentioned about "losing out on the big move" in the above entry. That was a bad attitude. I remember that feeling in J.U. too. I'm happy I noticed that it was a bad attitude back then. We need to come to the place where we just do what is right because it is right (not because it might get us somewhere).

I ended up leaving Grace Christian Assembly and began attending Christian Center Church in neighboring South Bend, Indiana. I came to the conclusion that I needed to go on a long sabbatical from leadership and learn from some real elders. It was a big church, which made it easy for us to "hide" in the midst of so many people. Christian Center was a great place to heal, and our stay there was enjoyable and encouraging. The services were uplifting and Pastor Sumrall was an inspiring preacher.

CHAPTER 26

THE NORMAL CHRISTIAN LIFE

TRIALS, TEMPTATIONS, AND BLESSINGS

On September 2, 1984, Val gave birth to the first of our two children, a son. A fine son! We named him Joel. We put his crib upstairs in our old small two-story farmhouse. The house was practically impossible to keep warm. I found out how cold it was upstairs one day when I noticed something shining on the slanted ceiling above Joel's crib. When I looked closer, I was amazed to find icicles forming all along the ceiling above his crib. Time to find a new home.

We found a small two-bedroom house on the other side of Niles. When we moved in and put Joel in his own room upstairs with its own heater, I said to Val, "My son will never again be cold at night!" Joel got his first cold two weeks later. He was perfectly healthy for the first six months of his life when he slept in the sometimes-freezing cold house.

After I worked my new programming job at Dayco for about a year, I was promoted to head engineer and very much enjoyed that job for four more years. Then, with the approval of my boss, I started a part-time business doing some metal stamping in the evenings in an old factory building near downtown Niles.

THE SPIRIT OF ERROR AND THE SPIRIT OF TRUTH

October 5, 1985

As You know, Lord, I've been setting up a business. I feel a peace, but I still am a bit afraid. I pray that if You don't want me to go into this business, You will close all the doors. As I pray, I feel it is Your will for me to do this. It has come to me. Yes, I have worked at it, but it has not been hard on my mind or full of strife. It is clear to me that I am being carried in this endeavor. The contacts are coming to me and all problems are getting worked out. It would be a thrill to work with You, Father, on something like this. I will pursue it to its fullest extent. I will trust You to take care of me and my family.

Our new home was located quite a distance from Christian Center Church, so we stopped attending regularly while we searched for a church closer to home. Christian Center served as a great place to worship, heal emotionally, and get fed spiritually. But it was now time to get back to serving God in a local congregation.

Thursday, October 24, 1985

I haven't gone to church much lately. I feel bad about that, but I don't feel spiritually down at all. I would like to get more spiritual stimulation, so I should go someplace.

About this time, a few of our friends invited Val and me to their church, raving about their minister's innovative preaching techniques. They said he often used unique methods such as preaching while lying down on a hammock or teaching from a rowboat that he lugged into the church. After we attended for a while, it became clear that this minister's main message was *Jesus!*

January 25, 1986

As You know, Lord, Val and I have been going to the Community Evangelical Free Church here in Niles. I feel rather comfortable with the format and the general direction of that church. Father, I pray that you will confirm it to Val and me if this is the place that You would like us to get involved.

God confirmed it, and Val and I have been attending and serving God at that same Evangelical Free Church ever since.

September 12, 1986

Father, I thank You for blessing our business. Now the big issue is when to quit Dayco. Since early in the year, I have felt the urge to go full time in this business. I have been struggling about when to make the break.

The big problem came when I had no energy to write any more, and so the book was not going forward. It has become clear to me that I cannot go on with a successful business, stay at Dayco, *and* fulfill my commission to write a book about the SPIRIT OF ERROR.

Yes, I now feel it is time to quit. I judge this by the same feeling I had when I went into business at the start. I was not sure of that decision either, but I remember the peace in my spirit about doing it. Now I feel that same peace in my spirit to quit Dayco.

The problem is that I see how much money it takes to run this business. Although I have built up a small reserve, I feel it is an enormous risk. So I think it is clear from a *practical* standpoint that I should not leave Dayco. But from a *spiritual* standpoint I feel God saying, *Yes, go for it. I will bless you!* So that is what I am going to do today.

I must go to work now. I trust You, Father, that You will give me wisdom when I talk to the president of Dayco and give him my notice.

October 6, 1986

Well, I did it. I gave Dayco my notice. This is the second week on my own. My own . . . ha, ha. It is clear to me, Father, that I need You more than ever. I thank You, Lord, for the peace in my heart. It is so exciting to be in this with You. For the first time in my life, I must see Your hand in order to survive. I am looking forward to knowing You better.

December 26, 1986

It is so interesting as I work on my journal and book. I just finished typing up the December 14, 1976 entry. That was 10 years ago. I was pleading with You, Father, to deliver me out of my rut at Dayco and put me back into a timeless lifestyle. Now I am there. Well, at least the opportunity is there. I seem to have put myself on a strict business office routine. Father, I thank You for answering my prayer of ten years ago by delivering me out of Dayco.

Many times, God came through at the last minute to enable me to pay bills and make payroll. His mighty hand has guided and blessed this project from day one.

In the following account, Val and I had been praying for a two-year-old boy named Morgan Wiesler who was struggling to recover from a near-drowning incident. He developed pneumonia and was close to death. We had met the Wieslers on our vacation to Florida the month before this journal entry, and we had become friends with them.

March 3, 1987

This is the beginning of the fourth day of our fast for the Morgan Wiesler situation. Father, I thank You for giving me the strength to fast. I pray that You will give us one or both of the following:

1. Morgan's complete healing.
2. Wisdom about this situation (insight into what Your will is for Morgan and the Wieslers).

I feel that it is Your perfect will for Morgan to be healed. I feel that it was an attack of the enemy that caused this crisis and that You will use it for Your glory. I pray for the gift of faith or miracles so that You can perform Your mighty work on Morgan.

As I was reading in Your Word last week, I felt You say to me, *This kind can come forth by nothing, but by prayer and fasting* (Mark 9:29). So we are doing only what Your Word says. I have no desire to afflict myself—especially if it is not necessary—but the situation seems critical. Please answer our prayers and especially those in Florida who are praying. *Move by your mighty hand! You are God!*

I had always believed in the power of God, and I had been expecting to see more of His power manifested ever since I became a Christian. I looked to God and prayed that He would show himself strong in the situation with Morgan Wiesler. Then Morgan died.

May 21, 1987

Morgan didn't make it. Well, Morgan made it, but he didn't make it on earth. He went to heaven on the fourth night of our fast. I was and am somewhat confused as to why or how this could have happened.

Lord, I don't understand how Morgan could have died. I see nothing in the Word to support this outcome. Obviously there is, because it happened. But there appears to be some real contradictions here. I know it happens all the time, but now that it has happened to us, it brings the problem closer and demands an explanation.

This situation greatly discouraged me and shook my faith in God's ability or willingness to take care of my family and me. I also began to seriously wonder about God's provision to take care of *any* of His children in hard times and for healing. From what I knew about the Bible, God should have moved to heal and deliver when His people fasted and prayed. But this time God didn't deliver. I fell on my face and cried out for understanding.

When you're struggling with a situation in your life, you can always pray and seek God and, as Jesus said, if you keep on seeking, you will find. The following journal entry includes a prophecy that I felt God spoke to me at that time. Please bear with me as you read it. This word to me was part of the answer to my question of "why" when bad things happen to good people. If tragedy strikes your life, you may get a different part of the answer, but God will answer you if you keep seeking Him. I ask that you not jump to any conclusions until you read my explanation of the prophecy.

May 21, 1987 (continued)

Right now, God, Val and I feel this is what happened: It was Your will for Morgan to be healed. I *still* feel that it was Your perfect will. But I never felt the *assurance* that You would heal him. So I cannot say that You let *me* down. But what I don't understand is that I read, and still read in the Bible, that Morgan *should* have been healed.

So I prayed for the assurance of that healing, because I didn't feel or perceive Your Word to my heart. (I didn't feel You agreed with our prayers for Morgan's healing.) This is the only out I have to still be able to trust You. But isn't the Bible supposed to be the final authority?

No, Larry. The Bible is often misinterpreted. My Spirit witnesses to the heart what is truth. And My written Word will always bear witness to what the Spirit says. It was My perfect will for Morgan to be healed. There were circumstances surrounding this situation that prevented Me from allowing him to be delivered on earth. Sin. Not necessarily the sin of the parents, but of the body of Christ in general. These are not sins unto death, but they do hinder the workings of the manifestation of My power at your will. If the body of Christ would continue to seek Me, I would manifest My power. In the meantime, it will have to wait until I decide to pour out an abundance of grace.

Lord, I thank You for Your love, Your grace, and Your wisdom. I will continue to trust You for my protection and sustenance.

Bear with me here while I explain what I think God was saying to me. He was gently saying that my interpretation on the subject in question was right in one sense, but I was missing some details that made the final interpretation flawed, and He explained some of those details. He indicated that my attitude toward the Bible was flawed because I put the "dead letter" (dry, legalistic, Holy Spirit void words) above the Holy Spirit (see 2 Corinthians 3:6).

On the subject of "the manifestation of My power at your will," this is about what Jesus said in John 15:7: *If ye abide in me, and my words abide in you, ye shall ask what ye will, and it shall be done unto you.* I suppose this is a state of mind/being where one is so in tune with the Bible and the Holy Spirit that one would only pray for manifestations that God wants and intends to do. I certainly wasn't *totally* in that state when I was fasting and praying for Morgan.

So what (or who) is the final authority on earth? *God* is the final authority. He manifests that authority by His Holy Spirit. The Holy Spirit speaks to the heart of the believer, and the believer interprets this speaking and acts accordingly. When a person is not being honest with what the Holy Spirit is saying, or if he resists the Holy Spirit, then he goes astray. We can also be led astray by believing interpretations of the Bible that are not guided by the Holy Spirit.

Yet the Holy Spirit does not act independently. *Howbeit, when he, the Spirit of truth, is come, he will guide you into all truth: for he shall not speak of himself but whatsoever he shall hear, that shall he speak: and he will show you things to come* (John 16:13). The Spirit is truth and the Bible in its purest form is truth. They work perfectly together as the final authority on all issues of life (see 1 John 5:6, John 17:17).

The Bible is important to all believers, but it is *especially* important to the newborn believer as the dominant voice of God. The Bible should be studied until the believer has become *familiar* with all of it. After that, we should continue to study it, because there is no end to the nuggets of truth, understanding, and wisdom that comes from studying the Bible. Eventually, we grow into an understanding of how to walk in the Spirit, having our senses exercised to discern good and evil (see Hebrews 5:14). The dominant voice of God becomes the Holy Spirit, which is in complete harmony with the correct interpretation of the Bible.

Our end goal is not to know all of the Scriptures. That might be *a* goal, but our *end* goal is to know God better and walk closer and closer to Him. The Pharisees in Jesus' time knew the Scriptures, but they didn't know God. We should be taught to trust the Scriptures, not trust *in* the Scriptures. That is, we should teach that the Scriptures are from God and can be trusted. They tell us about God, how to know Him, and how to walk in the Spirit. Jesus related this concept to the Pharisees when He said: *Search the Scriptures; for in them ye think ye have eternal life: and they are they which testify of me* (John 5:39).

The Pharisees worshiped the Bible, trusting in the knowledge of it, but they resisted the Holy Spirit and His ministry and manifestations. As believers, we can fall into the same trap if we miss this truth. Unfortunately, much of the Church today *has* fallen into this trap of worshiping the Bible and resisting the Holy Spirit. They do this in a similar fashion as I did in Morgan's situation. I stubbornly held to my interpretation of the Bible and resisted the Holy Spirit's gentle witness of God's mind about Morgan's matter. As I continued to seek God on the issue, the Holy Spirit spoke to my heart in the above prophecy, gave me a better understanding of the situation, and showed me that my interpretation of certain Scriptures was wrong.

Often, our set interpretations of the Bible become like a formula. But the Holy Spirit witnesses to the providence of God, His perfect will, and His permissive will at any point in time. He often dispels our formulas.

During Jesus Unlimited, we always held to the belief that the Bible was the final authority, yet we still got off into many deceptions. So our error was not rooted in disrespect for the authority of the Bible but in misunderstanding our inward witness of what the Holy Spirit was saying to our hearts.

Through our experiences, our Heavenly Father tries to teach us what the Spirit is saying. If we think back to when we made important decisions in our lives, or if we think about our present doctrinal positions, we can sense a feeling about them. As believers, the Holy Spirit is constantly witnessing to us what is truth, and (hopefully) we eventually understand what the Spirit is saying. The Holy Spirit brought great peace and understanding into my walk with God by speaking to me in the above prophecy. It helped to restore my faith in the written Word and trust in God's provision and protection.

Since Morgan's death, I have come to understand that most of us cannot handle an abundance of God's blessings. We are all growing in grace and still have sinful tendencies. Therefore, we often cannot handle prosperity or sensational spiritual blessings without falling into pride. Because of this, God often holds back the manifestation of His power for our own good. May our God grant us the grace to live in the midst of His power in a greater degree! I pray that I will see and experience that greater power on a regular basis. I really *do* expect to see it.

This book is partially about learning that you cannot justify your lifestyle just because God blesses you with a miracle or other forms of prosperity. When things are going well, there is more of a temptation to say, "I must be pleasing God, so that is why He is blessing me." Or, "I'm involved in a great ministry, helping many to be saved and healed. Therefore, I must be living right before God." That is a dangerous way to think. Eventually sin and resisting the Holy Spirit catches up to you.

God knows our hearts, and it seems clear throughout history that wealth and other forms of prosperity can cause us to stray. I'm thankful that Jesus loves us enough to withhold prosperity many times in order to keep us looking to Him and growing according to His plan for us. The Bible sums up this concept by saying:

Two things have I required of You; deny me them not before I die: Remove far from me vanity and lies: give me neither poverty nor riches; feed me with food convenient for me: Lest I be full, and deny You, and say, Who is the Lord? or lest I be poor, and steal, and take the name of my God in vain.

(Proverbs 30:7–9)

Just remember that if blessings begin to abound, continue to walk close to Jesus and be sensitive to the Holy Spirit's warnings. God is a God of love. He truly knows what is best for us and acts accordingly every time.

January 21, 1988

> God has blessed our business. Not to the place in which we have abundance—but the bills are all paid, the business is out of debt, and there are several very good jobs pending. All the prayers concerning the business have been answered. I thank You, Father, for your faithfulness.

In May, Val put in forty hours of labor (in less than two days) to deliver our second son, Micah. Another fine son, a nine-pounder! One of our favorite memories is watching Joel and Micah playing together with a clothes basket. Micah would get into the basket, and Joel would push him around the kitchen with Micah laughing and having a great time with his brother.

About this time, the owner of Dayco began to sell off many of his assets and things his company was no longer using. I bought one of his storage racks filled with a lot of old press dies and other obsolete tooling. At my shop, I started going over all the stuff that came with the rack and saw something that just melted my heart.

As I looked through all the stuff on the rack, my eyes came to rest on three punch-press dies that looked familiar. Then I realized that these were the same three dies that I used that night ten years earlier when I prayed for deliverance! Those dies represented my bondage in 1978, but now they were mine! God had placed those dies in my control! I *owned* them! God clearly answered my prayer for deliverance, but it never could have happened that way unless I had followed His advice, which was:

1. Be open to deliverance *within* Dayco
2. Serve that company as a service to God.

At the time, it had been a bitter pill to swallow because I just wanted *out* of Dayco. God wanted me to learn the business and prepare for the future. I still have those three dies, and I have used two of them on some of my own jobs. They remind me of God's faithfulness and love for His children—and that sometimes it takes time for His good plan to unfold for us. Be patient, trust in Him, and He will bring it to pass!

April 3, 1989

Father, I need to see your hand at work. I feel an unbelief sneaking in—that You are not really in control or involved personally with my life. I don't believe that. I would like to be in the center of Your will and to see You work. I feel I should ask You for something and wait for Your response. Money is too cheap and I feel you will bless me anyway, so I pray for the salvation of a soul. I never have been a soul winner, so a real miracle to me would be to lead someone to You. I ask You to lead someone to me who is ready to believe. Please give me the wisdom and words to respond correctly to clearly open doors during a conversation with this person.

Ever wonder how the Israelites constantly backslid from God, even though God did so many miracles for them? I think we are similar to them. We all need regular reminders about God's faithfulness, no matter how often we see His miracles. That's why we need to gather regularly with other believers to pray together and encourage each other about God's faithfulness. In the above entry, I was feeling like God wasn't very close to me or involved. Of course, He was, but at the time it didn't feel like it.

Several weeks later, a former coworker from Dayco was readied by the Spirit to give his life to Jesus. He sought me out, and after some meetings and a golf game, he prayed to accept Jesus as His Savior with me and two other friends.

313

November 7, 1991

> I had to lay off my workforce a month ago. It was very hard to do. I felt as if God had forsaken me. After looking at my personal situation, I could easily see that He hadn't forsaken me at all, but it still seemed that my employees were forsaken. I felt so much like a failure when I had to lay them off. However, if I give them one day of work, in addition to their unemployment, they take home about what they normally do. So I guess that God really hasn't forsaken them either.

I should comment here about finances. Experiencing financial blessings doesn't necessarily equal God's endorsement, and lack of finances doesn't mean that God has abandoned us.

Tough times are often a blessing in disguise, allowing us to learn spiritual things that we otherwise would not learn during prosperity. We need to heed Paul's warning to Timothy about *men of corrupt minds, and destitute of the truth, supposing that gain is godliness: from such withdraw yourself. But godliness with contentment is great gain* (1 Timothy 6:5–6). Don't serve the god of money. Love Jesus and seek godliness with contentment, whether he blesses you with good fortune or you struggle financially.

May 13, 1992

> Since last December, You have blessed us with so much business! I praise and thank You the most for peace in the midst of busyness and stress and bad news, and I also praise and thank You for this blessing that has begun to fall on us.

During the next four years, Val and I enjoyed our family life with our two boys, filled with first-time experiences such as riding the bus to school, field trips, parent/teacher conferences, softball games, and vacations to the ocean and Yellowstone Park.

And then . . .

January 4, 1996

Business is bad again. I have decided to just pray and seek God until I get direction. I already have heard one bit of direction. I felt I should work on this book at least one day per week. I started last week. I felt God say, *You work on the book, and I'll work on your business.* That is what I'm going to do, even though it makes me feel a little bit slothful in my business practices.

Father, I pray that You will bring in good work before our money runs out. I will work on the book as You have directed. Lord, I really need to see Your hand. Please show Yourself strong. I will proclaim Your power and Your provision and Your mercy.

January 24, 1996

Business is picking up. Not enough to pay the bills yet, but it is encouraging.

January 31, 1996

We are getting swamped with business! So much that I was tempted to not stay home today to work on the book. My engineer can't keep up with the engineering, so I have to help.

June 16, 1998

I've been praying about how to end my book. It seems like a never-ending story. While I was praying, I asked God how it will end. I thought I heard God say: *It will end at the beginning.* I am not at all sure what that means, but it could mean that I will end up being involved with a small group again and that God will begin to move again with a revival spirit in our midst. We'll have another chance to move with Him and hopefully be a lot more faithful to His ways.

Along those same lines, I hope that the mystery of Mark's disappearance will also be solved when I finish this book. I have felt that Mark is not alive. I hope I'm wrong and that he is still alive and will someday come to his senses and remember who he is. But either way, I have a feeling that Mark will be found shortly after this book is published.

We have now come to the end of my journal. *Wow!* A 25-year experience. I have attempted to take you along with me in those experiences to feel what I felt, to think like I thought, to be confused as I was confused, and to come out of it as I came out of it.

In addition to your knowledge of God's written Word helping you to know what is true, Hebrews 5:14 talks about having your senses exercised to discern both good and evil. I pray that reading this book has brought you one step further in having your senses exercised and that you will be less likely to fall into the traps of the SPIRIT OF ERROR.

Have you ever thought about discerning or "feeling" the spirit of something? Here is a little exercise: Think about and feel the spirit of the beginning of this book. Compare that spirit or feeling to the spirit of Chapter 14 (Personal Revelations) and 15 (The Ax). Then feel the spirit of Chapter 24, (Rebuilding). If you think about it, you can feel a distinct difference between these chapters.

Often, you come into a group or situation where you feel something is wrong, but you don't know exactly *what* you feel or what it means. You are sensing something, but you are just not sure what it is or what you should do. Remember this: In Christian circles, most of the time there are good *and* bad things happening at the same time, just like in my story. So don't jump in and condemn too quickly without praying and seeing clearly first. If you are going to pull anyone out of this type of fire, you must first acknowledge the good being done, or you will lose your audience.

The strength of any deception comes from the truth that is present within it. It is not the lies that give it strength. *It is the truth.* You need to do what Aquilla and Pricilla did for Apollos (see Acts 18:24–26). They *expounded unto him* [Apollos] *the way of God more perfectly.*

CHAPTER 27

THE SHOW

*P*eople *want* to see God move. They *want* to tell others about His moving. This is normal and healthy. However, we often want to see Him move so much that we exaggerate. Some ministers want so much for people to see God move that they learn to act. They begin to exaggerate and *add* to God's moving. Sadly, some preachers even cheat and lie to get people to support them.

God is misrepresented when people exaggerate or when preachers cheat and lie. God is often credited with and blamed for things He really didn't do. It happens all the time. I call it "The Show."

Many years ago while vacationing in Lee Funt's hometown in Florida, he called me up and could hardly contain his excitement. (Remember Lee? I became a Christian at his parent's house.) He said, "Larry, we're having a real revival at my church. I want you to come and hear this visiting preacher."

I really didn't want to "go and see," because I have done it so much, with so many disappointments. I was tired of running to the altar because of false religious guilt or from a desire to see, feel, and experience God's power. I have come to the place in which I just believe that God is and that He can and will manifest His power to deliver when He is ready.

Although I still enjoy seeing God's power manifested, I don't *have* to see it anymore to believe it, and I will patiently wait for the greater manifestation that I *do* expect to see someday. As I stated in the Introduction, I believe we should be seeing more of the manifestations of the Holy Spirit as listed in 1 Corinthians 12:7–11, including gifts of healing and miracles. I fully expect to see more (a lot more) of these manifestations in my lifetime.

Val and I ended up going with Lee and his wife, Ruth Ann, to their large church the following Saturday night. We found the place packed—with standing room only—so we stood against the back wall. The service had already started, and I was immediately impressed. The man who talked up front was so peaceful and plain. I was expecting a lot of flamboyant music and a "let's crank it up and praise God!" pushy type of atmosphere.

Don't get me wrong. I *love* to praise God, worship in Spirit, and get loud about it when I feel the Holy Spirit moving me from my heart. I *don't* like the crank it up, get it up atmospheres. What I saw was a music leader off to the side who was softly singing some worship songs and a person in the center who was commenting on what was happening.

When Lee told me that the man in the center was the main speaker, I was surprised in one way but not in another. I was surprised that the revivalist was a soft-spoken, simple, plain-looking and plain-acting person. I was not surprised because I figured that for revival to really come, it takes a *large dose of reality*. This man looked and acted real.

He decided to minister to people during the song service. Usually this takes place after the message. People came up to the front, and the revivalist and his team laid hands on them and prayed for them. Many fell down under the power of God. The man said he felt that they were to minister to young people under the age of twenty that night. During this prayer time, my hands began to burn or tingle like they were asleep, yet with full feeling at the same time. Everything was done decently and in order in the meeting.

A few people began to laugh out loud after someone prayed for them. This did not feel at all offensive to me, and I was surprised that it was not distracting either. I sensed the joy that these persons were experiencing and actually felt my heart leap for joy. You could hear the people laughing but not be distracted from the thoughts and exhortations of the speaker. I wanted to go up front, but I was well over the age of twenty.

After an hour or so, the man shared his message about emphasizing Jesus and not ourselves. During the message, the speaker said that sometimes a sign that God wants to minister to you is if your hands start to tingle. When it was time to go, I felt a little sad that I didn't have a chance to go up front and that I had missed a blessing from the Lord. But overall, I was blessed and encouraged by the night's activities and message. This definitely was reality!

We didn't go to church Sunday morning, but on Sunday evening Lee called and invited me to go to his church again. The revival team had left. The service started with some songs, like the night before. Then during the song service, the pastor got up front and said that he felt we should begin to minister to people, even though it was a little out of the ordinary.

People began to go up front for prayer. I began to reason that just because the revivalist was not there didn't mean that God wasn't there. Since I missed out the night before, I went up front. A man from the church's ministry team began to pray for me. I think it was his life's work to knock me down (in the Spirit). He kept pushing on my forehead and clearly acted like I ought to fall down. After five minutes or so, I said to myself, *This guy is not going to quit until I go down.*

Then I did something I hope I'll never do again. *I'm embarrassed to say this*, but I fell down for the purpose of getting this guy away from me. What I *should* have done was just say thank you and go sit down. But I didn't want to embarrass him or make a scene. What I *did* was to encourage him in his folly and create some unbelief in many honest onlookers. By God's grace, I'll never do anything like that again.

319

After I prayed on the floor for a while, I went back to my seat with Lee. The rest of the service was a copy of the night before, except I felt the air was full of the "trying to get the Spirit moving" atmosphere. The preacher seemed to be trying to copy the actions of the revivalist. It just wasn't the same, even though the outward actions looked the same. This is what I call "The Show." I believe I saw this because the two nights were back to back and the contrast was very evident.

"The Show." It's what so many people hate about church. However, God sometimes moves in the midst of it and does mighty things, blessing people with His presence and power. I, along with many other churchgoers, endure "The Show" to occasionally enjoy God's presence. It is a reasonable tradeoff, but I would like to be relieved from having to tolerate it in order to experience some truth.

By the way, it's better to endure The Show peacefully than to develop pride and a judgmental attitude about it. We need to cut the ministers some slack. They are giving it their best shot most of the time, and God honors that part. Peter said, *And above all things have fervent charity among yourselves: for charity shall cover the multitude of sins* (1 Peter 4:8). Paul said, *Knowledge puffs up, but charity edifies* (1 Corinthians 8:1).

The Truth About Confrontation

It is often said that the truth hurts. That is only a half-truth. Jesus said that knowing the truth will make you free (see John 8:32). That is my experience too. Why should we change the truth of God into a half-truth and *only* say it hurts? The truth may reveal some unpleasant consequences of past actions that may be uncomfortable (and painful), but that truth still makes you free when you understand and embrace it.

Why do I believe this over the traditional "the truth hurts"? Because Jesus *said* the truth will make us free, and I have experienced it. Truth answers questions and solves problems.

The truth *especially* hurts when it is coupled with some selfish motives or lack of wisdom from the person who is revealing the truth. What are some selfish motives?

1. A desire to get even or strike back at a person who has hurt you.
2. A desire to get people to validate your methods or beliefs.
3. A desire to get people to validate your job position.
4. A desire to get people to fear you.
5. A desire to get people to follow you.

Unfortunately, the truth comes forth with mixed motives most of the time. The "baby" Christian usually cannot sort out the selfish motives from the good ones, but he or she can usually sense them.

The spiritual adolescent will be able to sense and often will see and define the selfish motivations of their spiritual leaders and elders. This is a crucial time, because they can use the leader's selfish motivations as an excuse to walk away from God. They often become critical and angry.

It can be a real test and refining of the spiritual adolescent's faith. If they continue in Jesus' Word, they will eventually become more understanding and loving. They will purge themselves of their own selfish motivations as they follow Jesus, and they will begin to love their fellow Christians with a more perfect love.

Most of the pain, humiliation, anguish, frustration, and confusion that I experienced at J.U. was the result of either an outright lie, the twisting of truth, or exaggeration in the form of adding to or subtracting from the truth. These unpleasant experiences usually were the result of people trying to do the right thing. Sometimes they were the result of someone exaggerating the truth so they would be accepted; sometimes so they could have power over someone or manipulate him or her. Usually the person did these things subconsciously. There was almost always an element of truth in every confrontation.

Leadership Should Lead, Not Control

God's method of leading is front wheel drive. That is, He *draws* us toward Him. He doesn't push. When Jesus walked the earth, He had all authority yet he didn't *push* people to follow him. He led people. He taught us to serve, to *lead*, to *draw* people into the Kingdom. Good leadership *draws* people and controls things. Bad leadership not only controls things, but it also pushes and tries to control people.

One of the first things that a new dynamic prayer group does is form a church. They try to form an organization as close to the biblical description as they can and still be legal and get tax-deductible status. The use of the ecclesiastical corporation is not wrong in itself, if it is looked at as a tool. Corporations should be tools to manage and control *property*. But the typical mistake is that people start church organizations and begin to manage and control *people*. It is very hard not to fall into this trap.

This is one of the biggest mistakes we made in J.U. We started the J.U. organization to manage and control the original camp property vision. We ended up feeling it was our duty to manage and control people. Very few churches understand this principle. Occasionally, you see a large church organization that is full of life and freedom in Jesus and being very fruitful. This is usually the result of a dynamic leader leading people and letting others control the property. Or at least, the leader doesn't confuse the concepts of leading people and controlling property.

The home church movement generally looks down upon organizations but doesn't understand that the downfall of the organized church is its control of people. You can just as easily fall into that sin in a home church setting. Pooling resources together for larger projects is not wrong, and forming a corporation helps to keep large sums of money accounted for in specific ways. So in some cases, the right thing to do is to form a legal corporation entity.

The mandate of the church is to spread the Word of God, not try to control the people who hear it. Governments are ordained by God to restrict and control the lawless persons in their country. I don't believe the church has *any* responsibility for restricting lawlessness, except that individual Christians may participate in enforcing the (just) laws of the government, in accordance *with* those laws. But remember, we are talking about restricting lawlessness, not playing Holy Spirit and controlling the creativity of people. So let's lead people, control our property, and do our part to uphold the just laws of our land.

The Bottom Line

I have put together a teaching syllabus that deals with the eight lessons I learned during the Battle of J.U.:

1. Seeking God's Power in a Healthy Manner
2. How to Judge Apparent Manifestations of God's Power
3. Doing Things in Your Own Strength versus God's Strength
4. The Demon of Exclusiveness
5. Motivation: Ungodly Fear Compared to a Healthy Fear of God
6. How to Avoid Blind Following
7. How Deep Deception Creeps In
8. Handling Failure

In the future, I hope to teach these lessons in seminars across the world. But in the meantime, you may be wondering: what's the bottom line? What *is* the SPIRIT OF ERROR? What *is* the SPIRIT OF TRUTH?

- The SPIRIT OF ERROR is about "The Show."
  The SPIRIT OF TRUTH is about waiting on God's timing to do what He wants, even if the waiting seems embarrassing, boring, or out of the norm.

- The SPIRIT OF ERROR makes us feel that we won't be safe unless we join a particular group.
  The SPIRIT OF TRUTH recognizes that there are many places in the world where we can fellowship.

- The SPIRIT OF ERROR involves leadership applying fear in order to motivate us and selfishly using us to make themselves feel better in some way.
  The SPIRIT OF TRUTH teaches a healthy fear (reverence) of God, which will motivate us to serve Him.

- The SPIRIT OF ERROR is about thinking we are justified in *all* our ways just because God is using us in *some* good ways.
  The SPIRIT OF TRUTH teaches that we are all works in progress and can be used by God even while we're imperfect. Just because we are operating gifts of the Holy Spirit and being used of God, it doesn't mean that *all* of our actions, ideas, and statements are right and pleasing to God.

- The SPIRIT OF ERROR *uses* the Bible.
  The SPIRIT OF TRUTH *confirms* the Bible.

- The SPIRIT OF ERROR is about being afraid to humbly judge the actions of a person who is being used by God.
  The SPIRIT OF TRUTH recognizes that no person is perfect in word and deed, and Scripture encourages us to lovingly confront people (even leadership) at appropriate times (see 1 Timothy 5:1; Galatians 2:11–21; 6:1).

- The SPIRIT OF ERROR is about compromising our own sense of right and wrong out of fear of being left out of a group.
  The SPIRIT OF TRUTH teaches us to please God, not men (see Galatians 1:10).

- The SPIRIT OF ERROR involves someone capitalizing on our natural desires to experience God and His supernatural power.
  The SPIRIT OF TRUTH allows God to work without manipulation and "hype."

- The SPIRIT OF ERROR is about using the truth for selfish reasons.
  The SPIRIT OF TRUTH always confirms that love "does not seek its own" (see 1 Corinthians 13:5). It is concerned about the welfare of others.
- The SPIRIT OF ERROR is more about exaggeration and deception than a flat-out lie.
  The SPIRIT OF TRUTH is about telling the simple truth out of a motivation of love, without exaggeration.

The SPIRIT OF TRUTH is just that: being truthful, telling the truth, and simply being *real* when you do it. Jesus never exaggerated or did anything just to be accepted. He simply told the truth, with no selfish motives.

The Circus Vision

During some of the better times in J.U., one of the leaders had a vision. I judged it then to be of God. I still judge it to be from God. This is how he described it:

I saw a bright stairway leading up into the clouds. Part of the way up the stairway was a circus tent off to the side. People were walking up the stairway and going into the tent. The door to the tent opened for me, and I viewed what went on inside. I felt confusion and a lot of things flashed in front of my face; things that didn't seem to be important or didn't have any meaning. It was just plain havoc.

As the people came out of the tent, they would all shake their heads. Some turned and started to go back down the stairs. I thought to myself, *Man, where are you going?* But they just kept going down. I looked up again to see the beauty of the clouds and felt the drawing in my heart to go on, but I also had the feeling that it seemed such a long way, miles and miles.

Other people began to come out and show the same confusion on their faces, but they would turn and go up the stairs and continue their journey toward the beautiful clouds, even though it seemed so far away. And even when you reached the top, you didn't know what was really behind those clouds.

Somewhere between the circus and the clouds, there was a man hanging off the edge of the stairs by only a few fingers. He seemed to have lost heart. I asked, "Why?" I felt God say that the man simply needed to overcome that feeling and pull himself up and go on. Then I felt the man's feelings. He felt complacent but also felt a drawing in his heart toward God, and there seemed to be a battle inside him. He did not want to fall but needed strength.

He asked for strength, and God was pleased that he had the will, even though he lacked the strength. The strength was granted, and he pulled himself up and felt a *new strength*. Then he continued up the stairs, and the vision ended.

The stairs represent our individual walks with God. The activity in the circus tent represents the things that Christians do that are contrary to God's will, including "The Show." The clouds represent our eternal reward in heaven.

Are you confused by the circus? Are you tired of the confusion? Do you hate "The Show"? Will you quit and walk down the stairs, or will you look up and ask God for the strength to continue to seek Him?

A Scripture comes to me now: *And they overcame him [the Devil] by the blood of the Lamb, and by the word of their testimony* (Revelation 12:11). What does that mean to us? *Jesus* made it possible for us to overcome through His sacrifice on the cross. We believe it and say, "Jesus, You are God, and I believe You will help me to continue my walk with You and to overcome."

What Will You Choose To Do About It?

You have read this story and probably heard a lot of confusing things about God in your life. But what are you going to do? Do you sense that God is calling you to walk with Him, continue to walk with Him, or to walk closer to Him? Do you sense that God is real and that there is just something right about Jesus? If so, then choose to follow Him. Turn from the things that God is calling you away from. Choose to continue to follow Jesus, even if you hate "The Show," even if you are confused. He is the way, the truth, and the life (see John 14:6).

If you have never committed yourself to God, I encourage you to repent and just do it. That is, turn away from what you know is wrong. God will forgive you, and you can be born again with a whole new outlook on life. Ask Him to reveal Himself to you. Ask Him to forgive you for your sins. Ask Him to help you do what is right. Learn how to read and study the Bible. Gather together with other believers to learn more about God. If you keep on seeking, you will find the answers, and you will enter into greater and greater freedom and peace.

Peace I leave with you, my peace I give unto you.

(John 14:27)

Seek, and ye shall find . . . .

(Luke 11:9)

And ye shall know the truth, and the truth shall make you free.

(John 8:32)

CAST OF CHARACTERS

Mick Ahrens—Mick was one of the ten leaders of J.U. Mick seemed to have an advanced spiritual growth rate early after his conversion. He hired on in leadership as a prayer warrior in early 1975 and then became an elder later that year. Mick married my wife's younger sister in 1975. They divorced around 1979.

Val Barrett—My wife. I met Val at Boulder's Chapel in 1972, shortly after my conversion to Christ.

John Beal—The Riverside Camp coordinator for the Methodist Church. John was in charge of selling the camp for their denomination. He lived in Grand Rapids, Michigan.

Mark Bechtel—The main character and leader of J.U. He was one of my best friends in high school and college.

Christi Bechtel—Mark's wife. They met and got married during J.U. She was about 17 years old when she left high school and married Mark.

Jeff Bechtel—Mark's older brother and one of the ten leaders of J.U. He was skilled in hunting, trapping, and basic survival techniques. Jeff's first wife left him after two years at J.U. and went back to South America, where her family lived. Jeff remarried a few years later to a girl he met at J.U. They are happily married today and have successfully raised two children.

Phil Bechtel—Mark's oldest brother and one of the ten leaders of J.U. Phil was divorced before J.U. started. Shortly after J.U. began, Phil started dating and eventually married a pleasant young lady named Sandy Henderson. She was tall, blond and close to ten years younger than Phil. Val and I moved in with Phil and Sandy when our finances got tight, and we lived with them for one year. Phil reminds me of the typical stereotype of the apostle Peter. He is big and burly with black hair, and is always ready to boldly stand up for God. Phil loves the Lord fervently and is a successful businessman involved in beekeeping supplies and selling honey. He is also a communications consultant.

Wilt Bechtel—Mark's dad, also known as "Brother Bechtel" or "Brother Wilt." Brother Bechtel started a church shortly after he and a few other families left Boulder's Chapel. Wilt is still a faithful pastor of that church and is regularly involved in community-wide prayer meetings.

Mom and Dad Calldean, Terry, Sally and her two sisters—Friends of my wife whom I originally met at Boulder's Chapel. We still communicate occasionally, and they all are serving God in one way or another. I became a Christian after I read a little gospel booklet that Val and the Calldeans handed out at the musical *Jesus Christ Superstar*.

Greg Curry—Greg was one of the ten leaders of J.U. He was gloriously saved from a rough life and was not ashamed to tell his story! I think Greg could be described as a modern-day prophet. He had a keen sense of right and wrong. Greg reported many visions that made sense and are applicable to the church today.

Rusty and Penny Evans—Rusty was one of the ten leaders of J.U. Rusty, Mark, and I were the original charter framers of the J.U. church organization. Rusty started full-time as a pastor at J.U. and later became an elder and one of Mark's right hand men. Penny and Rusty were married near the beginning of J.U. They were good friends with Val and me before J.U., and we hung around together. Penny and Rusty are serving Jesus together in another state. We are still friends and enjoy each other's company.

Al Fletcher—"Brother Al" was the pastor at Boulder's Chapel Church of God while Val and I attended there. He performed our marriage ceremony and was a great minister of weddings. The best! Brother Al retired around 1989 and is enjoying his retirement.

Jim Flood—Jim was one of the ten leaders of J.U and one of the pastors. Jim married Mark Bechtel's sister, Melody, at a double wedding at the camp with Mark and Christi, and he's been a faithful husband ever since. Jim is tall—seemingly twice as tall as Melody.

Lee Funt—One of my best friends in high school and college. Lee and I met on our walk to school when he was in kindergarten and I was in first grade. I became a Christian after a wild party at his house. Mark, Lee, and I were best friends, and for several years we hung around each other constantly. Lee continues to be one of my few lifelong friends.

Dick Holdin—Dick was at the first meetings of J.U. and was with us for the first six months or so. He played the guitar and led worship almost all the time. Dick told me recently that he left J.U. because Mark told him he was singing too many fun songs and needed to do more serious songs.

Pastor Murphy—Pastor Murphy was an associate pastor at Christian Center Church in South Bend, Indiana. My hometown of Niles, Michigan—where this story takes place—is only seven miles from the Indiana border and about 14 miles from this church. Pastor Murphy was an energetic man, had lots of faith in God, and was always encouraging us to walk with God.

Bill Norten—Bill was one of the ten leaders of J.U. He was one of the elders and known as "pretty smart." He helped Mark write and organize most of the teaching materials. Bill had long, dark, bushy but well-kept hair, usually all combed into perfect place.

Bill Riggenbacher—Bill was one of the ten leaders of J.U. and a deacon. I considered Bill to be one of the kindest, gentlest, and most liked of all the leaders. Bill seemed a bit slow and could have been voted most likely not to succeed. After J.U. however, Bill went to a chef school and now has a good job with a lot of responsibility in the food service industry.

David Wilkerson (and his vision)—David is the author of over twenty-five books, including *The Cross and the Switchblade* and *The Vision*. In the early 1970s, he had a vision from God about what was coming in the future. It included bad weather extremes, a worldwide depression, persecution of Christians, and an unbelievable moral decline in the United States. Some of David's vision has come to pass, especially the part about moral decline. (I remember thinking at the time that such immorality would never be seen on television. I remember thinking, *XXX rated films on cable TV after midnight? Never!*)

LIST OF PLACES AND ORGANIZATIONS

ACA—The American Canoe Association. They bid on the Riverside Camp, which was sold to them in 1974.

Boulder's Chapel—The church in Niles where Mark, Lee Funt and I started attending shortly after our conversion to Christ. We left Boulder's Chapel to become involved with J.U. There has been a miraculous change at Boulder's Chapel that has taken place in the past few years. Not only have they have abandoned the exclusiveness attitude, but they have embraced healthy ecumenical activities around town. They have been leaders in a local movement called the "Church of Niles" that actively promotes the idea that God wants Christians everywhere to be able to worship together. A large number of the local churches gather at a different church once a month on a Sunday night. Although Brother Al has retired as pastor, he faithfully attends Boulder's Chapel and is still involved in some of the ministry and Church of Niles activities.

Christian Center Church—A church located in South Bend, Indiana. The Christian Center Church is a fruitful ministry that sponsors television and radio ministries in the Michiana (Michigan and Indiana) area and around the world. Dr. Lester Sumrall was the senior pastor (he passed away in 1996), and Pastor Murphy was an associate pastor there.

FGBMFI—Full Gospel Business Men's Fellowship International is a Christian organization comprised of about 500 chapters in the United States and 5,000 worldwide, touching 160 nations. FGBMFI consists predominately of laymen and business owners who gather regularly for meetings of encouragement and various ministry endeavors.

Front Street Building—We rented this building after our plastic structure was blown off the side of Bechtel's garage in early 1975. This 5,000 square foot rectangular building was conveniently located in a non-crowded area within two blocks of downtown Niles. It was a rather plain single-story dark gray steel building with two doors and a loading dock facing the street. For an old warehouse, it was pretty clean inside with relatively short ten-foot eaves (walls). There was no drop ceiling, so the steel beams stretched across the building, with two gas space heaters hanging down in the center. The space heaters were pretty noisy and distracting when they came on in the winter.

Glory Barn—A church in northern Indiana about one hour's drive from Niles. The Glory Barn ministers heavily preached a "faith message" and were of some renown in the charismatic world during the 1970s. Apparently, they took their message to the extreme. They seemed to indicate that it was wrong to go to doctors, and several people died—including some children—because they went without medicine. After visiting a few times, Mark felt warned by God that the Glory Barn had dangerous doctrine. I believe the Glory Barn closed during the 1980s.

People of Praise—A charismatic group of Christians that my parents started meeting with in 1972 in South Bend, Indiana. Roman Catholics mostly attended, but it was open to people of all denominations. The People of Praise were part of the "Charismatic Renewal" of many mainline churches in the 1970s.

Prayer Shack—Ron Binks built this "one room with a loft" near the back of his parent's rolling, wooded 17 acres. It was about the size of a small one-car garage. As you walked in the door, you saw an old wood stove to the left with the loft over your head. The back wall of the shack was lined with windows, and a stuffed chair or two were in the corners. Carpet hid the dirt floor, and the place was kept reasonably clean. The loft covered half of the room and could accommodate up to ten people.

Riverside Camp—A camp near Buchanan, Michigan, about five miles from Niles. The beginning of J.U. centers on this camp. Riverside Camp was a church camp owned and operated by the United Methodist Church. There were two levels on the property. The top level consisted of several little cabins, the tabernacle, and a large mess hall building. To get to the lower level of the property, you had to go down a hill with many cement steps, cross a narrow public dirt road, and then negotiate another long set of steps. At the bottom of the steps, there was a large field, then the big swimming pool, and a bunch of little cabins in the midst of many trees. At the back of the cabins and trees you came to the vesper bowl facing the wide St. Joseph River. In the 1980s, the camp was leveled and subdivided into lots. Today, there are many nice homes on this property.

Tabernacle—A large, rectangular, unheated wood building that was located on the upper portion of the Riverside Camp property. Large assemblies of people used it for worship and other meetings. All along the sides of the building were large wooden doors that would swing out and open up each side of the building like an awning.

Vesper Bowl—A cement amphitheater located on the lower level of the Riverside Camp that faced the river. This was the site of many memorable J.U. moments. At the bottom of the bowl, in the center along the ledge by the river, was a big cross that was made from a telephone pole. The vesper bowl is still there, but the old rugged wooden cross—which was such an inspirational part of it—is now gone.

GLOSSARY

Anointed—A term used to describe someone whom God has specially inspired and equipped to use gifts and talents in a powerful, authoritative, and captivating way to communicate truth. It is also a term used to describe a situation where the Holy Spirit comes upon a person and gives him or her an "anointing" to minister at that particular moment. God's anointing teaches a person all things that are true (see 1 John 2:27). It's also used to describe the process of putting oil on someone's head—as a symbol of the Holy Spirit's power—just before that person is prayed for; "to anoint with oil."

Antichrist Justification—A J.U. term that meant being deceived by the Devil into thinking that religious good works alone are the basis for righteousness, instead of trusting in the grace of God through the sacrifice of Jesus.

Apostle—Someone sent on a mission by God to preach the gospel and start churches, as in Christ's original twelve disciples; the first prominent Christian missionary to go to a region or group. I considered Mark an apostle because I felt he was called and sent by God to start a new and unique ministry in J.U. The New Testament references over twenty apostles.

THE SPIRIT OF ERROR AND THE SPIRIT OF TRUTH

Apostle's Fund—This was a fund that we started among the ten leaders. We began to sell our assets and give the money to this fund. It was not tax-deductible and could be distributed any way we wanted. The fund eventually grew to more than $12,000. We used the money to fund certain needs among the body, mostly among the leaders. The bulk of the fund went toward vans for ministry. When J.U. broke up, Mark got one van, and I believe Jeff got the other one. (Jeff certainly deserved to get a van, because he contributed the most money into the fund.)

Binding—This usually refers to a feeling of awkwardness coupled with a lack of ability to express feelings and ideas freely. Sometimes it refers to controlling evil spirits, "binding them up" for exorcism.

Buffet—To strike blows against; to make conditions difficult (physically or spiritually).

Body—The church people; used for either the universal body of Christ or the local church body.

Bore Witness in Our Spirits (or "My Spirit Bore Witness")—This is a phrase that really means we checked what we felt our spirit was telling us, and the thought in question was true. Thus, if you said, "I think that the Lord wants us to get more sleep," and I felt the same way, I would say, "My spirit bears witness with that." When a person is born again, his human spirit changes and becomes born of God according to what Jesus said in John chapter 3. When this happens, that person can learn to "hear" what his pure reborn spirit is saying (or witnessing) to him. It is a lifelong process of learning that voice, with many errors in judgment along the way. Paul refers to this in Hebrews 5:14 as having your *senses exercised to discern both good and evil.* The written Word (the Bible) and pastors help you to stay out of trouble on this issue.

Breaking of the Outer Man—A religious term that describes the process of dying to your own selfish will and then letting God live out through you.

Burden—A strong inward desire inspired usually from the Holy Spirit to do something; an intense interest about something and a feeling of deep concern.

Call of God—A person having full assurance that God is leading him or her to a certain path of service to Him. A missionary might say, "God called me to be a missionary in Papua, New Guinea, four years ago." Once you "hear" the call from God regarding salvation or service, you must decide how you will respond.

Charismatic—In the Christian world, this usually describes a person who believes in the baptism of the Holy Spirit and endorses moving in manifestations of the Holy Spirit such as healing, miracles, speaking in tongues, knowing things supernaturally, and so forth. The technical dictionary definition describes a person who is full of charisma, enthusiasm, and personal magnetism. Mark was charismatic by both definitions.

Convicted—A state of mind in which you feel guilty. I used this word wrongly sometimes in my journal because the *real* conviction of God includes a clear understanding of what God wants you to do *and* peaceful direction as well. Most of the time, I was referring to just a guilty feeling.

Deacon—A person in a church leadership position whose responsibilities are mainly to take care of the temporal (physical) needs of the church, such as facilities and money management. Most times, the Greek word in the New Testament is translated either "minister" or "servant."

Deliverance/Delivered—This is a term to describe exorcism or the casting out of demons. People who are set free from demonic possession or demonic oppression are "delivered" from the demons. Of course, sometimes the word is used to describe being set free from drugs or other habits that may or may not be directly related to demons.

Discernment—Although this term is usually associated with the phrase "discerning of spirits" or else perceiving something wrong, we began to use this term at J.U. to also describe an interesting physical feeling (as described early in Chapter 16).

Elders—People in official positions of leadership in a local church whose responsibilities and qualifications are listed by Paul in Titus 1:5–14 and by Peter in 1 Peter 5:1–4. Also, an "elder" means one having respect and authority by virtue of age and experience and wisdom in the Christian life. At J.U, we used the term "elder" to describe a position of spiritual authority and ministry such as preaching, teaching, and solving spiritual problems that came up in the church. The J.U. elders had authority over the deacons.

Establishment or Established Heart—A determination to begin or continue serving God in a particular area.

Exhorted/Exhortation—To give encouragement, strong advice, or a warning as led by the Holy Spirit. We must do this *with all long suffering and doctrine* (2 Tim. 4:1–4).

Fall out/Falling out—In J.U. we used this term usually to describe the experience of going into a mild state of being "slain in the Spirit" (see that term below). In the "fallen out" state, persons would normally receive information or a vision from God.

Fruit—The results of a person following God's will for his or her life. This could include seeing people get saved or renewing their faith in God because of this person's witness. Or it could be the fruit of the Spirit evidenced in that person's life (see Gal. 5:22). Jesus said, *Herein is my Father glorified, that ye bear much fruit* (John 15:8).

In the Flesh/Flesh/Fleshly—A term to describe our human sensual desires. Also, trying to do things in our own power instead of God's power.

Intercession—In most Christian circles, intercession usually means praying for people who have sinned and need God's forgiveness and mercy. In J.U., we also used this word to describe the following type of prayer: A person would pray for an afflicted person—but also at the same time enter into that person's situation—and feel a bit of the pain or anguish that the afflicted person was going through.

Sometimes the person praying would seem to act out what the afflicted person was going through.

One time at a prayer meeting, one girl began to flail her arms around, and later she reported that she felt like she was drowning. Later we found out that Evel Knievel had just missed his famous Snake River Canyon jump and almost went into the river below. Mark felt that the girl was praying for Evel Knievel's safety, keeping him from drowning. Evel's parachute carried him back across the canyon and set him down on the bank, next to the raging river. Although some of our bouts with intercession were exaggerated, I do believe that intercession is a legitimate ministry.

Inward Witness—A peaceful, inward direction from the Lord (not a literal voice).

Jacob Fighting—In Genesis 32, Jacob "wrestled with the angel of the Lord" all night and, according to that story, Jacob "prevailed with God." At the end of Jacob's wrestling, the angel said to Jacob, "Your name shall no longer be called Jacob, but you shall be called Israel, for as a prince you have power with God and with men, and have prevailed." We began using the term "Jacob Fighting" at J.U. to mean to prevail in prayer or to continue to pray until God responded.

Laid Hands On—A custom of putting one or both hands on people while praying for them. This practice is demonstrated and encouraged throughout the Bible. Sometimes many people will gather around a person who has a need or is sick and put their hands on him or her while they pray for the need.

Pentecostal—I use this term to describe people or churches that believe in the activity of "speaking in tongues" or "speaking in other languages."

Personal Crucifixion—A religious term used to describe the process of dying to your selfish will.

Pillars—Spiritually mature people who help keep the church strong and doctrinally sound. They faithfully support the church with their time, talent, and treasures through good and bad times.

Plunder—To thwart someone's plans; to cause a person with wrong motives or working from the SPIRIT OF ERROR to be unfruitful in his or her attempts to serve God.

Prophesied (*prah`-fah-sighed*)/Prophesy (verb)—When people speak by the inspiration of the Holy Spirit. It is a manifestation or gift of the Holy Spirit. In the New Testament, when one prophesied, it seldom meant to foretell the future. New Testament prophesying is described by the apostle Paul in 1 Corinthians 14:3 as *speaking to men to exhortation, edification, and comfort,* inspired by the Holy Spirit. John said in Revelation 19:10, *The testimony of Jesus is the spirit of prophecy.* Although one may prophesy, operating that gift alone would not automatically make him a prophet.

Prophet—One who has visions and dreams from God and shares them with the church. A present-day prophet will help define God's will (see Acts 13:1–3), encourage and strengthen believers (see Acts 15:32), and predict the future (see Acts 21:10–11). Whereas all may prophesy according to 1 Corinthians 14:31, all will not necessarily be prophets, according to 1 Corinthians 12:28–29.

Rapture—An event that many Christians believe will take place to remove all the believers from earth suddenly, just before God pours out His wrath on the world. Based on 1 Thessalonians 4:13–18.

Revelator—A J.U. term that we used to describe a person who received revelations and visions from the Lord on a regular basis.

Saint—Our modern culture often refers to saints as special Christians who were very holy and near perfect. But the Bible refers to saints as normal Christians (for example, Paul's words in Ephesians 1:1).

Saved—A word used in the New Testament to describe someone who is a Christian and saved from an eternity of suffering and punishment in hell (see John 3:16–17)

Self-righteous—A person who constantly tries to attain righteousness (right standing with God) through works rather than trusting in Jesus and faith in God. *Not* doing things (*touch not; taste not; handle not*) is usually the center focus of the self-righteous, like those whom

Paul spoke of in Colossians 2:20–23. It is also used to describe the repelling superior attitude that person has toward others who aren't as "mature" as he or she.

Sheep—Several years after J.U. began, we started referring to people who were not leaders in the congregation as "sheep" (as Jesus called His followers in John 10).

Slain in the Spirit/Slayed/Slayed in the Spirit A term that we used at J.U. to describe when a person was prayed for and then was so overwhelmed by the Holy Spirit that he or she seemed to faint and fall to the ground. After a while, the person became fully conscious. While the person was "out," the Holy Spirit usually administered some type of emotional or physical healing. Sometimes, the Spirit simply communicated a message. Unfortunately, the practice is overdone and exaggerated in many Christian circles (See chapter 27), but it takes place legitimately and often throughout the world. From my experience and study, these occurrences always end up being a positive experience when the Holy Spirit is really at work. In the Bible, these occurrences have been referred to as becoming "as dead" (see Revelation 1:17).

Speaking in Tongues/Tongues—A manifestation or gift of the Holy Spirit. It means to supernaturally speak in other languages. There appear to be two major types of tongues in the Bible: One is speaking earthly languages for the purpose of communicating the gospel to unbelievers; the other is a heavenly or prayer language that St. Paul spoke of in 1 Corinthians 13:1.

Travail—A J.U. term that meant a type of prayer that sounds a lot like moaning. The person praying can feel an urgency inside his or her body, similar to the urge to cry.

Vessels—People who are willing to be used by God to reach others with the love of Jesus Christ. The Lord referred to Paul as a "chosen vessel" in Acts 9:15.

Vision—In this book, there are two types of visions mentioned. The first is an understanding of what God wants for you to do, such as my vision to share my message of the SPIRIT OF ERROR. The second type of vision is a supernatural experience where a person sees into the spiritual world. This type of vision is fully explained in my journal entry dated July 7, 1975 in chapter 12.

To obtain more copies of this book,
or to contact the author about speaking at your church or conference,
please go to *www.SpiritOfErrorSpiritOfTruth.com*

To order additional copies of this title call:
1-877-421-READ (7323)
or please visit our web site at
www.winepressbooks.com

If you enjoyed this quality custom published book,

drop by our web site for more books and information.

www.winepressgroup.com

"Your partner in custom publishing."